HEALTH SYSTEMS RESEARCH

Edited by W. van Eimeren

G. López-Casasnovas (Ed.)

Incentives in Health Systems

With 22 Figures and 49 Tables

Springer-Verlag
Berlin Heidelberg New York
London Paris Tokyo
Hong Kong Barcelona
Budapest

Dr. Guillem López-Casasnovas
Facultad de Ciencias Económicas,
Departamento de Hacienda Pública,
Universidad de Barcelona,
Avenida Diagonal 690, 08034 Barcelona, Spain

1st European Conference on Health Economics,
Barcelona, 1989

ISBN 3-540-53933-6 Springer-Verlag Berlin Heidelberg New York
ISBN 0-387-53933-6 Springer-Verlag New York Berlin Heidelberg

Library of Congress Cataloging-in-Publication Data
European Conference on Health Economics (1st: 1989: Barcelona, Spain)
Incentives in health systems/[edited by] G. López-Casasnovas. p. cm. – (Health systems research)
"1st European Conference on Health Economics, Barcelona, 1989" – T.p. verso.
ISBN 3-540-53933-6 (alk. paper). – ISBN 0-387-53933-6 (alk. paper)
1. Medical economics – Congresses. 2. Health behavior – Economic aspects – Congresses. 3. Insurance, Health – Congresses. I. López-Casasnovas, G. Guillem), 1955– II. Title. III. Series.
[DNLM: 1. Delivery of Health Care – economics – congresses. 2. Economics, Medical – congresses. W 74 E89i 1989]
RA410.A2E89 1989 338.4'33621–dc20 DNLM/DLC 91-4815

Printed in Germany

Typesetting: International Typesetters Inc., Manila, Philippines
19/3130-543210 – Printed on acid-free paper

Preface

This volume contains selected papers from the First European Conference on Health Economics, held in Barcelona on 19–21 September 1989. The meeting was organized by the Spanish Health Economics Association (AES) and chaired by L. Bohigas. The following groups participated: the English Health Economists' Study Group, the Associaçao Portuguesa de Economia de Saüde, the Scandinavian Health Economics Group, the Vereniging voor Gezondheidseconomie and the Association Française d'Economie Sociale.

Incentives in Health Systems offers a wide view of the topic. Research and policy implications come together in the analysis, offering the reader important insights for understanding some of the most prominent reforms in health care management.

This book takes a new view of the topic. It includes analyses of consumers' behaviour (diet, lifestyle, etc.), providers' activity (professional practice, ethics, financial incentives and some aspects of the organizational reform) and intersectorial measures for health targets. Financial as well as organization and mode of practice policies are also analysed. Thus the authors take not only a financial view of the issues: intersectorial factors and agents behaviour are also considered with a view to improving efficiency in health services.

Some of the existing proposals for health system reforms ("Willingness to Change" by the Dekker Commission in the Netherlands, "Working for Patients" in the UK, Enthoven's proposals for the United States health system reform, etc.) can be analysed from the perspective offered by this book, in focusing on the K factors to be addressed for implementing changes in health care.

The meeting was sponsored by Generalitat de Catalunya (Department d'Economia i Finances and Department de Sanitat i Seguretat Social), Ministerio de Sanidad y Consumo, Ajuntament de Barcelona, Universitat de Barcelona, Patronat Català Pro Europa, Collegi d'Economistes de Catalunya (Comissió d'Economia de la Salut) and Sociedad Española de Salud Pública y Administración Sanitaria. The Congress had the support of the World Health Organization.

I am grateful for the assistance of Esther Martínez (Universidad de Barcelona), Juan Rovira (A.E.S. and Universidad de Barcelona), Paula Bagés (Soikos), and the members of the Spanish Health Economics Association Josep Fité, Juan Cabasés, Fernando Antoñanzas, Marisol Rodríguez, Carlos Murillo, Vicente Ortún and Josep Flaquer.

Barcelona, August 1991

Guillem López-Casasnovas

Chairman of the Scientific Committee

Table of Contents

Part II: Research on Health System Incentives

Theoretical Developments

Case Studies

List of Contributors

Birch, Stephen
Department Clinical Epidemiology and Biostatistics,
McMaster University,
1200 Main Street West, Hamilton, Ontario L8N 3Z5, Canada

Breyer, Friedrich, Prof. Dr.
FernUniversität Hagen,
Postfach 940,
W-5800 Hagen, Federal Republic of Germany

Casas, Mercè
Institut Municipal de la Salut,
Plaça Lesseps 1, 08023 Barcelona, Spain

Culyer, Anthony John, Prof.
Department of Economics, University of York,
Heslington, York Y01 5DD, United Kingdom

Doorslaer, Eddy van
Department of Health Economics,
University of Limburg, Limburg, The Netherlands

Gerritse, Ronald, Dr.
Instituut voor Onderzoek,
Orangestraat, 8, 2514 JB The Hage, The Netherlands

Graeve, Diana de
University of Antwerp,
Prinsstraat 13, 2000 Antwerpen, Belgium

López-Casasnovas, Guillem, Dr.
Facultad de Ciencias Económicas,
Departamento de Hacienda Pública,
Universidad de Barcelona,
Avenida Diagonal 690, 08034 Barcelona, Spain

Maynard, Alan, Prof.
Department of Economics, University of York,
Heslington, York Y01 5DD, United Kingdom

Neudeck, Werner E., Dr.
Institut für Wirtschaftswissenschaften, Universität Wien,
1010 Vienna, Austria

Pekurinen, Markku, Dr.
Health Services Research Unit,
National Public Health Institut,
Elimäenkatu, 25 A, 00510 Helsinki, Finland

Risa, Alf E., Dr.
University of Bergen, Institute of Economics,
Jonas Reingstr. 19, 5008 Bergen, Norway

Rochaix, Lise, Dr.
Universite Claude Bernard, CNRSV a 934, bat. 101,
43 Bd. du 11 Nov. 1918, 69622 Villeurbanne, France

Rovira, Joan, Dr.
Soikos, S.L.,
Arizala, 1–3, entlo. 1ª, 08028 Barcelona, Spain

Schneider, Thierry
Cepninserm Unité 240,
BP 48, 92263 Fontenay-aux Roses, France

Stoddart, Greg. L., Dr.
Centre for Health Economics and Policy Analysis,
McMaster University,
1200 Main Street West, Hamilton, Ontario L8N 3Z5, Canada

Ven, Wynand P.M.M. van de, Prof.
Department of Health Policy and Management,
Erasmus Universiteit,
PO Box 1738, 3000 DR Rotterdam, The Netherlands

Williams, Alan, Prof.
Department of Economics, University of York,
Heslington, York, Y01 5DD, United Kingdom

Incentives in Health Systems: Introduction and Outline

G. López-Casasnovas

The issue of incentives in health systems has been receiving greater attention in recent literature on health economics. This is not surprising since several problems appear related to this topic. Typical examples are provider-induced demand, consumer abuse of health care services, lack of cost-consciousness management and system inefficiency.

Most of the problems described above seem to be independent of the health systems, although they do reflect some organizational and financial aspects of the particular way in which health services are delivered. Hence, they do not have a universal solution and their treatment requires a problem-specific approach.

The central issue of incentives in health care arises from the fact that the behaviour of physicians blurs the relationship between health targets and instruments. Health care requires coordination among health professionals (in short periods and over time), consumers (consuming goods and not "bads") and policy-makers (health-related policies) from the public and private industry at large. Regarding these groups, the interests and motivations of the parties in the health care sector are not always incentive compatible. Even when all parties share a common goal, their view of what is "the best" for patients may not be similar.

Financial considerations, for instance, often confront policy-makers and physicians. The former group is concerned with overall health expenditure to achieve certain targets. The latter group is also concerned with individual disposable income. However, physicians' incomes add most to health expenses. Therefore, one of the basic issues on incentives is how to reconcile the primary interests of these confronted parties, particularly if we take into account the strong power of the medical guilds in health care delivery.

These issues are neither particular to the health sector nor new. Some of them are similar to the ones faced by organizational theory when information asymmetries prevent perfect monitoring of contracts. Problems like team production and task assignment may also exist in large firms. Resources are often allocated with no clear claimant entitled to the residual or reward. Moreover, in some organizations like bureaucracies, the threat of being dismissed from the team (as a penalty for poor performance) is also precluded.

In addition, once money rewards and job satisfaction are considered in physicians' rational behaviour, health care appears as an economic good – and not only as a citizen's right – open to be traded for other utilities.

In the context of the "adversarial economics" of the neoclassical theory, the solution to these problems results from the balance between the bargaining powers of the parties. This balance is usually reached at the level of health authorities (acting on behalf of the citizens and not just of the patients) and in the medical profession. However, they do not bargain in isolation. Individuals play a major role. They may adopt attitudes in support of society's restraint on health resources, or strengthen support of health professionals' claims for additional resources.

Individuals thus may pursue rather different goals depending on the role they play: as members of the community at large, as contributors (or taxpayers), or as patients. In any of these situations, health authority policies are more likely to succeed if the way in which the financial restraint is imposed on health care resources is clear-cut. The questions of how resources are allocated, how much they amount to, what their relative share is, and how they are spent in practice, do indeed matter. They shape patients' expectations of health care, and may provide a sense of cost-consciousness among consumers and providers in managing care.

In public health systems, this expenditure rationality becomes particularly relevant. In the absence of this, no opportunity costs, or foregone benefits, from increases in health expenditure may be established. By paying "once and for all" taxes, consumers may have the feeling that any required health expenses are guaranteed.

Moreover, at the time of consuming health services, those foregone benefits are much more diluted. Patients are more concerned with the poor quality of care. And this poor quality is more likely when professional dissatisfaction is present, as may be the case when income policies are wed to restrain expenditure.

Health care managers may also be highly responsive to the restraint rationale. In some countries, the idea that a "good" health manager easily overcomes financial constraints, making life easier for the "health community" in still fairly common. Savings in health expenses are considered money lost for the sector. In this situation, providers may view the aggregate level of expenditure without any sense of rationality. This is a very weak starting point from which to expect efficient management of health resources to follow.

In summarizing the argument so far, we notice that a clear identification of the relationship between social interest and individual patient motivation is missing in health care consumption. This erodes public policies – supposedly adopted on behalf of the community – and reinforces the power of health professionals. In this context, many decisions have been left to trust and ethics, and efficiency and equity targets may not be properly addressed. New approaches are needed. The theory of organizational design and optimal contracting may prove helpful for this purpose. Some of the most promising areas of research open by this book are outlined in what follows.

Supervision and Output Sharing

As is well known, uncertainty and risk aversion, information asymmetry and asset specificity are common features of health care, as they are of other areas of economic activity. They provide the conventional arguments in favour of the agency theory, in which output-shared contracts or output-based budgets offer, from a theoretical point of view, the optimal agreement for incentive policies.

In addressing this particular relationship between the principal and the agents – that is, between the patient in private systems or the health authority on his or her behalf in public systems, and the health professionals – two different types of methods can be used.

Internal methods consist basically of "trust contracts" and internal monitoring. Hierarchical supervision and decentralized budgeting techniques – from a regulatory and a financial point of view, respectively – are the most representative instruments in pursuing this approach. *External* methods include organizational changes (market simulation, regulated competition, etc.) hoping that these policies will supply personal incentives in the organization (from rewards to dismissal, from making business to bankruptcy).

Contract arrangements are mostly limited to the development of financial instruments. Researchers are commonly attracted by the design of internal budget mechanisms, following the tradition of the Soviet macroeconomic incentive models. Their results are limited, since it is difficult to fulfil the sufficient rather than the necessary conditions for interest compatibility.

The former approach, based on budgetary strategies, may be complemented by the analysis of optimal governmental structures. The purpose here is the design of organizations that minimize joint production and transaction costs. The latter costs may be very important in health services since, in Leibenstein's words, health agents have the possibility of defining pace, time and effort in their regular activity. This gives enormous power to doctor's side and weakens the organizational structure. Despite this, there have been few advances in the recognition of plausible models of organizational behaviour since the original contributions, in the past decade, by Newhouse, Harris, Pauly and Reddisch.

A *second* area for research on agency theory has focused on the relationship between patient and physician. This has been the preferred area of study in health microeconomics. Internal markets and behavioural incentives (consumer "tickets" and productivity-related agent remuneration) are examples of this growing area of research. Note, however, that is very difficult, in public health systems, to put much faith in consumer payments whenever supplier-induced demand is present.

In both types of approach, some models seem to exhibit an ex ante rigorous analytical construction no matter how far from reality they are. Alternatively, other models are built on extremely "ad hoc" assumptions and although they derive implications which are closest to reality, they offer very low generalization properties. The natural step in the analysis has been to introduce thereafter, changes in the models aiming to end up by affecting the agent remuneration for a given work-effort. However, they have very often failed to take into account the policy context in which practices take place and which turn out to be decisive.

Finally, a very promising area of research is that on decision analysis in health services. Researchers in this field commonly take an experimental view based on case studies. This microapproach focuses on practice styles and providers' care management. Results may then be related to some observed individual and environmental characteristics – other than financial aspects – such as age, codes of practice, available information and risk spread. Hence, paths for motivating behavioural change can be proposed.

The descriptive nature of these studies – that is, the reference to specific treatment processes and to particular settings where activity takes place – allows us, moreover, to relate some organizational variables to the observed differences, and to test their influence in reality.

In building these models, decision trees may be used. They require the definition of alternative strategic options, the adoption of choice analysis given the associated risks and expected benefits of the options, including outcome and side effects and, finally, the specification of outcomes in terms of patients' health states. Whenever possible, a cost-effective practice may be identified, compared to the actual choices, and further related to organizational characteristics, regulation, environment, access to services, etc., of different systems of health delivery.

Incentive Policies

This book aims to provide a wide view of the state of research on incentives in health systems.

The papers cover the main areas of the topic as defined by the Scientific Committee of the First European Conference on Health Economics, held in Barcelona in September 1989.

At the end of the Conference, more questions than answers arose, as is usual in economics. The main contributions may be summarized as follows. In the first paper, Culyer gives a precise account of the basic questions which arise in studying incentive policies. Thus, Culyer's analysis offers an excellent introduction to the topic. To ask the right questions is a necessary condition for obtaining the correct answers. Research on incentives should be more precise about which "roles" and agents need to be identified and about how they act in the health care sector, if it is to induce action in the appropriate direction.

As Culyer points out, actual patients, citizens as potential users, experts (medical or others), politicians, policy-makers, and society at large have different roles in the health care field. They may be present as advertizers, applicants, diagnosers, priority setters, researchers, treatment assigners and electors. The recognition of this diversity offers different paths for incentive policies according to the target group.

The second and very illuminating paper is the one by Williams on incentives, ethics and clinical freedom, which provides a set of general considerations delving into the core of the issue. In public health systems, economists (the ugly face of incentive policies) and physicians (much nicer!) are at the end of the day in the same front line of battle: There is no such thing as the kingdom of benefits – based on the principles of clinical freedom and ethics – and the kingdom of costs – derived from the economic efficiency criteria. Economists work with the same ethical code as health professionals if they share the same objectives: the health of the population as a whole. This view rules out the conflict, at least in principle. In practice, however, the financial restraint on health activity creates problems of incentive compatibility that need to be faced.

Gerritse and Vrancken explore the theoretical basis for the analysis of providers' behaviour in health care. As the authors point out, the traditional Marshallian approach ignores some relevant aspects of the operation of health care markets. A more productive framework may then be one based on decision theory, which nests demand from the actual behaviour of the provider. In this approach, unequal information, uncertainty, institutional and technical constraints on resource utilization, etc., need to be taken into account if incentive policies are to be implemented. This seems to the authors to be the appropriate context for incentive analysis, and decision analysis would be the appropriate field for experimental research.

Maynard's contribution provides relevant insight into the agent–principal relationship in health care by analysing the contents and purpose of incentive contracts in the reform of the National Health Service. The study of the proposals for reform of the British NHS (the "Working for Patients" Report) offers a review of theory as well as information about the workings of incentive contracts from an analysis based on labour economics. The implications of incentive contracts are derived by developing the traditional economic paradigm and introducing the postulates of bounded rationality and game theory. Social norms are very important in this context. They set the culture of the organizations and, through determination of what is acceptable and unacceptable, legitimate or illegitimate, can provide a decisive contribution to efficiency.

Maynard seems to favour these considerations over others related to the neoclassical theory based on the economics of confrontation, self-love and individual utility maximization. Mutual good may in fact reduce transaction costs and facilitate investment, information exchange and the enhancement of quality. These factors may then be considered for designing alternative incentive contracts in health care.

This view favours the strongest criticism in evaluating the NHS reform. Current aims are mostly based on Adam Smith's beliefs on individuals' self-interest (and not on "the benevolence of the butcher, brewer and baker") rather than on his beliefs on the moral imperatives derived from the sense of duty "correcting the misrepresentation of self-love, concerning what is fit and proper to be done". (I quote from Maynard). Note in any case that both quotations are postulated by A. Smith, the "architect of rationality", providing a rather ambiguous approach to the issue.

Rovira looks at the role of several agents commonly precluded in the "health contract": citizens as consumers of health and the society at large. Rovira's paper focuses mainly on incentives for healthy consumer behaviour and intersectorial measures for health targets.

From a basic microeconomic framework, the author first analyses the effects of three different types of incentives for healthy behaviour: price incentives, information and persuasion. Secondly, proposals from outside the health sector for policy and research on intersectorial actions on consumer behaviour are examined. In the past, this has probably been a Cinderella topic in health economics, despite the fact that it is well recognized that the health of individuals is much affected by the consumption of hazardous goods and by the effects of the behaviour of other social agents, and not only by the consumption of health care. As Rovira points out, a new multidisciplinary approach is needed for further research in this area.

The first part of the book ends with Stoddart's paper on incentives and health system reforms. Coming from Canada as an invited speaker to the Barcelona Conference, Stoddart brings a cold breeze from the North Atlantic by examining the Canadian experience. According to him, incentive policies must not be looked at as a "panacea". Given the nature of the objectives pursued in health systems, we should have moderate expectations about what incentives may achieve. Two particular points are emphasized by Stoddart. First, economists (and non-economists) should keep an open mind concerning the toolbox for incentive policies: "if the hammer is the only tool (as usually happens with financial incentives), it is more probable that problems will tend to be looked at as nails".

Secondly, the paper suggests that the feeling of enjoying "clinical freedom" is very important for physicians: This perception in itself provides an implicit incentive to "live" within the financial constraints. As an unwritten and tacit compromise which influences the clinical practice of Canadian physicians, it seems to have helped, overall, to keep public health expenditure under control. To take not only a financial view of incentives can, in this sense, be an important component in the management of the health system.

The *second part of the volume* is divided into two sections. The first one contains papers dealing with theoretical developments in incentive analysis. The second offers some selected experiences on implementing incentive policies.

Contributions of the first of these sections include those of Neudeck, Risa, Breyer, Van de Ven, Van Dorslaer et al. and finally the paper by Birch and Stoddart.

One of the policies to be analysed from the incentives' perspective is that of rationing health services. Neudeck's paper on quantity rationing in the physician services market analyses the actual workings of the Austrian Social Insurance funds. He studies the paradox that excess supply of physicians and excess demand from patients (waiting lists) appear at the same time in ambulatory care. In the Austrian health system, fees for services, with different payment levels according to the type of services covered, provide the basic structure to the financial relationship between users and physicians. In this context, Neudeck's analysis offers an interpretation of the economic nature of some forms of quantity rationing. His view is that the coexistence of overworked physicians and unemployed physicians who are willing to work, together with price rationing for users, is optimal. By rationing the supply of contracts, the positive relationship between fees and quality of services is enhanced. According to Neudeck, this result cannot be taken as a proof to support charges on health services. It provides, however, an explanation of the persistence of the Austrian rationing system in the primary care market. The neutralization of the unwanted effects of the fee-for-service structure may still need to be considered.

The public-private debate is next in the analysis. Risa provides a theoretical view of the effects of the coexistence or private and public health care. The paper focuses on the impact of public policies for health care on the individual agents' demand for private care. From the analysis he derives the observation that the total resources allocated to health care seem to be larger in mixed systems (public/private) than in exclusively public or private ones.

This result is derived from the standard model on moral hazard, in which individual agents maximize the expected utility of health treatments in the context of a not fully known medical technology. In this framework, the supply of public health services generates a positive income effect on individual health demand. Consequently, the income effect increases the total resources spent on health care whenever individuals can freely demand private health services. The empirical evidence from the countries of the Organization for Economic Cooperation and Development (OECD) according to the author, cannot prove the case fully , since several forms of rationing are present in the market for private health services. The data seem to offer support to this observation.

Breyer's paper is the first of three which study the effects of social health insurance systems on incentives. A theoretical insight on the distributional effects of defining alternative coinsurance options is provided.

In contrast to the traditional assumption that the provision of copayment mechanisms destroys the solidarity transfers which are implicit in the rating of community health insurance contributions from low-risk to high-risk members, Breyer's paper shows that this is not necessarily the case under certain conditions. In fact, it is possible to design copayment options in health insurance systems in order to increase welfare in Paretian terms even for those who remain in the standard plan.

In obtaining this result, one must be careful to consider perfect risk separation through the choice of sickness funds (that is, all funds should be obliged to offer supplementary plans at fair premiums). For this purposes, one must take account of the programmes offered by the sickness funds and the potential discrimination among the subset of those demanding the supplementary coverage. If no separation of risks occurs and zero administrative costs are present, it is no longer valid – as Breyer points out – to assert that optional copayment in social health insurance systems necessarily results in making high-risk individuals worse off. This is an interesting result which deserves, perhaps, more attention from a policymaking point of view.

The reform of health insurance systems in a more systematic approach is first analysed by Van de Ven and then by Van Dorslaer and their colleagues. The reform under study in both papers is that of the Dekker Commission for the Dutch Health Insurance system. Van de Ven presents a detailed analysis of the incentives policy behind the "Willingness to Change" report of the Netherlands. Two major issues in this proposal are: (1) the introduction of a (basic) health insurance programme on a nationwide scale, and (2) the regulation of "competitive tendering" between insurers and providers. Health insurance incentives for consumers, as well as for providers, are at the heart of the reform. Van de Ven's analysis puts forward some caveats about the successful implementation of the reform. Mainly, doubts remain about how to develop the right formula for budgeting the insurers, how to abolish all the existing differences between sickness fund insurance and private health insurance, and how to develop and enforce an effective anticartel policy in health care. If these problems are not properly addressed, more competition between insurers than between providers is likely to result. The final result of the efficiency-improving measures contained in the reform proposals is then, overall, unknown, as are the side effects of cartel policies on consumer information and the preferred risk selection which may be produced.

The "Changes Assured" report for the Netherlands opens, therefore, an interesting field for experimentation. Van Dorslaer and colleagues analyse the reform from the equity point of view. For this purpose, their paper reviews first different measures of vertical equity (Kakwani's Reynolds' and Smolensky's, Suits' and Pfähler's progressivity indices) and applies them to the changes contained in the Dutch reform. Different policy scenarios are previewed for this purpose in a forecasting exercise which is not free from problems, as the authors recognize. According to the results, the effects in terms of the values of the progressivity indices, seem in fact to be extremely sensitive to the assumptions made. However, the authors emphasize the convenience of including the analysis of the equity implications of the reform in policy discussions. The search for efficiency may have a cost in terms of equity which needs to be considered.

Birch and Stoddart, from McMaster University, focus on consumer behaviour. Their analysis explores a standard economic model of consumer behaviour from which the optimal level of individual participation in health-related activities is derived. The paper deals, in this sense, with the individual consumer's behaviour and the impact of alternative lifestyle patterns on future health and, consequently, on the individual well-being. The authors strongly emphasize the need for understanding the health-related behaviour of the "victims" of poor health, so that the appropriate health policies can be implemented. They strongly oppose blaming individuals for not responding to the opportunities to behave in other more healthy ways. Thus, if inequalities in health are to be reduced, according to the authors, policy makers need to look for the individual behavioural change within the best-interest framework of the individuals concerned. This is a more realistic approach than adopting a paternalistic "outsider" view, assuming irrational individual behaviour. Policies aimed at changing the population's health status should then first consider what the implications of the changes are for individual utility.

The second section of the second part describes some experiments on the design of health system incentives.

The first study analyses the impact of drug price information on physicians' cost-consciousness. De Graeve and Carrin refer to the results of improving drug information in the prescription practices of a large sample of Belgian general practitioners. The analysis focuses on four patient categories: patients with high blood pressure, patients with acute sleeping disorder, patients with throat infection and patients with a heart complaint.

In addition, the relative importance of criteria used by physicians in prescribing is analysed. These criteria include information on effectiveness, contraindications and undesired effects, methods of administration, the reputation of the pharmaceutical company, and price and reimbursement categories.

The relative importance attached to each of these criteria in the actual costs of prescription practices are correlated to the characteristics of the general practitioners: age, workload (number of consultations per week) and time spent on scientific work, courses, and reading scientific journals containing drug information.

The results are not always the ones expected. Moreover, regression analysis hardly explains the high dispersion observed in the prescription costs for these patient categories. The authors strongly emphasize the important variability in the behavioural patterns observed and their importance in terms of the related costs of prescription practices.

Pekurinen, Vohlonen and Sintonén report the main results of the economic evaluation of the "Personal Doctor Programme" in Finland. This is a large demonstration project which aims to restructure primary care by general practitioners (GP) within publicly operated health centres. The goal of the programme is defined as the achievement of the clinical advantages and performance incentives resulting from enrolling each citizen on a specific GP's list, but within the broader responsibility of a team-based community health centre. The Finnish demonstration project experiments with the incentives derived from the organizational change (consisting of setting practices in health centres) and from the financial remuneration systems by substituting public salaried physicians for private GPs. Pekurinen and his colleagues conclude that having adjusted for an equivalently structured reimbursement framework, the "personal doctor approach" of the project seems to offer higher quality primary medical care at lower cost.

Primary care is also the subject of Rochaix's contribution, which presents an analysis from the theoretical and applied viewpoint of the Quebec experiment in ambulatory care.

This experiment consists of a policy which combines price and quantity regulations. Under the responsibility of the Quebec provincial authority, fees are negotiated between the sickness fund and representatives of the medical profession. Since 1976, a global cap has been placed on total GP expenditure. Consequently, an average income per physician is negotiated and the global fee increase necessary to achieve this income is then worked out. If the resulting global amount earmarked for GP services is surpassed, a collective sanction at the end of the period is adopted in the form of a reduction of the global rates of fee increases in the next period.

In order to avoid, in part, the adverse effects of high activity rates of some GPs on the rest of the GPs, their representatives have adopted an income ceiling which entails a reduction of 75% of the fee paid for any service provided over and above the initially stated benchmark. This represents, in fact, an individual cap on the overall quantity of services provided per physician. Rochaix then analyses the resulting joint price and quantity regulatory strategy with a formal model of the utilization of the physician services, and applies the model to the data of the Quebec sickness fund.

Incentives in hospital health care are covered by Casas and Spagnolo, who describe a hospital reimbursement experiment in Spain. They analyse the incentives and equity effects using different alternatives for hospital financing. Four models of hospital reimbursement are tested for this purpose. The first is based on the payment of a fee per day of stay with a single tariff for all the hospitals. The second one (the one actually applied to reimburse private and non-profit hospitals in the public health system for Catalonia) consists of a payment per hospital day too, but with tariffs differentiated according to hospital complexity levels. Hospital reimbursement results here from the joint determination of a maximum value for hospital's average length of stay and a maximum index of activity (defined as basic units of care) per year, these being specified in terms of equivalent days of hospitalization. The third and fourth models are based on a payment "per patient". In one case, patients are classified according to diagnosis-related groups, DRGs, defined by similar average length of stays for the five hospitals included in the experiment. In the other case, DRGs are weighted by actual US Medicare costs.

The simulation of these models allows for the testing of the differences in resource distribution with respect to case mix definition. Casas and Spagnolo conclude that systems of payment per day favour hospitals with a more complex case mix. The differences introduced by current tariffs, supposedly related to hospital complexity, are much greater than those due to the actual patient categories in reality. The authors conclude, then, that the budgetary systems applied in Catalonia introduce incentives for adverse selection of simpler pathologies by paying relatively lower fees for them.

Finally, the issue of intersectorial measures for health targets is treated by Schneider from the French Research Centre for Nuclear Risk Assessment and

Management and Francis Fagnani of the French National Institute of Health and Medical Research. The authors' contribution focuses on the influence of the financial allocation of responsibility for occupational injuries and diseases and on the consequences of breaking the direct relationship between the costs of prevention and compensation in work-related injuries. The study deals, particularly, with the problem of achieving compatibility between employers' objectives (essentially, the economic profitability of the firm) and social objectives concerning health policy and the acceptable level of safety. The case study applies to work-related injuries in France, where the imbalance, after the 1970s, in the financing of the system has disrupted the incentives for firms to adopt safety measures. This has created a situation in which the safety level does not equalize anymore the marginal cost of prevention to the marginal benefit expected from the decrease in compensated risks. The authors then explore the financial policies of risk insurance using various approaches (mutualization and capitalization) to calculate the employer's rate in order to determine the optimal safety incentive mechanism.

Part I
Policy Issues

Incentives: For What? For Whom? What Kind?

A.J. Culyer

In trying to set an agenda I have interpreted my brief as one entailing more the asking than the answering of questions. I shall therefore endeavour to suppress my own strong feelings as to what the answers ought to be, though I dare say I shall be less than fully successfull in the attempt.

The discussion is divided into three major sections, each corresponding to a broad issue that needs to be settled before the detailed consequential questions can be properly addressed: what purposes are to be served by incentives? whose behaviour is to be targeted? and what types of incentives should we be considering?

Incentives: For What?

Where you stand on questions of incentives depends on where you sit. There is more than one perspective. Thus, taking the converse side to the politician's perspective, which often emphasises public expenditure restraint, from the other side of the national income accounts this looks like *income* restraint. Whatever the ultimate purpose or purposes, therefore, of any changes in a system's incentive structure, the possibility of making such changes can be made or broken on grounds of the financial interests of major income- or rent-receiving politically organised groups (dressed up, though these interests will typically be, in the sheep's clothing of patients' welfare).

Less parochial views on perspective abound, however, and it is important to identify which of these other various possible contexts may be in the minds of those seeking change. Two broad alternatives are the idealised rival perspectives investigated in Culyer, Maynard and Williams (1981). The first (viewpoint A) considers access to health care to be essentially similar to access to all the other good things in society (such as food, shelter and leisure pursuits) which are purchased in markets out of personal incomes and which themselves form part of society's reward/penalty system. The second (viewpoint B) regards access to health care as a citizen's right, like access to the ballot box or courts of justice, which should not depend mainly (or even at all) on an individual's income and wealth. Such goods are sometimes referred to as primary goods (e.g. Tobin 1970) or merit goods (Musgrave 1959).

The view taken of the appropriateness of various incentive structures will clearly be highly conditional on whether one espouses viewpoint A or B. If A, then the standard interpretational framework of individualistic neoclassical welfare economics seems appropriate. A conventional, Paretian, view of the social welfare function conditions the concept of "efficiency" and hence the evaluation of the contractual relationships that ought to exist between economic agents, the appropriate reward/penalty framework that conditions their behaviour, and the impediments to efficiency (such as market failures) that require remedial action. If B, then an alternative, perhaps non-welfarist, interpretation of social welfare becomes appropriate (e.g. Sen 1979; Culyer 1989a). The objective function may be interpreted to be, say, the maximisation of "health", somehow defined (Culyer 1989b), and the appropriate reward/penalty structure is evaluated by reference to this maximand. Likewise, the concept of "efficiency" becomes redefined and a different view is likely to be taken of the sorts of contractual relationship that ought to exist between economic agents and the impediments (other kinds of market failure) that require remedial action.

There are therefore (at least) two views of efficiency. But whichever view you take, the evaluation of different incentive structures will depend also on the degree to which the pursuit of efficiency is to be constrained by equity (or the pursuit of equity by efficiency). Under standard welfarism, this takes one into issues of first, second and third best welfare theory (e.g. Ng 1983). Under (say) health (rather than welfare) maximisation the possibility arises that greater equality of access to health care is itself a necessary condition for efficiency because of the well-known theoretical (post Grossman 1972) and empirical negative association between income and health status (Culyer 1988). Equity, like efficiency, is however no unambiguous notion. Equality of access (for equal need) is but one. Mooney (1986) offers six others: equality of expenditure per head, inputs per head, inputs for equal need, utilisation for equal need, marginal net need, and health itself. Each of these is likely to imply a different assessment of the appropriateness of incentives, and several raise other important issues (such as the definition of "need") to which it is possible to give more than one answer (such as depth of suffering, ability to benefit, expected value-of-health-added).

What I am therefore suggesting is that there is a considerable thicket of fundamental conceptual issues raised by a forest of possible "view-points" which need to be hacked through before attempting any appraisal of incentive structures. The differences between commentators are likely to be as much the product of differences of viewpoint and differences in claimed general objectives for the health care system as they are the product of an a priori or empirical assessment of the predicted behavioural and resource allocation consequences of different incentive structures. If commentators do not themselves "come clean" on the former set of issues, their viewpoints need to be inferred as best one may. This is necessary because the answer to the question "how efficient or equitable is the incentive structure of one system (or changes in it) according to that system's pretensions?" is quite different from the question "how efficient or equitable is the incentive structure of one system (or changes in it) according to *another* system's pretensions?" (Culyer et al. 1981). To demonstrate that the incentives embodied in one system worked against its own ostensible values would be a devastating criticism (provided that alternative incentives were available that worked *for* its ostensible values). To demonstrate that the incentives embodied in one system worked against the values embodied in *another* system is far less impressive – and particularly so if they worked rather well in pursuit of the values of the system in which they *were* embodied.

Incentives: For Whom?

It is natural, in addressing questions to do with targeting incentives, to categorise the key actors in the health care system and then discuss the positive and normative implications of both specific incentives and those provided by the general property rights framework, in terms of their impact on the key actors, preferably in a general equilibrium framework that would encompass interactions between the actors. Obvious candidates include: people generally, patients (viz. those who have lost "people" status), physicians (perhaps further subcategorised as primary care or hospital care physicians), other health care professionals who are allied to medicine, other health service workers, health service managers, supply industry firms and politicians.

Given the still undeveloped state of economic theories of organisations in the health care industry, the positive analysis of incentives must, at the theoretical level, depend heavily on the fundamental law of demand that emerges from the theory of constrained utility maximisation: the idea that compensated demand curves have a negative slope. In my judgement this is much less of a handicap than may at first appear. After all, every choice is a constrained choice and all compensated demand curves do have a negative slope. In the analysis of predicted behavioural responses to changes in penalty/reward structures, the essential key that unlocks the analysis is the identification of the way in which an incentive or disincentive changes the relevant constraint. Once this can be done, the qualitative analysis of the impact of a change in the relative "price" attached to each postulated argument in the utility function may go ahead. To this will need to be added the imaginative skills necessary to identify the likely knock-on and feedback effects in an interdependent system and the empirical skills needed to estimate the quantitative size of the theoretical predictions. Indeed, to have done all this is effectively to have created an appropriate model of the relevant "institution". But doing it explicitly is much to be preferred than doing it implicitly, partly because greater explicitness brings with it greater rigour, partly because greater explicitness brings with it the possibility of identifying reasons why theoretical predictions are not empirically sustained, and partly because the explicit demonstration that an explicit analysis of a particular incentive or system of incentives is or is not consistent with the central core of behavioural economic theory is inherently to be encouraged, at least by those of us who are scientifically committed to that central core as our *Econ Modl* (Leijonhufvud 1981).

This task is much harder when one is addressing general systemic changes, of the sort that may be well characterised by the British government's proposals for "provider markets" within the publicly financed National Health Service, or by wholesale shifts from fee-for-service to capitation methods of physician remuneration, than by changes to small bits of the system that leave its "constitution" intact (for example, changing the fee schedule within a fee-for-service system, or the capitation rate with a capitation system). There seems to be much to be said for formal experimentation on a limited scale (limited, for example, by geography) in connection with major systemic changes where the theoretical underpinning, especially with regard to its general equilibrium characteristics, is usually much weaker and the downside welfare consequences of systemic "mistakes" are potentially catastrophic. However, this consideration needs to be tempered by difficulties to be discussed later.

A linguistic subtlety is to be noted here. The use of a utility-maximising behaviour-generating modelling approach in positive economics is quite consistent with the rejection of individual utilities in normative economics. (Positive) utility theory is of great potential use even to non-welfarists like the health-maximisers (e.g. Williams 1988) and even though (a further subtlety this) operational non-welfarist measures of health are often termed "utility measures" by their developers (e.g. Torrance 1986).

It is an irony that the greatest amount of intellectual effort and empirical estimation into incentives has taken place at the level where it is arguably least important: consumer responses to user-charges and copayments: least important in the sense that, from an expenditure control point of view, the low elasticities typically found do not suggest that disincentives for first-contacts or subsequent utilisation are major instruments in the battle for cost-containment. They are, of course, important in the sense that any disincentives operating at this point may have important consequences in the shape of rising quantities of undetected and untreated disease, and for equity. In particular, incentive (or rather disincentive) systems that effectively deny access to care to large segments of the population because of inability to afford insurance, adverse selection or loss of employment status are likely to be both highly inefficient and highly inequitable.

Behavioural responses by other targeted groups as their constraints change have been far less carefully analysed and measured: that of physicians in respect of changes in preset budgets, or changes in fee schedules, or changes from fee-for-service to capitation or salary (though much of the literature on health-maintenance organisations has a bearing on the latter); that of managers in respect of: changes in their accountability and authority over physicians, introduction of performance review and performance-related pay, changes from being "administrators" to enterprise managers (an exception here is the now well-developed research programme into the effects of prospective reimbursement systems such as diagnosis-related groups in United States hospitals); that of supply industries in response to the exercise of monopsony purchasing arrangements and other regulatory measures; that of politicians and central service managers and planners at the highest level to changes in their functions and public opinion. Indeed, this latter crucial group is almost entirely an empty box from the research point of view. Since a great many of these responses can be expected to be "culturally" conditioned there is also a great need for more country-specific studies rather than placing reliance on the exportability of (usually) United States results.

Incentives: What Kind?

It is extremely partial (not to say crass) to focus attention only on financial incentives in health care systems. One of the reasons why many economists are opposed to fee-for-service systems of remuneration is because of a belief that they contaminate the working of a fully professional relationship between the agent, the patient and the insurance system. Independently of where one stands (or sits) on the Supplier-Induced-Demand debate, the idea that adequate professional rewards which are independent of workload enable freer and more effective rein to be given to the exercise of professional judgement should not be dismissed on either a priori or empirical grounds as fanciful. There has been far too little analysis of the ways in which changes in a professional's professional environment can provide effective incentives for professional behaviour to serve more efficiently the objectives set for the system. Such factors include peer review, promotion prospects, practice style (for example frequency of surgical practice), in-service training opportunities and professional recognition for professional excellence. All of these are much talked about but where is the theory, and what is the evidence?

There has likewise been far too little good analysis on the effect that information may have on behaviour. In some areas, it seems as though the mere provision of information has little effect. For example, United Kingdom studies of the effect of cost information to hospital doctors seems to have had small impact (if any) on medical decision-making and the demand for (e.g.) diagnostic workups (Wickings et al. 1985). In the political arena, however, it seems that at least in one case some well-documented information (McLachlan and Maynard 1982) directly affected the outcome of political debate (the book itself was debated in the United Kingdom House of Lords) and effectively saw off an incipient political movement for the introduction of health insurance in the United Kingdom.

A grossly under-researched area (at least by economists) concerns the effect of health education on the behaviour of individuals (especially people and patients). Although consumption of addictive substances (especially tobacco products) has been fairly well analysed, reliable information of the effects of, say, information about healthy diets on the demand for health care and on the health of populations is vanishingly thin, despite the tremendous passions these consumer effects arouse (perhaps, however, such passions are chiefly to be found in areas where evidence is weakest, where faith may generally be expected to be substituted for knowledge).

Closely related to the questions involving choice of type of incentive is the question of motivation. After all, incentives operate on the arguments of utility functions whose contents, whether positively or negatively signed, are the motives in economic theories of behaviour. In health economics this has probably been most fully discussed in the context of supplier behaviour and, in particular, with respect to for-profit and non-profit hospitals, both of which are to be found in the private sector but typically only the latter exist in the public sector. A common expectation has been that for-profit behaviour is to be expected under conditions of competition in the product and capital markets. In the limit, the price of non-profit related arguments in managerial utility functions is driven to infinity (e.g. Alchian and Kessel 1962) so that surviving utility-maximising management is driven to profit-maximising, the latter thus becoming a special case of the former. Here, then, is an example of how incentives can affect the ostensible motivation of individuals. Associated with this line of argument has been the idea that non-profit hospitals, like other non-profit firms, will tend towards X-inefficiency (e.g. Clarkson 1972; Frech and Ginsburg 1981). However, the empirical data are extremely hard to interpret (not least because of failure to control for case-mix and case-complexity in unit cost comparisons) and Stoddart and Labelle (1985) were able to conclude in their review that the evidence did not substantiate (indeed it refuted) claims that privately owned for-profit hospitals operated more efficiently than did non-profit hospitals. Whether this is because the theory is wrong, or the circumstances under which its predictions are generated (viz. competition in capital and product markets) did not apply, is impossible to say. If the latter types of competition were grievously absent, the theory cannot of course be held to have been tested at all.

The United Kingdom provides an interesting case study in the shape of the forthcoming introduction via provider (or internal markets) of a major systemic change in the pattern of incentives, whose purpose is precisely to promote efficiency within a cash-limited and largely egalitarian system, on the grounds of a generalised belief in the beneficial effects of competition and contestability in markets and on the sophisticated (but implicit) idea that the system *need not choose* between for-profit and non-profit, or private and public hospitals; rather it need provide only the right environment in which the successful can thrive (whatever their motivation and ownership) and the unsuccessful will be driven out by economic natural selection and evolution (Alchian 1950). Whether the inefficient would ever be permitted really to go out of business under the new supply-side competition in the National Health Service is of course much to be doubted. The changes to occur will place hospitals in a position of dependence on revenue earned from the successful winning of service contracts from client health authorities and capital borrowed from the state or on the open market. As remarked above, this sort of systemic change seems to be a likely candidate for experiment prior to wholesale implementation. But this view has not found favour with the British government, which is determined to proceed with the proposal without formal experimentation. One reason for this may be a political judgement that experimentation can too readily serve as the instrument of those who oppose change and can sufficiently prolong a final verdict well beyond the expected political life of the Administration. Another reason, more problematic for the research community, lies in the difficulty of controlling such massive experiments sufficiently so that reasonable inferences can be drawn about the effects of the changes they embody (and their ultimate desirability) independently of any other changes that will inevitably be taking place within the experimental group and within its comparators. It is certainly true that those in the United Kingdom who advocated such experiments (e.g. Institute of Health Services Management 1988) gave little attention to these difficult questions of research design.

In the end, however, I have little doubt that the major focus will be on financial incentives as the chief engine for promoting efficiency (of whatever kind) and equity (of whatever kind) if only because of the ready fashion in which they can be incorporated into extant behavioural models and because they lend themselves to ready quantification for econometric purposes. These are reasons of convenience rather than substance, though I would not wish anyone to infer that I believe that financial incentives are of inherently second-order importance. The truth is that I do not know how significant they are (at the margin) relative to incentives that operate outside or at one remove from direct financial incentives.

Conclusions

I shall set out my conclusions as a set of ten short questions:

1. To what extent do the criteria used to evaluate the desirability of the particular incentives or systems of reward/penalty under consideration depend on what you are trying to accomplish?
2. Do the incentives under consideration promote efficiency and equity, and how contingent is the effectiveness of these incentives on a particular view of what it is to be efficient or equitable?
3. To what extent do changes in the behaviour of one group of actors in the system affect the behaviour, health and welfare of others?
4. Do patients have to bear the brunt of incentives designed to control costs?
5. Must the absence of widely accepted institutional models of medical "firms" deter us from applying the compensated demand theorem?
6. May one use utility theory as a behaviour predicting theoretical tool while rejecting its normative interpretation in the evaluation of the effects of incentives?
7. While the behaviour of patients in response to user charges and copayments, and that of hospitals and hospital physicians to prospective payment systems, has been extensively studied, is it true that many incentives for many actors in the system are still largely unresearched?
8. May the incentives effects found in one culture over one period transfer to other cultures or other periods?
9. Are non-financial incentives potentially at least as important as financial ones?
10. Should empirical experimentation necessarily always precede policy implementation?

References

Alchian AA (1950) Uncertainty, evolution and economic theory. J Polit Econ 58:211–221
Alchian AA, Kessel R (1962) Competition, monopoly and the pursuit of money. In: aspects of labor economics. Princeton University Press, Princeton, pp 157–175
Clarkson KW (1972) Some implications of property rights in hospital management. J Law Econ 15:363–384
Culyer AJ (1988) Inequality of health services is, in general, desirable. In: Green D (ed) Acceptable inequalities? Institution of Economic Affairs, London, pp 33–47.
Culyer AJ (1989a) The normative economics of health care finance and provision. Oxford Rev Econ Policy 5:34–58
Culyer AJ (1989b) Commodities, characteristics of commodities, characteristics of people, utilities and the quantity of life. In Baldwin S, Godfrey C, Propper C (eds) The quality of life: perspectives and policies. Rout ledge, London, pp 9–27
Culyer AJ, Maynard AK, Williams A (1981) Alternative systems of health care provision: an essay on motes and beams. In: Olson M (ed) A new approach to the economics of health care. American Enterprise for Public Policy Research, Washington, pp 131–150
Frech HE, Ginsburg PB (1981) The cost of nursing home care in the United States: government financing, ownership and efficiency. In Van der GAAG J, Perlman M (eds) Health, economics and health economics. North-Holland, Amsterdam, pp 67–81
Grossman M (1972) The demand for health: a theoretical and empirical investigation. Columbia University Press, New York
Institute of Health Services Management (1988) Working party on alternative delivery and funding of health services: final report. IHSM, London
Leijonhufvud A (1981) Schools, "revolutions" and research programmes in economic theory. In: Information and co-ordination: essays in macroeconomic theory. Oxford University Press, Oxford
McLachlan G, Maynard AK (1982) The public private mix for health: the relevance and effects of change. Nuffield Provincial Hospitals Trust, London
Mooney GH (1986) Economics, medicine and health care. Harvester, Brighton
Musgrave RA (1959) The Theory of Public Finance. McGrawHill, New York, pp 9–14
Ng Y-K (1983) Welfare economics: introduction and development of basic concepts. Macmillan, London
Sen AK (1979) Personal utilities and public judgements: or what's wrong with welfare economics. Econ J 89:537–558
Stoddart GL, Labelle RJ (1985) Privatization in the Canadian health care system. Ministry of Supply and Services, Ottawa
Tobin J (1970) On limiting the domain of inequality. J Law Econ 13:447–463
Torrance GW (1986) Measurement of health state utilities for economic appraisal: a review. J Health Econ 5:1–30
Wickings ID, Childs T, Coles J, Wheatcroft C (1985) Experiments using PACTS in Southern and Oldham HAs: a final report to the DHSS. King Edwards Hospital Fund, London
Williams A (1988) Ethics and efficiency in the provision of health care. In: Bell M, Mendus S (eds) Philosophy and medical welfare. Cambridge University Press, Cambridge

Incentives, Ethics and Clinical Freedom

A. Williams

I wish to begin my contribution with a parable which although drawn from the Bible (St. Matthew, Chap. 22, verses 15–21), was not there presented as a parable, but as straight narrative.

> Then the Pharisees went and took counsel how to entangle him in his talk. And they sent their disciples to him, along with the Herodians, saying, "Teacher, we know that you are true, and teach the way of God truthfully, and care for no man; for you do not regard the position of men. Tell us then, what you think. Is it lawful to pay taxes to Caesar, or not?' But Jesus, aware of their malice, said 'Why put me to the test you hypocrites? Show me the money for the tax'. And they brought him a coin. And Jesus said to them, 'Whose likeness and inscription is this?' They said, 'Caesar's'. Then he said to them, 'Render therefore to Caesar the things that are Caesar's, and to God the things that are God's'.

I do not wish to pursue too strongly the analogy between the people in that biblical episode and the present situation facing the medical profession in Europe, but do want to emphasise the long-standing tensions between what doctors feel they owe to God (i.e. to their consciences) and what they owe to Caesar (i.e. to those who provide the money both to pay their salaries and to provide the facilities they need in order to practise medicine).

The conscience of the medical profession has been formalised in a code of ethics, of which a clear and succinct summary has recently been provided by the Stanford University Medical Center Committee on Ethics in the *New England Journal of Medicine* (1988). They identify six distinct principles, as follows:

> A basic principle of medical ethics is obviously the preservation of life, which is frequently tempered by the second principle, the alleviation of suffering. A third is the injunction that physicians 'first do no harm ...'. A fourth principle [is] respect for the autonomy of the individual patient .... A fifth fundamental principle is the concept of justice, exemplified by the effort to ensure that medical resources are allocated fairly. The final principle is truth-telling .... Because medical practice often brings these principles into conflict, resolving such conflicts is central to the art of medicine.

Resolving these conflicts is indeed no easy matter, because it is rarely that a course of action will enable a medical practitioner simultaneously to (a) preserve life, (b) alleviate suffering, (c) do no harm, (d) respect the autonomy of the patient *and* (e) tell the truth. Usually it is possible to ease the latent conflict by regarding each injunction as operating "on balance" or "within reason". Alternatively one might interpret the injunction to "do no harm" as *not* excluding a course of action just because it carried some *risk* of doing harm, since some such risks (but not all) are to be regarded as "acceptable". Likewise, respect for the autonomy of the patient may be limited by the consideration that the patient is too upset to know where his or her true interests lie. And telling the truth does not mean telling the whole truth, but only so much of it as is thought best for the patient [so as not to cause unnecessary suffering, say, following injunction (b)]. These principles have come to be so well internalised in professional thinking that they become seen as the dictates of conscience. But because the principles are all *relative*, equally conscientious doctors may on occasion disagree about their precise bearing on a particular decision or action.

Lately, however, a further principle has been added to the list, namely: (f) deal fairly with patients. Unlike the others, this is a principle of distributive justice, not only simply guiding ethical behaviour by a powerful professional adviser when confronted with a trusting and vulnerable patient. It adds five more potential sources of conflict (one with each of the previous five), but ones with which the profession is as yet relatively unfamiliar, at least in the rather formal guise in which these conflicts currently manifest themselves. Medical practice has always recognised that there were limits to what might be done for one particular person, especially if that limit was due to sheer lack of scientific knowledge, or lack of time to mobilise the necessary resources, or, in a fee-paying system, if the patient or his family could not afford to pay for any more treatment. Only in dire emergency was it acceptable to adopt a triage system designed to concentrate the limited resources where they would do the most good.

But the enormous advances in medical practice over recent decades have now outgrown our capacity to generate the extra real resources needed to support them, so we are in the fortunate, yet painful, situation of having at our disposal more beneficial activities than we can afford. This is the reason why health economics is coming to play a more influential role in health care policy at all levels, and why the recommendations of health economists are seen by some doctors *both* as unethical *and* as a threat to their clinical freedom. Let me deal with each of these (related) concerns in turn.

First of all, on the ethical issues, health economics operates within exactly the same code of ethics as medicine. We too are seeking to preserve life and to alleviate suffering, to minimise the risk of harm, to respect the wishes of patients, to tell the truth, and to ensure that the provision of health care is equitable and just. Resolving the possible conflicts between these principles is just as central to the art of *health service management* as it is to *medical practice*, and health economists have concentrated a lot of attention on *measuring* the consequent "trade-offs" between them as a practical contribution to that conflict resolution. How is it then that some doctors still imagine that clinicians and economists are in irrevocably opposed roles?

Consider for example the views of an American MD published in the *New England Journal of Medicine* in 1980. He wrote:

> Of late an increasing number of papers in this and other journals have been concerned with 'cost-effectiveness' of diagnostic and therapeutic procedures. Inherent in these articles is the view that choices will be predicated not only on the basis of strictly clinical considerations but also on economic considerations as they may affect the patient, the hospital, and society. It is my contention that such considerations are not germane to ethical medical practise . . . A physician who changes his or her way of practising medicine because of cost rather than purely medical considerations has indeed embarked on the 'slippery slope' of compromised ethics and waffled priorities.

The sharpest expression on this alleged conflict is to be found in the contrast between the following two propositions:

Viewpoint A. It is the doctor's duty to do all he or she can for the patient no matter what the cost.

Viewpoint B. It is the doctor's duty to take costs into account when deciding what course of action to recommend for the patient.

The key to resolving this conflict is to recognise that "costs" mean "sacrifices borne by other people". In the context of health care systems with (unavoidably) limited resources, the *explicit* decision to devote resources to one patient is inevitably an *implicit* decision to deny them to somebody else. Having a "clinical policy" is one way of formulating such priorities, referral practices are another, waiting lists, fee schedules, and even appointment systems and the opening times of clinics are yet others. But the essential point which needs to be recognised in the context of a debate about the *ethics* of counting costs, and of letting costs influence priorities, is that these costs represent sacrifices of health which are suffered by other people. To ignore costs is to ignore the risks to others of premature mortality and avoidable suffering. Not to care about the health of anyone other than the person in front of you is hardly an ethical position, and it is in direct conflict with the ethical injunction to deal fairly with patients. People who act regardless of costs are usually termed "fanatical", *not* ethical, and fanaticism is just as dangerous in medicine as it is in other walks of life. Thus I would argue that it is those who *refuse* to allow costs to influence their actions who are behaving unethically. Ethical medical practice requires a balancing of the interests of different patients (or potential patients) and this means counting the costs of each and every decision that is made. Because not all beneficial things can be done, it is necessary to restrain the humanitarian impulse to do everything that is *possible* for the person in front of you, because unless yo do show that self-discipline, some greater good which might have been done to someone else will be denied that other person. And in making that excruciatingly difficult judgement, and putting it into practice, the medical profession is being called upon to reflect the (admittedly) very poorly articulated notions of justice or fairness held in the community they serve.

So let me turn next to the related theme of clinical freedom. I will start with the views of an eminent British Professor of Cardiology. John Hampton, as published in the *British Medical Journal* (Hampton 1983):

> Clinical freedom is dead, and no one need regret its passing. Clinical freedom was the right – some seemed to believe the divine right – of doctors to do whatever in their opinion was best for their patients. In the days when investigation was non-existent and treatment as harmless as it was ineffective the doctor's opinion was all that there was, but now opinion is not good enough. If we do not have the resources to do all that is technically possible then medical care must be limited to what is of proved value, and the medical profession will have to set opinion aside.
>
> Clinical freedom dies accidentally, crushed between the rising cost of new forms of investigation and treatment and the financial limits inevitable in an economy that cannot expand indefinitely. Clinical freedom should, however, have been strangled long ago, for at best it was a cloak for ignorance and at worst an excuse for quackery. Clinical freedom was a myth that prevented true advance. We must welcome its demise, and seize the opportunities now laid out before us.

As I have myself observed in a rather long disquisition on this subject published in the *British Medical Journal* last year (Williams 1988), I think Hampton's rather unkind obituary notice for clinical freedom was in fact premature, for if indeed clinical freedom is dead it seems reluctant to lie down. It is still frequently paraded before us (rather as with the corpse of El Cid?) in defence of some medical practice which is being challenged by a non-medical person on grounds of its doubtful effectiveness, or its undoubtedly high cost, or both.

The essence of the problem here seems to be the belief that asking doctors to have regard to costs will destroy the doctor-patient relationship, which in turn is based on the belief that doctors have always exercised their clinical freedom in such a way that *only* the interests of the patient are taken into account. This is formalised in the view that the doctor is in a principal-agent relationship with the patient, in which the patient is the principal, and the doctor is the agent. For the doctor to be a *perfect* agent their relationship would have to be as follows:

> The doctor is there to give the patient all the information the patient needs in order that the patient can make a decision, and the doctor should then implement that decision once the patient has made it.

If you find that description of the relationship a bit odd, try reversing the respective roles of the doctor and the patient so that it now reads:

> The patient is there to give the doctor all the information the doctor needs in order that the doctor can make a decision, and the patient should then implement that decision once the doctor has made it.

Does that sound more like it actually is? The point is that doctors are not perfect agents, and because of that they have quite a lot of discretion over what they take into account in exercising their so called "clinical" judgement, so that the distinction between "strictly clinical" and "extraneous" factors is a fuzzy one. They will frequently take into account the competing demands on their own time when deciding how much of it to spend with one patient or another, or how much of it to spend on the practise of proven therapy as opposed to the conduct of research, or on training the next generation of doctors, or on going to conferences to improve their own future skill and knowledge. They will frequently be influenced in their clinical decisions by the availability of hospital beds and operating theatre time, and by their good or bad relationships with those colleagues to whom they might refer patients. They will be influenced by the impact of a patient's condition, or its treatment, upon the general welfare of the patient (e.g. in terms of ability to work, or the fact that there are young dependent children to be thought about). All of these are "extraneous" social or economic considerations, not strictly *clinical* considerations. And I do not think that anyone would regard it as at all unreasonable, or indeed unethical, that such "extraneous" considerations were taken into account, so I am not criticising doctors for doing so. I am merely observing that they *do* do so, and hence have *not* used their clinical freedom in the very narrow way some of them claim.

This was explicitly recognised in a recent monograph on *Clinical Freedom* by Professor Raymond Hoffenberg, Immediate Past-President of the (British) Royal College of Physicians. In his view (Hoffenberg 1987, pp. ix, x, 13, 18, 35):

> There is no such thing as clinical freedom, nor has there ever been. Nor, for that matter, should there be . . . . Absolute freedom to make clinical decisions without taking into account the preferences or wishes of the patient could not be countenanced. It is therefore proper that personal, moral, ethical and even legal constraints should be observed. To these must now be added the constraint of limited resources.

Later he notes that this additional constraint requires doctors to help in rationing access to health care and asks:

> Does acceptance of this function compromise our clinical freedom? It is not easy to identify or isolate the part played by awareness of costs when individual doctors . . . decide whether or not to investigate or treat a patient. The open and direct opinion 'This would cost too much', is rarely expressed and, I suspect, not often consciously entertained as a discretionary factor. Even if it were it would be regarded simply as one of the factors that needed to be taken into account in order to establish a course of action. It would not often be seen as detracting from the doctor's clinical freedom. Whether or not he was influenced by costs would be entirely up to him; his autonomy would be unimpaired. A more

important question from the point of view of clinical freedom is doing something they wish to do for their patients, by an authoritarian embargo, based on resource considerations, which is in conflict with their professional judgement.

This comes close to saying that only doctors have the right to determine what the effect of resource constraints should be (which, if true, might explain why clinical freedom is invoked against health economists, who also think they have something to say about how best to respond to resource constraints). But this does not appear to be Hoffenberg's intention, for he goes on to consider limited list prescribing and the carefully controlled dissemination of heart transplantation in the United Kingdom as cases where, despite "the authoritarian encroachment on clinical freedom", there seems to have developed:

... a widespread acceptance by the public as well as the profession that resources are not unlimited and that the doctor has a responsibility to Society – through a thoughtful allocation of scarce resources – as well as the individual patient.

This seems to be a much more constructive role for the clinician to see himself in, and one which accords fully with my suggestion that both economists and doctors are working within the same ethical code and towards the same objectives, namely the preservation of life and the alleviation of suffering. Those objectives can only be realised *ethically* by accepting that compromises (*or* as we economists say, "trade-offs") are necessary when ethical principles conflict, and that one of these compromises is the balancing of benefits between one group of patients and another. In order that such a balancing may occur, clinicians need to know what the costs of their actions are, and need to be placed in a situation where they are properly motivated to act on that information, alongside the clinical information available to them. Cost minimisation in isolation from any consideration of benefits is as nonsensical and unethical as benefit maximisation in isolation from any consideration of costs. *Both* benefits *and* cost must be considered. That is the underlying theme of this conference, and that is why the search for appropriate incentives is so important *and* so difficult. But since the health of the millions of people who depend on our respective health care systems depends on our finding a suitable way forward, it is an enterprise which is worth a great deal of our effort on our part. And it is not one which will be helped forward if any of us claims moral superiority over the others. After all, if my reasoning is accepted, the biblical example with which I opened this paper may not be as threatening as you might have thought. For my argument is essentially that it is perfectly possible to render unto Caesar that which is Caesar's *without* sacrificing those things that should be rendered unto God. There is nothing immoral about becoming more efficient.

References

Hampton J (1983) The end of clinical freedom. Br Med J 287:1237–1238
Hoffenberg R (1987) Clinical freedom. Nuffield Provincial Hospitals Trust, London
Loewy EH (1980) Cost should not be a factor in medical care. New Engl J Med 302:697
Ruark JE and the Standford University Medical Center Committee on Ethics (1988) Initiating and withdrawing life support. Principles and practice in adult medicine. New Engl J Med 318:25–30
Williams A (1988) Health Economics: the end of clinical freedom?. Br Med J 297:1183

Provider Behaviour in Health Care: Some Notes on Theory

R. Gerritse and P. Vrancken

Introduction

Health care is an intricate system of both individual and collective choice. Individual demand and supply meet in an environment that is strongly – if not decisively – influenced by institutional arrangements, legislation and public policy. Our health care systems thus bear the distinct social, economic and cultural imprints of society. Within the health care systems and their institutional frameworks, the nature of consumer and producer behaviour is a major influence on the access of provisions and on the use, quality and cost of care. The effects of behavioural incentives in critical areas such as consumer cost-sharing, physician reimbursement, hospital budgeting or the details of insurance system are some of the issues which lie at the heart of much economic research and public debate on the development of health care and health care policy. In fact there is some degree of policy reorientation in a number of countries, aiming to increase the scope for incentives in an attempt to gear patient wants more efficiently to a cost-effective provision of care. Provider incentives are a "slice", as it were, of the circumstances defining the intricately entangled relations between supply and demand in the health care system. Since medical care providers (and physicians in particular) are pre-eminent decision makers in the process of allocation of medical services, provider incentives are certainly a *major* slice of the health care economic environment: i.e. in terms of its impact on the quantity, quality and costs of medical care.

In this paper we will outline some of the basic theory on provider behaviour in health care. It needs to be emphasized from the outset, however, that, in spite of an ever-growing mass of speculation on the characteristics and determinants of medical provider behaviour in the international literature, there is actually very little coherent theory on the subject and (worse perhaps) there is little convincing empirical evidence to sustain clear-cut and unambiguous hypotheses on the nature and effects of provider behaviour. Therefore this paper is largely on theory (and the lack of it). But "theory without measurement", to borrow Tjalling Koopmans' phrase, leads us only to endless dispute. We will conclude, therefore, with a few suggestions for a research strategy that may lead us to more explicit evidence on the nature and consequences of provider behaviour in the intricate markets of medical care.

First, we will examine some of the basic characteristics of supply and demand in the health care markets, which will be a starting point for the interpretation of different theoretical angles to the issue of provider incentives. We will then, only roughly, consider the more or less "neoclassical" theorizing on the characteristics and outcomes of allocative processes in that market, including what we perceive to be variants of that archetypical view, such as the supplier-induced demand theories. We will argue that – in our perception of the health care market – this approach really leads us nowhere. Next, we will, in passing, take a look at some of the econometric attempts to grasp the health care markets explicitly as the "Gordian knots" of supply and demand that we hold them to be. The econometrics of the entangled determinants of health care, we will conclude, is much "measurement", however, and little "theory". Finally we reach the point that, we feel, *should* be tackled: the theory of choice, and its specific characteristics in health care decision-making.

Supply: The Interpretation of Nested Demand

The time when we may have felt that resource allocation in the market for medical services expressed unambiguous – or even sovereign – consumer preferences has long since gone. If we ever adhered to the naive view, it must by now have been effectively undermined by a few decades of systematic reflection on the essentials of supply and demand for health care.

To begin with, it must be recognized that the time-dimensional concept of demand for health care is derived from the individual's stock of "demanded health" (Grossman 1972). That concept of "demanded health" is best interpreted in terms of the intangible inventory of personal capital that structures the "household production function" of any individual (Muellbauer 1981). "Demanded health" is a concept of structured objective needs, biased by subjective wants and preferences (Krashinsky 1981), and it must be specified in terms of the characteristics of an individual's welfare function. Demanded health is a preferred state of being. It is *not* a quantity of use values demanded in discriminate periods of time. It does not even necessarily *generate* a discriminate quantity of "derived demand" in those terms. On the contrary, the demand for health care that originates in "health demanded" is essentially the individual's unspecified demand for *aid and care* pure and simple, given his or her perception of illness, handicaps or needs generally. If such demand is subject to considerable uncertainty, and if it is therefore not simply structured by a set of risks that may be discounted by any probability standards, as Kenneth Arrow (1963) argued in his classical article more than 25 years ago, the demand for medical care becomes quite *indeterminate* in terms of the services actually bargained for. Under uncertainty, demand for aid and care will intertwine with anxious and virtually insatiable demand for *information*.

One may perhaps be inclined to infer that all this would simply mean that the elasticities of the demand for medical care (i.e. given some sort of opportunity costs in terms of relative prices or time prices, or whatever) should be expected to be high, and presumably rising with a perceived deterioration (or "depreciation") of the "health stock" of any individual. But that is all too simple. The hardcore conclusion must be that the concept of "consumer demand" itself (if that is to be defined along any schedule of alternative consumer choices between use values in relation to opportunity costs) is becoming rather shaky altogether. Given indeterminate consumer demand, it seems to make little sense to describe consumer behaviour in terms of actually determinable tangent points of indifference curves and production possibility frontiers, i.e. by any demand schedule from the upper-left to the lower-right in the type of graphs that economists favour (Wagstaff 1986). Even if there were unambiguous prices or other opportunity costs to be specified in the demand functions, there may be no demanded quantities to be pinpointed. So what we have is a generally unspecified "demanded health" on the one hand and the actual use of services and facilities on the other; but so far there is nothing to link the two.

The "missing link" in the economics of consumer behaviour in health care must be found in the behaviour of the one economic subject that is capable of restating (anxiously) demanded health in terms of the quantities and qualities of output that are apparently needed for preferred. It is the one agent that is able to re-evaluate the consumer's (subjective) uncertainties in terms of (objective) risks: i.e. the provider of medical services. Demand for health care is therefore essentially *nested in supply*. Supply is (almost always) derived from demand and all health care utilization is therefore basically "supplier-induced" (Birch 1988). The entangled knot of supply and demand, and of patient interests and provider choice, is what then should be at the core of any analysis of economic behaviour, and of the impact of incentives, in the health care industry.

Essential for the analysis of provider behaviour is the recognition, therefore, that consumer demand is not generally specified in terms of quantities of services requested. It is essentially an *unspecified* demand for information, and for aid and care pure and simple, easily driven by anxieties. And if inarticulate demand becomes a major parameter for provider choice, this implies that in the absence of effective environmental consumer constraints (i.e. for instance price or income constraints) demand may tend to push supply to its capacity limits. If, at the extreme, medical care providers are perfect "preference brokers" for health care consumers, they will tend to articulate anxious demand in terms of available or conceivable diagnostic and therapeutic options, and capacities will all too easily become the effective constraint to the use of health care. The economics of health care then become the *economics of shortage* in the sense given to that concept by Janos Kornai (1979): quantity adjustments clearing the market. It is not needed to assume or suspect that undesirable, or even perverse or unethical, provider incentives (perhaps the physician's income considerations) drive supply to capacity limits. It would suffice to have indeterminate, little constrained and anxious consumer demand, *and* providers acting as perfect "preference brokers" (i.e. to have truly concerned physicians) to produce precisely that effect.

Supply and demand, and the behavioural characteristics of consumers and producers, their driving and mitigating forces, become necessarily intertwined. The question that becomes crucial in terms of the costs and benefits of health care is whether provider decisions, feasibly along the edges of capacity, could ever warrant a more or less "Pareto-optimal" outcome of the process, i.e. an outcome providing the most benefits for all, given capacity. In fact, this seems unlikely: the interdependency of supply and demand implies in itself that little normative significance can be attached to the outcome of the health care market (i.e. in traditional welfare economic, rather than medical or ethical, standards).

Now essentially we have half the story so far. If demand tends to be limited by capacities, we ought to know what it is that determines capacity. In the market sector, consumer preferences are weighted by disposable income. Income there defines the capacity to appropriate scarce resources. In the health care sector, however, entitlements are not allocated by "dollars", but largely by "rights", simply because we feel that "money shouldn't buy some things" (Okun 1975; Wolfson 1985), least of all aid and care. Where dollars rule the market, we hope that rights – and not dollars or ECUs – govern the distribution of entitlements to health care. That of course does not mean that prices cannot or should not play a part in the allocation and rationing of the use of medical provisions, but it does imply that access to health care must somehow be warranted by non-market arrangements: i.e. primarily by government or quasi-government regulation and/or social insurance.

The generation and allocation of supply capacities are therewith governed by the social and political standards that structure public policy. And with the consumer willingly caught between politics and the medical profession, the health care market becomes governed by political and supplier decisions:

1. Because provider decisions, driven by inarticulate and anxious consumer demand, tend to take supply to its capacity limits
2. Because capacity limits are under the persistent inflationary pressure of the social "promises" that are embedded in the basic social right to have full access to health care.

What should have us worried with those conditions is the possibility that the health care market characteristics may (paradoxically) lead to shortages and waste in terms of social, i.e. collective, standards. For any individual the medical services that are provided may be beneficial (as marginal benefits to consumers may be felt to be positive). And consumers may have actually bargained for the services provided (because often marginal cost to the individual is practically zero). Finally, within capacity limits, the services will indeed be provided (because benefits to suppliers are positive). But nothing warrants that the health care benefits are optimally distributed in terms of consumer needs as a whole or that they are in some sense less than total social cost (Aaron 1981).

In fact there are a few persistent observations that have been made in the international literature that may have us worried in this respect, and that have actually been the raison d'être of the various studies of supplier behaviour, and of the impacts of provider incentives, in the economic literature on health care.

1. There are large (regional) variations of per capita utilization that cannot be explained by variations in background characteristics of patients, medical needs or health apparently produced (Enthoven 1981; Eisenberg 1986).
2. There is substantial evidence of low or zero individual marginal productivity in (some areas of) health care (Enthoven 1981; Fuchs 1985).
3. There is the simple logic of potential physician behaviour under conditions of rigid entry requirements and occupational licensure (Maynard and Ludbrook 1981), framed within systems of renumeration and hospital budgeting characteristics that would allow for income-targeting (Roemer 1962; Glaser 1970; Rutten 1978; Reinhardt 1985).
4. There is a persistently growing variety of ad hoc evidence to suggest that the actual availability of capacities and provisions induces treatment, without there being an evident impact on health produced or on the efficiency of care provided (Maynard 1979; Hofland and Wilms 1984).

If medical service providers are the "preference brokers" of patients, if inarticulate and quickly anxious consumer demand induces a resource-constrained provision of care through provider decisions, if such decisions lead to market clearing through quantity adjustments, and (especially) if such a process leads to a distribution of provisions that cannot apparently be explained by initial health status differentials between consumers, there will be pressing welfare economic questions to be answered: questions with respect to the social allocation of individual benefits, and questions with regard to costs and the incidence of costs. And within that framework of welfare theory, the impacts of provider incentives in terms of social (i.e. allocative and distributional) cost-benefit standards will have become one of the major issues for the economic evaluation of the health care industry.

The Marshallian Deadlock

The early attempts to deal with provider behaviour were attempts to formulate and test the so-called "supplier-induced" demand hypotheses. To this end theoretical models have been developed on the basis of various hypotheses regarding some sort of constrained utility maximation by health care producers (see Pauly 1980; McGuire 1985). Within such frameworks, the perception of the "demand inducement" problem was essentially laid down in the hypothesis that demand curves in the health care markets may be shifted "to the right" by suppliers, actively inducing an additional willingness to pay by consumers in order to maintain supplier incomes with increasing numbers of suppliers (e.g. Evans 1974; Fuchs 1978; Richardson 1981).

The basic test for the existence of supplier-induced demand in this sense is not simply that utilization would rise with rising supply. That it may do so is quite compatible with traditional neoclassical models as well, as prices decrease in reaction to enlarged supply (Reinhardt 1978). The existence of supplier-induced demand would, more strictly, want to see the apparent unit price elasticities with respect to the number of suppliers to be non-negative. But the problem is that this outcome need not be produced per se: i.e. demand may shift, but less than enough to produce non-falling prices. It would all depend on the slopes of (segments of) supply and demand curves and on the extents of the changes foreseen. Moreover, the required outcome of non-falling prices may still be compatible with traditional neoclassical assumptions regarding market behaviour. All that is needed is to allow for the assumption that consumers would react to changing densities of provider (physician) supply. If, for instance, increasing numbers of physicians were perceived as an improvement of quality or as an enhancement of accessibility, an effect on demand could easily be predicted. Therefore one of the problems with the supplier-inducement theory is that it fails to produce original predictions (see Reinhardt 1985; Birch 1988). The target income hypotheses, moreover, that seems to be its backbone, would also be quite consistent with any straightforward "satisfying" behaviour that fits the standard models of utility maximation perfectly, or may be quite compatible with profit-maximizing models under monopoly conditions (e.g. Stano 1987). The, basically North American, supplier-induced demand theory does not in any case appear to fit large sectors, of health care in Europe. Assume that in *our* world we have price-insensitive demand, or fixed prices, or consumer prices not playing a role at all: all of this leaves us little to be explained in terms of hypothetical consumer demand curves.

More fundamentally, it does not seem to make much sense to attempt to model supply and demand in the health care sector along the (upward and downward sloping) lines of confronted aggregate producer and consumer behaviour in reaction to alternative quantities of medical services, which cannot be defined unambiguously and which would need to produce results in terms of prices that are not there. "Quantities" and "prices" in this market are not the same to producers and consumers of health care. And it is not at all evident what could ever clear the market under the conditions that prevail in the health care sector, i.e. anything other than straightforward provider decisions at effective capacity constraints: leaving us to wonder what has happened to consumer benefits and social costs.

In short, supply and demand in the medical market are not separate schedules of consumer and producer alternatives in mutually comparable terms, to be confronted and equilibrated at some point of market clearing opportunity costs and income per unit. The health care market is principally a "Gordian knot" of supply and demand interaction that cannot simply be untangled by the brutal force of "Marshallian" economics, interpreting provider and consumer behaviour in terms of the supply and demand curves that economists have grown fond of. That, of course, does not mean that consumer and producer behaviour cannot or should not be analysed specifically, but it means that we must do so within a theoretical framework that differs radically from the neoclassical, Marshallian view of separate demand and supply decisions in the market.

A consideration of the supplier-induced demand theory leads us to the recognition that in the empirical analysis of health care use we are up against a very fundamental problem of *identification.* What we may actually measure are the different rates of utilization of various types of capacity at different points of time or at various locations. From the data we cannot, however, know what it is we are measuring other than apparent outcomes. The outcomes reflect the one scenario of mixed supply and demand impacts that happened to become reality. We may of course attempt to break down the mongrel function of "supplied demand" into the various determinants of conceivable supplier and consumer characteristics and behaviour: essentially by standardizing the consumer, generally in robust terms (e.g. by age, sex, occupation and the like), and checking the residuals for assumed supply-side effects (Rutten 1978; Van der Gaag 1978; Van Vliet 1988). But a substantial drawback of much of this type of (econometrical) work on health care use is that it allows only inferential comments on the underlying doctor-patient interaction, on the resource constraints that are locked up in the doctor-hospital relations or on the characteristics of medical decision-making within that framework (Eisenberg 1986).

What we do not have is a more or less coherent model of consumer-producer interaction along the lines of an explicitly non-Marshallian theory of "nested demand" for health care. We have too much measurement without falsifiable theory. However, with recent progress of the analysis of small-area variations and with the generation and analysis of sets of detailed microdata (Wennberg 1984), the empirical ground begins to be cleared for a serious undertaking of falsifiable model building. Once we are able to use microdata, the question of how to model economic behaviour comes to the fore much more sharply than it has in the years that we had to cope with unrefined aggregate data.

Economics of Medical Choice

If there is agreement that provider behaviour, and the incentives conditioning that behaviour, are in the core of the process of health care allocation, we ought to have attempts to model medical care in terms that may do justice to the decision problem that providers face with each major choice that is to be made. That decision problem is to be structured in terms of the options that are actually there, given the health status of patients and given the technical and institutional facilities that build up capacity. In a nutshell, the gradual elaboration of a coherent, realistic and falsifiable theory of provider behaviour in medical care should come to incorporate the following elements as we go along.

1. If the health care market tends to be a "resource-constrained" dynamic system, capacity regulation must be modelled. Within that framework the genesis and evolution of technical and behavioural incentive structures is to be outlined in model terms. In such more or less "macro" models (e.g. of hospital planning and budgeting or of sheltered monopoly markets and reimbursement systems for physicians), we may need to incorporate elements of *game theory*. Moreover, in particular it may be very useful to develop and test the *principal-agent models* (see Jensen and Meckling 1976) that are more generally being used to understand the asymmetrical relations between government (the principals) and its negotiating parties in the quasi-autonomous non-government sector (i.e. the agents), along

with all the "moral hazards" that come with the fact that the agents are generally much better informed about technical efficiencies and costs. In the Netherlands a principal-agent model has been used by De Groot (1988) to analyse regional government decision-making with regard to capacity reduction of hospitals. In general, the modelling of capacity and supply regulation must allow for a recognition of the existence of "collective failures" or structural public policy deficiencies (Wolf 1979) and should ideally include an assessment of the effectiveness of the operation of pressure groups in this sector (Hofland and Wilms 1984)

2. The next step is to model provider behaviour within the framework of capacity constraints and existing incentive structures at a more micro-level. Such "micro" models of provider behaviour are descriptions of actual provider choice within the settings of capacity constraints and given the nature of incentive systems. Within that framework provider behaviour is to be interpreted as the articulation of demand in terms of the available diagnostic and therapeutic options and strategies that are specific to any given institutional setting. Microeconomic models of provider behaviour are therefore institutionally biased (which makes an interesting case for international comparison).

In order to model actual provider choice as the nexus between supply and demand, we thus need a theory on how supply constraints come about, and how incentives are generated: those are the "macro" questions to be answered. And geared to an explanation of capacities and the nature of incentives, we need to model actual choice: this is the "micro" issue.

The microeconomics of provider choice should essentially specify *both* the technical options for choice, i.e. the alternatives available, *and* the behavioural stimuli governing actual choice within that framework. This implies that any such model can only be formulated specifically for a more or less definite case mix or diagnosis-related group (DRG) and along the range of episodes of such case mixes (Feldstein 1967; Stoddart and Barer 1981; Aaron and Schwartz 1984). What we would want is a modelling of "best practice" alternatives, given capacity, and a theory of how "average practice" comes about, given incentives. Such an analysis, although it may perhaps be modelled in abstract terms, can only lead to testable results for particular DRGs. That is where, in our view, the emphasis should be in further research on the microissue of provider behaviour and provider incentives.

It will also be necessary to broaden the concept of the medical care provider from the physician who has received so much attention in the literature, to the range of providers, actually present in the industry and the possibilities of complementation or substitution between them. Health care providers may need to be classified into ambulatory care physicians and specialists, nursing staff, physical therapists, and pharmacists, each within their specific intramural or extramural settings and given the varieties of conceivable interactions between them. Within such a framework the lead decision-maker in each "market" is to be identified. But the recognition that, e.g. physicians and medical institutions are not uncommonly "joint suppliers" of medical care accentuates the necessity to deal explicitly with the interrelations between provider behaviour in those combined settings. The analysis would therefore also need to focus on the alternatives for care and cure in hospitals, in nursing homes, by means of ambulatory care or community services. That is all essential in the analysis of actual provider choice. The extents to which decisions by providers in one subsector of health care affect, set or limit the options for efficient provision of health care in other sectors, shift costs and affect benefits to patients is the essence of what the analysis of provider behaviour ought to be about.

A research strategy which may actually make us wiser with regard to the impacts of provider behaviour and the influence of (provider) incentives should focus on the analysis of provider behaviour for specific diagnoses-related or treatment groups. It aims to formulate the "best practice" of alternatives open to the provider and to explain the origin of the alternatives in terms of the macroanalysis we have been referring to. Here we must find the link with the literature on the microeconomic evaluation at treatment levels, i.e. with cost-benefit and cost-effectiveness analysis (e.g. Drummond et al. 1987), with much of the more recent work on QUALY estimations (e.g. Maynard 1987), and we may take in account the information that is generated by consensus conferences (see Wennberg 1984).

Within the framework of alternatives, microeconomic behaviour must be modelled on "average practice" or actual choice. This actual choice between alternatives will be made within the setting of the provider's perception of costs over benefits, and all the probabilities and risks associated with the evaluation of these costs and benefits, and given capacities and institutional and technical constraints. There we have the archimedic point in any model of medical provider choice. And here *decision theory* may be a good framework for analysis: it allows for a tentative formalization of the alternative strategies the provider may adopt when confronted with (what is perceived to be) a given case, and it is in fact standard fare in the theories of medical choice (e.g. Albert 1978; Weinstein and Fineberg 1980; Doubilet and McNeil 1985). Provider behaviour essentially falls into the class of decisions and problems under risk (Wennberg et al. 1982; Eddy 1984) For any "given case" there is a decision tree of feasible alternatives and probable outcomes. If supplier behaviour "nests" demand, consumer preferences enter the provider's decision problem as the interpretation of the "case" (and its social dimensions) that is to be dealt with in this particular instance *and* affecting the utilities of alternative treatment strategies discounted by that provider.

Decision theory may be applied normatively, but for our purposes it must above all be a descriptive tool to structure technical options and best-practice alternatives in relation to actual choice. It would allow for an analysis of the impacts of imperfect information, risk aversion and behavioural thresholds in decision-making. It allows for the study of physician behaviour in terms of the "multi-attribute utility problem" that the provider faces with each choice: i.e. in terms of the trade-off of assigned utilities (affected by both provider and consumer interests) to probable outcomes of the existing diagnostic and therapeutic options. The actual choice is between a limited number of discrete alternatives. Here a multinominal logit framework (Amemiya 1981), which is consistent with the standard model of utility maximization (see Frank and Kamlet 1989), may specifically be of use. Within such a context provider incentives also fall into place. They structure the provider's decision problem, basically in terms of the utilities (i.e. the net benefits) assigned to the outcomes of technical alternatives. It is the average practice that actual choice produces that is then to be charted against the (normative) background of best practice alternatives as the economically relevant counter-factual, given capacity at large.

Taking the microeconomic angle and interpreting provider behaviour in terms of medical choice that may be biased by capacity constraints and incentive structures we believe would be the appropriate way to elaborate a methodology for the analysis of provider choice, methodology that leads beyond the Marshallian framework of traditional supply and demand analysis. The microeconomics of medical choice is a field of research that is worth developing step by step, not only because it is a major intellectual challenge, but above all because our understanding of provider behaviour, of its determining factors and of its economic and social consequences are of the utmost importance for the evaluation of our policy options in health care.

References

Aaron H (1981) Economic aspects of the role of government in health care. In: van der Gaag J, Perlman M (eds) Health, economics, and health economics. North Holland, Amsterdam

Aaron H, Schwartz WB (1984) The painful prescription. The Brookings Institution, Washington

Albert DA (1978) Decision theory in medicine, a review and critique. Milbank Mem Fund Q/Health Soc 56:362–401

Amemiya T (1981) Qualitative response models: a survey. J Econ Lit 19:1483–1536

Arrow KJ (1963) Uncertainty and the welfare economics of medical care. Am Econ Revi 53:5

Birch S (1988) The identification of supplier-inducement in a fixed price system of health care provision. J Health Econ 7:129–150

Doubilet P, McNeil BJ (1985) Clinical decision-making. Med Care 23 (5):648–662

Drummond MF, Stoddart GL, Torrance GW (1987) Methods for economic evaluation of health care programmes. Oxford University Press, Oxford

Eddy DM (1984) Variations in physician's practice, the role of uncertainty. Health Aff 3:74–89
Eisenberg J (1986) Doctors decisions and the cost of medical care. Michigan University Press, Michigan
Enthoven AC (1981) The behavior of health care agents: provider behavior. In: van der Gaag J, Perlman M (eds) Health, economics, and health economics. North Holland, Amsterdam
Evans RG (1974) Supplier induced demand: some empirical evidence and implication. In: Perlman M (ed) The economics of health and medical care. J Wiley, London
Evans RG (1984) Strained mercy; the economics of Canadian health care. Butterworths, Toronto.
Feldstein MS (1967) Economic analysis for health service efficiency econometric studies of British National Health Service. North Holland, Amsterdam
Frank RG, Kamlet MS (1989) Determining provider choice for the treatment of mental disorder: the role of health and mental health status. Health Serv Res 24:(1) pp 83–103
Fuchs VR (1978) The study of surgeons and the demand for operations. J Hum Resources 13 (Suppl)
Fuchs VR (1985) The 'rationing' of medical care. N Engl J Med 311:1572–1573
Van der Gaag J (1978) An econometric analysis of the Dutch health care system. North Holland, Amsterdam
Glaser WA (1970) Paying the doctor, systems of remuneration and their effects. Johns Hopkins Press, Baltimore
De Groot H (1988) Decentralization decisions in bureaucracies as a principal-agent problem. J Public Econ 36 (3):323–338
Grossman M (1972) The demand for health: a theoretical and empirical investigation. National Bureau of Economic Research, New York
Hofland J, Wilms PJM (1984) Onder behandeling: strategische keuzen bij de kostenbeheersing in de gezondheidszorg. Institute for Research on Public Expenditure, The Hague
Jensen MC, Meckling WH (1976) Theory of the firm: managerial behavior, agency costs and owner structure. J Financ Econ 3:305–360
Kornai J (1979) Resource-constrained versus demand-constrained systems. Econometrica 47:4
Krashinsky M (1981) User charges in the social services: an economic theory of need and inability. Ontario Economic Council University of Toronto Press, Toronto
Maynard A (1979) Pricing demanders and the supply of health care. Int J Health Serv 9 (1):121–133
Maynard A (1987) Incentives for cost-effective physician behaviour, Health Policy 7 (2):189–204
Maynard A, Ludbrook A (1981) Thirty years of fruitless endeavor? An analysis of government intervention in the health care market. In: van der Gaag J, Perlman M (eds) Health economics, and health economics. North Holland, Amsterdam
McGuire A (1985) The theory of the hospital: a review of the models. Soc Sci Med 20 (11):1177–1184
Meulbauer (1981) Household production theory, quality and the hedonic tehcnique. Am Econ Rev 64:6
Okun A (1975) Equality and efficiency; the big trade off. The Brookings Institution, Washington
Pauly MV (1980) Doctors and their workshops: economic models of physician behavior. Chicago
Reinhardt UE (1978) Comment of competition among physicians. In Greenberg W (ed) Competition in the health care sector: past, present and future. Aspen Systems Corpor. Germantown Md, Maryland
Reinhardt UE (1985) The compensation of physicians: approaches used in foreign countries. Q Rev Bull 14:366–377
Richardson J (1981) The inducement hypothesis: that doctors generate demand for their own services. In: van der Gaag J, Perlman M (eds) Health economics, and health economics. North Holland, Amsterdam

Roemer MI (1962) On paying the doctor and the implications of different methods. J Health Human Behav 3:4–14

Rutten FFH (1978) The use of health care facilities in the Netherlands; an econometrical analysis. Leiden

Stano M (1987) A further analysis of the physician inducement controversy. J Health Econ 6 (3):227–238

Stoddart GL, Barer ML (1981) Analyses of demand and utilization through episodes of medical services. In: van der Gaag J, Perlman M (eds) Health economics, and health economics. North Holland, Amsterdam

Van Vliet RCJA (1988) Hospital utilization, performance measures and health status; econometric analysis of Dutch Micro Data. Offsetdrukkerij Kanters BV, Alblasserdam

Wagstaff A (1986) The demand for health: theory and applications. J Epidemiol Community Health 40:1–11

Weinstein MC, Fineberg HV (1980) Clinical decision analysis. Saunders, Philadelphia

Wennberg JE (1984) Dealing with medical practice variations: a proposal for action. Health Aff 3 (2):6–32

Wennberg JE, Barness BA, Zubkoff M (1982) Professional uncertainty and the problem of supplier-induced Demand. Soc Sci Med 16:811–824

Wolf C (1979) A theory of non-market failure: framework for implementation analysis. Law Econ 20:107–139

Wolfson DJ (1985) Criteria in engineering social justice. In: Terry G, Culyer AJ (eds) Public finance and social policy. Homewood, Irwin, Detroit

Incentive Contracts

A. Maynard

Introduction

Rather than risking repetition and reviewing existing evidence about the effects of incentives on the behaviour of consumers and providers, the intention of this paper is to concentrate on the supply side of the market and:

1. To review how one country, the United Kingdom, intends to reform its health care system, the National Health Service.
2. To examine how the incentives inherent in these reforms are believed to work.
3. To challenge these beliefs by highlighting the paucity of theory and evidence about the working of competing incentive contracts.
4. To argue that the traditional economic paradigm may be too narrow and, if reforms about to take place in England and elsewhere are to be designed and evaluated efficiently, a broader theory of economic behaviour needs to be created.

Reforming the National Health Service

In late 1987 a chorus of public protest about the "inadequate" funding of the National Health Service persuaded Prime Minister Thatcher to establish a review of the NHS. The terms of reference of this review were never published and may not have existed in an explicit and agreed form. There was no public call for written or oral evidence and the selection of evidence given and the views they presented to the Review are unknown. The review group was chaired by the prime minister and included the Secretary of State for Health, his junior minister, Treasury ministers, together with political advisers and civil servants. NHS personnel entered and left the Review group over its 1 year life.

This undemocratic and quixotic enquiry into the NHS transformed itself from an initial response to demand factors, especially a plea for additional funding, to a proposal to reform radically the supply of health care (Working for Patients 1989). The fundamental proposal is that the budget holding (demand) side of the market should be separated from the provision (supply) side with buyers and sellers being induced to trade in relation to market signals. The public (tax) finance of the NHS is to be unaltered. Radical, innovative and uncertain reforms are focused on changing provider's behaviour (Maynard 1989; Williams 1989).

In future there will be two sets of budget holders, who will act as the patients' guardian and, by spending, determine the pattern of services to meet local health care needs. The first group will be 192 district general managers (DGMs) in England. They will be given a cash limited budget with which to provide efficiently health care to meet the health needs of their local populations (of about 250 000). Care can be purchased from any public or private supplier and the budget holder will enter into contracts which will specify price, volume and quality, i.e. demand decisions will become more transparent and easier to review. The main incentive for these budget holders to act efficiently is the short-term nature of their contacts and the system of performance review which is in place. Aggressive use of these incentives could be a sharp discipline on behaviour.

The second group of budget holders that may emerge are general practitioners (GPs) who work in groups with a list size in excess of 11 000, a size which may worsen adverse selection problems. Such GPs will be able to elect to have cash limited budgets to finance certain cold (elective) surgery procedures, outpatient referrals and diagnostic tests. Again these budget holders can use their budgets to purchase care from public and private suppliers and this trading will be subject to explicit contracts about the nature of trading arrangements.

Trading will take place in three forms of contact – block, cost and volume, and cost per case – and each will oblige managers to produce better cost, activity and outcome information. A variety of problems are likely to emerge with such contracts. There may be perverse incentives at the interfaces of the contracts for hospital care (DGMs), primary care (GPs) and community care (the latter is itself the subject of a separate and similar reform). Arbitration arrangements, using "pendulum" settlement methods (i.e. the arbitrator has to decide in favour of either the purchaser or the provider with no compromise permitted), will require the provision of information about trading which the traders may be reluctant to provide if it is commercially sensitive.

Three other areas may create novel problems for managers. What if hospitals sell in excess of capacity like airlines, in order to maintain a high "load factor" and lower costs? If the hospital is contracted to provide care and has no capacity when demands are made, its managers will have to have side contracts, i.e. spot and futures markets in hospital beds may emerge, particularly in areas such as London.

Obviously managers will have to deal with monopoly and monopsony problems. The latter is well recognised: local hospitals may have monopoly power and seek to raise costs, causing inflation. However, buyers (e.g. DGMs) may form coalitions and use their sole buyer (monopsony) power to push prices down. Both monopoly and monopsony may induce cost cutting and quality erosion unless management is careful.

A final interesting problem arising from contracting is will the Government let hospitals, which fail to acquire contracts, go out of business? Clearly there will be a tension between the manager's role as a purchaser and the manager's residual role as an owner of the local NHS (non-self-governing) hospital. No doubt this problem can be mitigated by replacing the management of inefficient units.

Budget holders will be able to purchase care from two types of NHS hospital. In addition to existing NHS hospitals, which are managed by District Health Authorities, Self-Governing (Trust) Hospitals (SGHs) are to be created. The SGHs will have greater freedom in setting labour contracts and in determining capital investment. They will be able to make surpluses from trading and plough these monies back into the SGHs. These hospitals will own their assets and be free to raise new funds subject to Whitehall financial limits.

Consultant staff in all public hospitals will be subject to medical audit of the process, outcome and resource consequences of their work. The consultant's contract, at present ill defined and poorly monitored, is to be made explicit and reviewed regularly by District Health Authorities. If behaviour, or service provision, is at variance with the job description, the consultant will be subject to disciplinary controls. The system for distinction awards for consultant's pay is to involve management as well as peers in its allocation and awards are to be reviewed every 5 years.

In addition to the introduction of practice budgets, general practitioners will be subject to medical audit (presumably of process and activity) and indicative drug budgets will be introduced for all practitioners. The latter will augment the downward pressure on GP prescribing initiated by the limited list in 1985 and enhanced by an extended prescribing information feedback system (PACTs) in 1988.

The proposals for general practice set out in the NHS Review White Paper have been augmented by proposals for a new GP contract (Department of

Health and the Welsh Office 1989). The existing GP contract is extremely vague and requires practitioners "to render to their patients all necessary and appropriate medical services of a type usually provided by general medical practitioners". This circular statement, "a GP's got to do what a GP's got to do", is to be elaborated in the new contract with the attainment of specific targets for vaccination, immunisation and other preventive activities (e.g. cervical cytology) to be rewarded with payments rather than with piece rates at present. In addition, there is a marginal shift of emphasis in another aspect of remuneration with the average GP to get circa 55% of his or her income from capitation, as opposed to circa 47% now, in an effort to enhance the "patient responsiveness" of GPs.

To create a market, a network of buyers and sellers, in health care and to reform the GP contract will require large investments in information about costs, prices, activities and outcomes. No health care market exists which provides cost information let alone outcome data. The United States health care markets create some price data and no doubt the United Kingdom market will operate, especially initially, at high levels of aggregation if and when such information is available. At present, routine cost and outcome data are noticeable by their absence and this deficiency will cost a good deal to remedy even if there were proven methods of gathering and monitoring such data, which there are not.

Incentives and Beliefs

The beliefs informing those who have made these proposals are very familiar to any inhabitant of Thatcher's island. One of the apparent basic premises of Adam Smith was (Smith 1776, 1976; pp 26–27):

> It is not from the benevolence of the butcher, the brewer and the baker, that we expect our dinner, but from their regard to their own interest. We address ourselves, not to their humanity, but to their self-love, and never talk to them of our necessities but to their advantages.

A central belief of the liberal ideology is that self-interest (or self-love) will create the mechanisms from which efficient resource allocation and enhanced wealth will be produced.

The proposals in the White Paper *Working for Patients* and in the proposed new GP contract are designed to create market pressures which enhance the performance of the supply side of the health care market in the United Kingdom. The dominant ideology of the Thatcher Government is informing the beliefs behind these reforms, in particular, following Maynard and Williams (1984):

1. Financial surpluses (profits) for GP budget holders, self-governing hospitals and other hospitals, NHS and private, are deemed to be an appropriate and efficient way of motivating public and private suppliers to respond to the demands of budget holders, district general managers and GPs.
2. Priorities will be determined by the willingness and ability to pay of the budget holders, GPs and DHA managers, and by the costs of meeting their demands at the margin.
3. Suppliers will have a strong incentive to economise.

Even at a general level these propositions can be countered by the apparent results of market transactions:

1. Those services that create surpluses for GP budget holders, self-governing hospitals and other hospitals, NHS and private, may not be what the patients' guardian, the DGM and the GP, should be buying to enhance the patient's health status by the maximum amount at least cost. Suppliers typically advocate the use of unproven methods of providing health care, often high technology and preventive services, and budget holders are as ill informed as suppliers as to the cost-effectiveness of competing treatments.
2. Priorities will be determined by the extent to which budget holders can be persuaded to spend their money and by the costs of providing the care they choose for their patients. Professionals and industrial suppliers will have strong incentives to advertise their services and products widely and "educate" budget holders and patients, for whom they are guardians, about the merits (but not their costs!) of their goods and services.
3. The pursuit of surpluses will give suppliers a strong incentive to "cooperate" by forming cartels and using mechanisms such as market segmentation, price discrimination and tie-in agreements, to ensure that producers to the greatest extent possible "organise" and stabilise the "choices" of budget holders.

Thus, at this general level, the beliefs of the advocates of the market can be countered with evidence. Whilst the natural inclination of most economists is to favour market mechanisms as a means of allocating resources, it is difficult to create and sustain competitive market mechanisms in health care markets, and it may be possible that such mechanisms are not appropriate means of organising the efficient production of health. Sustained advocacy of competition by economists such as Enthoven (1981, 1985, 1989) have been relatively unsuccessful and accompanied by statements explaining previous failures in making progress with the argument that it has yet to be tried. Clearly, market competition in health care is like Christianity, about which the novelist G.K. Chesterton argued that it had not failed because it had not been tried!

Incentive Contracts: Theory and Evidence

The coverage of incentive contracts in labour economics textbooks is surprisingly sparse (e.g. see Ehrenberg and Smith 1982). The authors of these books offer detailed discussion of models and evidence concerning labour supply in particular and, from these, it is clear that wage rates do affect labour supply and that their impact on female labour supply is greater than that for males (e.g. Killingsworth 1983). This evidence on labour supply is imprecise and available quantitative estimates of the effect of wages on any given labour supply function, that is the elasticity, typically cover a wide range.

Whilst these issues have been the subject of extensive economic analysis, the formulation of models of incentive contracts and their testing has received less attention. Yet it is the specification of such contracts which are of considerable interest and importance to health care reformers. What are the effects of price rates on the behaviour of hospital doctors? Is the part payment of United Kingdom GPs by capitation efficient? The effects of alternative payment contracts on inputs mix, processes of care and outcomes appears to have been researched little in economics as a whole and in health economics in particular. Yet powerful beliefs exist about the appropriateness of particular payment systems of labour supply and the provision of health care. What is known about the efficiency of alternative incentive contracts? How do agents respond with more labour and output to additional compensation?

Incentives are necessary because people love leisure, and when confronted by work, may tend to shirk where possible. In order to persuade health care suppliers to provide their services, it is necessary to compensate them for their loss of leisure. However, the principal-agent relationship complicates this issue. The principal's problem is that, because of the asymmetry of knowledge, either the principal cannot see what the agent does or the principal cannot interpret the agent's actions, i.e. the treatment is unseen or, if seen, it is difficult to interpret.

To deal with these problems a variety of output or input incentives have been devised. One output incentive proposed for the resolution of the principal-agent problem uses a sampling approach to review the agent's work (Becker and Stigler 1974). Thus the politician or doctor can be required to post a bond and, if he or she is caught deviating from acceptable practice, the bond is forfeit.

An early example of an output orientated incentive contract was sharecropping. With this arrangement the land owner and the individual who farms the land contract to share the product of the land. This arrangement may lead to the farmer offering inadequate effort to maximise the product of the land, as part of this product goes to the owner, and if the supply of land is elastic, the farmer may increase his acreage until the marginal product is zero.

An obvious method of seeking a resolution to this problem is to rent the land and so induce behaviour where the marginal product and marginal cost of output is equated. However, the defect with this contract is that the farmer has not incentive to maintain the value of the capital stock, e.g. he may not fertilise the land and move to another plot when it is exhausted. Thus, sale of the land to the farmer may be the best solution if he has the capital to buy, the skill to manage it and is prepared to accept the risks associated with ownership.

Partnerships, which are prevalent in health care, exhibit problems similar to sharecropping. If the doctor can leave a partnership without penalty, he or she does not have the same incentive to maintain the partnership's capital, in particular its patient goodwill.

Piece rates are a special case of sharecropping. The hospital manager allows the doctor to use the medical facilities and pays the doctor in relation to output. A major advantage of piece rates is that it accepts worker heterogeneity, with the more able workers receiving higher levels of pay. One important problem with this method of payment is the definition of the unit of output and the maintenance of the quality of output. An associated problem is that the appropriateness of activity may be difficult to detect and, as a consequence, outputs of little or unknown value may be produced by the maximising doctor.

A predictable effect of capitation payments is that the doctor may, if list size is controlled, seek to maximise leisure within the list size constraint. This may mean that consultation periods are low but, given the paucity of evaluation, it is not clear what consultation duration is efficient to particular groups of patients. The new NHS-GP contract may provide a marginal incentive to increase list size but the effects of this on patient care processes (for instance, will there be greater or less substitution of capital and other labour for GP inputs?), the quality of care and outcomes are not known.

The efficiency of the use of salary or hourly payment systems depends on the relationships between time and effort. As workers can vary their work per hour, this incentive mechanism is an uncertain way of generating an appropriate supply of effort. Salary systems mean that the employer accepts the risk of variations in worker output (unlike with piece rates where the worker bears this risk). As a consequence, in an industry where piece rates and salary payment system are used, lower quality workers may be attracted to the firms paying salaries. Furthermore, output may not be increased by shifting workers from salary to piece rate payment systems because, as noted by Lazear (1987), such a move may waste resources on a potentially useless market signal.

If the quality of care is difficult to detect and the doctor is paid by the hour and instructed to produce goods of a given quality, he or she has every incentive to accept such rules. There is no incentive to rush the job but there is a need to monitor effort and quality cheaply.

In salary payment systems, there may be inadequate definition of providers' roles. This, in conjunction with the firm (or team) structure of producer teams in NHS hospitals, may lead to senior team members electing to do what is innovative and interesting rather than what is cost effective.

Knowledge about the impact of particular forms of compensation on labour supply and output is limited. The theoretical literature (reviewed in Lazear 1987) is based on the traditional maximisation approach of economics. This literature has not been developed and applied extensively in the health care market. Whilst there are beliefs that certain forms of compensation for doctors (and other health care workers) achieve particular ends, both theory and evidence are underdeveloped. How can this work be developed?

Developing the Economic Paradigm: The Implications for Incentive Contracts

The usual economic model assumes that the decision maker is rational, i.e. she appreciates the possible variations in the outcome of any chosen action, and behaves in a consistent and self-interest fashion. The game-theoretic framework clarifies the nature of winning, i.e. "gaining relative to one's value system, and this may be done by bargaining, mutual accommodation and avoidance of mutually damaging, behaviour" (Schelling 1960), p. 4–5, quoted in Sen 1985). However, these broad observations about how competitors can win have been incorporated into game theory slowly.

Let us assume, following Sen (1985), a situation where the players are assumed to have:

1. Goal completeness, i.e. each doctor's goal takes the form of maximising in relation to a complete order of resulting states and a completeness of consequential lotteries.
2. Goal self-regardingness, i.e. each doctor's goal is to maximise his or her welfare.
3. Goal priority, i.e. each doctor is assumed to pursue his or her goal subject to what is feasible and without regard to any other values.
4. Mutual knowledge, i.e. each doctor is well informed about the other goals, values and knowledge.

The well-known game of "Prisoners Dilemma" gives the two players, A (a surgeon) and B (an anaesthetist) two strategies, a_o and a_i for A, and b_o and b_i for B. Faced by the problem that one of their patients has died due to their failure to observe a treatment protocol and their propensity to innovate with new techniques, the two doctors are interviewed separately by their manager and a police officer.

The two doctors are to be investigated, tried and sentenced for providing unauthorised care which led to a patient's death, but their prosecutors have insufficient evidence. The prosecutors do have evidence of a joint minor crime. Each doctor is asked whether he or she will confess and the choice set is shown in Table 1.

If both doctors confess, they will be tried for the major crime but given a reduced sentence, say 10 years (options a_i and b_i). If neither doctor confesses, they will be sentenced for the minor crime a_o and b_o). If one doctor confesses and the other does not, then the "honest" practitioner goes free and his or her colleague gets 20 years in prison (either a_o b_i or a_i b_o). The preferences of the two doctors in the "Prisoner's Dilemma" are set out in Table 2.

Doctor A's preferred option is a_i b_o, where he or she confesses and B gets 20 years in prison. The second preference is to refuse to confess and receive sentencing only for a minor crime. A's third preference is dependent, mutual confession and the least preferred outcome is that B confesses and A does not, with the result that A gets a 20-year prison sentence. B's preferences are similarly dictated by self-interest: option 1 (a_o b_i) results in A being imprisoned for 20 years and getting B off free, option 2 (a_o b_i) no confessions, option 3 (a_i b_i) mutual confession, and option 4 "carrying the can" (a_i b_o).

The outcome of the "Prisoner's Dilemma" is that each would like mutual silence (a_o b_o) but because it is in the interest of each to break silence unless there is enforcement, they do not trust one another and prefer to opt for mutual, independent confession (a_i b_i). Thus in the absence of enforcement, each doctor is worse off as a result of rational behaviour.

Table 1. The prisoner's dilemma

		Doctor B (anaesthetist)			
		Confess (b_i)	Not confess (b_o)		
Doctor A (surgeon)	Confess (a_i)	10	10	0	20
	Not confess (a_o)	20	0	2	2

Table 2. "Prisoner's dilemma" choice orderings

Doctor A	Doctor B
$a_i b_o$	$a_o b_i$
$a_o b_o$	$a_o b_o$
$a_i b_i$	$a_i b_i$
$a_o b_i$	$a_i b_o$

Such competitive behaviour is, however, violated by players in many experimental games as well as in observations of real life events. This discrepancy between theory and behaviour can be resolved by either relaxing the mutual knowledge assumption [assumption (4) above] or by taking a practical reasoning approach which involves reference to ethics, social norms and reciprocity to and relaxation of assumption (3).

The first practical reasoning approach is the "Assurance Game", where there is a contract or professional code of mutual non-confession. Each doctor knows his or her colleague will do the "right thing" by remaining silent and there is no temptation to maximise individual self-interest. Such behaviour leads to "Assurance Game" preferences (which differ from the "Prisoner's Dilemma" preferences above) as shown in Table 3.

With the "Assurance game" there are two equilibrium points (a_o b_o, a_i b_i) and, because of assurance, the superior equilibrium may be reached. For this outcome to be achieved, the assumption of goal priority is violated.

Assurance would not be necessary if the doctors' preferences had the ordering shown in Table 4.

What Sen in 1972 called "other regarding" behaviour means that each would be determined not to let the other doctor down (see Sen 1982). The concern of one doctor for another helps to explain why they cooperate and succeed in avoiding penalties (e.g. the threat of long-term imprisonment in the "Prisoner's Dilemma" game). These behavioural norms may be particular to groups and societies and create a sense of "identity" which influences behaviour.

Table 3. "Assurance game" choice orderings

Doctor A	Doctor B
a_ob_o	a_ob_o
a_ib_o	a_ob_i
a_ib_i	a_ib_i
a_ob_i	a_ib_o

Table 4. "Other regarding" choice orderings

Doctor A	Doctor B
a_ob_o	a_ob_o
a_ob_i	a_ib_o
a_ib_o	a_ob_i
a_ib_i	a_ib_i

Sen's "other regarding" approach is derived from philosophical and physchological literature. Kant's categorical imperative was to act in a way you wish others to act: do as you would be done by. This approach is altruistic and rational. If an individual deviates from social norms her or she may be successful initially in a world of cooperators but eventually cooperators will defect, become deviant and turn the success of the initial deviant into failure.

Higgs (1985) reports a series of psychology experiments which show that people pay more attention to the evaluations they regard as more competent than themselves, identities once acquired are difficult to alter and to the extent they can be altered "the degree of change effected is inversely related to the amount of social support of significant others" (Webster 1975 quoted in Higgs 1985). Whilst much can be learnt from social psychology, the integration of these lessons into economic theory appears to be as yet limited.

The apparent architect of rationality and self-interest as the basis for economic action, Adam Smith the apparent apostle of self-love and atomististic maximisation, recognised the importance of social norms as a factor determining individual behaviour (Smith 1790, chapter IV, para. 12, chapter V, para. 1, pp 160–162):

> Those general rules of conduct when they have been fixed in our mind by habitual reflection, are of great use in correcting the misrepresentations of self-love concerning what is fit and proper to be done in our particular situation. . . .
> The regard of those general rules of conduct, is what is properly called a sense of duty, a principle of greatest consequence in human life, and the only principle by which the bulk of mankind are capable of directing their actions.

The importance of social values in motivating and explaining behaviour is evident from the analysis of the economic performance of different countries. Economic productivity is dependent on cooperation and teamwork in management and production. The extent to which people can be induced to work together and rely on each other for assistance in their individual activities can, thus, be of great importance. It has been argued that countries such as Japan (Morishima 1982) which emphasise social norms other than those of individual self-interest have been more successful economically.

Dore (1983) has also sought to draw lessons from Japanese behaviour. He points out that a cardinal sin in Japan is lack of sincerity and emphasises that goodwill is of crucial importance in all market transactions. Williamson (1979), who continually emphasises the importance of transaction costs in all contracts, has highlighted the existence of "obligational contracting" in which buyers and sellers maintain relationships based on goodwill. Such contracting is very different from the spot contracting familiar in western markets which Solow (1980) has likened to a one-night-stand rather than the long-term marriage inherent in obligational (Williamson) or relational (Dore) contracting. Yet such contracting arrangements may be more relevant in health care systems, where collaboration between patients and providers is an essential element of the health production function.

Inherent in Williamson's (1985) and Dore's (1983) analysis is that relational contracting reduces risks and transaction costs by exploiting a dislike of adversarial attitudes and a recognition of dutifulness. Morishima (1982) argues that such attitudes in the Japanese are the result of long-term religious influences which act as a guardian of the Government"s legitimacy and sanctify the legitimacy of the ruling classes. The west, being influenced by the individual ethic of Protestantism, has evolved adversarial market relationships. However, such relationships may vary within countries and across sectors (especially those related to caring mores) and the ethics of both east and west may change over time.

Social values may produce resource allocations which are apparently inefficient but produce rapid economic growth. Dore argues that the Japanese economy is riddled with misallocation, but relational contracting compensates for this by reducing X-inefficiency. Whilst relational contracting distorts the price system, it creates employment contracts in which workers are anxious to retrain as market needs alter and in which capitalists, when faced by declining demand, have a sharp incentive to produce new product lines. Thus, the feeling of mutual obligation facilitates new investment, the rapid flow of information and an emphasis on quality: quality assurance depends on trust. Such qualities are not unimportant in the health care market and impending reforms may undermine the relational contracts that exists between doctors and other care professionals.

Thus the simple self-interest maximisation assumptions may ignore important interactions between individuals and society (Hirschman 1970, 1982) and, as a consequence, such models may be inadequate and actual behaviour may be more complex. In evaluating standard models of rational behaviour, Sen emphasises the distinction between "representations of rationality" and "their usefulness in predicting actual behaviour" (Sen 1987, p. 71). An alternative is bounded rationality where choice is not a simple and all encompassing maximisation behaviour, but is a series of non-integrated choices based on limited information and little consideration. An advocate of this approach argues that (Simon 1983, p. 23, quoted in Sen 1987, p. 78):

> Rationality of the sort described by the behavioural model (of bounded rationality) doesn't optimise, of course. Nor does it even guarantee that our decision will be consistent. As a matter of fact, it is very easy to show that choices made by an organism having these characteristics will often depend on the order in which alternatives are presented.

Whilst such models of "bounded rationality" can be advocated with claims of greater plausibility in explaining behaviour, the unrealism of specific kinds of "irrational" action is comparable to the unrealism of rational behaviour. As

Solow argued; "a reasonable theory of economic policy ought to be based on a reasonable theory of economic life" (1980, p. 10).

Conclusions

The beliefs inherent in the United Kingdom proposals for health care reform arise from the adversarial economics of the neoclassical model in which individuals and institutions are assumed to be motivated by "self-love". Such narrow theories based on simple maximisation behaviour and atomistic competition have not been tested extensively and the area of incentive contracting has been relatively ignored by economists in general and health economists in particular. A consideration of this limited literature tends to underplay the role of "social norms" in determining behaviour. In health care markets, such unwritten rules may be of considerable importance. Mutual goodwill may reduce transaction costs and facilitate investment, information exchanges and the enhancement of quality. Issues such as these, arising from institutional economics, psychology and sociology, need integrating into the process of evaluating incentive contracts and new forms of health care structure. As it is, the process of health care market reform appears to be based on the narrow maximisation assumptions which Adam Smith did *not* believe in. Policy makers and politicians who are the slaves of defunct economists may find their "theories" (or beliefs) a poor basis on which to enhance the length and quality of life of patients at least cost!

One important consequence of these arguments for the reform of the health care is to throw doubt on the efficiency of competition as a resolution of cost inflation and resource misallocation. The production of health requires patients and health professionals to work cooperatively rather than participate in competition, a contest between rival buyers and sellers. The model of competition, involving adversarial relationships and striving for market shares, whilst central to much that is taught in economics, may be inappropriate if used alone as a basis for the efficient reform of the NHS and other health care systems.

References

Becker G, Stigler G (1974) Law enforcement, malfeasance and compensation of enforces. J Leg Stud 3:1–18

Department of Health and the Welsh Office (1989) General practice in the National Health Service: a new contract. Department of Health and the Welsh Office, London

Dore R (1983) Goodwill and the spirit of market capitalism, Br J Sociol (4):450–482

Ehrenberg R, Smith RC (1982) Modern labor economics: theory and public policy. Scott, Foremann, Glenville

Enthoven AC (1981) Health plan: the only practical solution to the soaring cost of medical care. Addison-Wesley, Reading

Enthoven AC (1985) Reflections on the management of the National Health Service. Nuffield Provincial Hospitals Trust, London, occasional paper No. 5

Enthoven AC (1989) The consumer-choice health plan for the 1990s. N Engl J Med 329 (1):29–37

Higgs R (1985) Identity and cooperation: a comment on Sen's alternative programme. J Law Econ Organisation 3 (1):140–42

Hirschman AO (1970) Exit, voice and loyalty. Harvard University Press, Cambridge

Hirshman AO (1982) Shifting involvements. University Press, Princeton

Killingworth MC (1983) Labour supply. Cambridge University Press, London

Lazear EP (1987) Incentive contracts. In: Ealwell J, Milgate M, Newman P (eds) The new Palgrave: a dictionary of economics, vol 2. Macmillan, London

Maynard A (1989) Whither the NHS? Centre for Health Economics, University of York, York (NHS occasional paper No. 1)

Maynard A, Williams A (1984) Privatisation and the National Health Service. In: Le Grand J, Robinson R (eds) Privatisation and the welfare state. Allen and Unwin London

Marishima M (1982) Why has Japan "succeeded"? Cambridge University Press, Cambridge

Sen AK (1982) Choice welfare and measurement. Blackwell, Oxford

Sen AK (1985) Goals, commitment and identity. J Law Econ Organisation 1 (2):341–355

Sen AK (1987) Rational behaviour. In Ealwell J, Milgate M, Newman P (eds) The new Palgrave: a dictionary of economics, vol 4. Macmillan London

Simon HA (1983) Reason in human affairs. Blackwell, Oxford

Smith A (1776/1976) An inquiry into the nature and causes of the wealth of nations. Campbell RH, Skinner AS (eds) Oxford University Press, Oxford

Smith A (1790/1976) Theory of moral sentiments. (Revised edn, Macfie R, Macfie Al, eds) Clarendon, Oxford

Solow R (1980) Theories of unemployment. Am Econ Rev 70 (1):1–11

Williams A (1989) Efficiency ethics and clinical freedom. Centre for Health Economics, University of York, York (NHS occasional paper No. 5)

Williamson OE (1979) Transaction cost economics: the governance of contractual relations. J Law Econ 22 (ii):233–261

Williamson OE (1985) The economic institutions of capitalism. Free Press, Macmillan, London

Working for Patients: the Health Service, caring for the 1990s (1989) Presented to Parliament by the Secretaries of State for Health, Wales, Scotland and Northern Ireland. HMSO, London

Incentives for Healthy Consumer Behaviour and Intersectorial Measures for Health Targets

J. Rovira

Introduction

The two concepts included in the title of this paper, intersectorial measures and individual incentives for healthy behaviour, do not form a logical unity; they are rather intended to embrace part of the field of health policy that is not directly involved with the provision and consumption of health care, but with activities of primary prevention and health promotion.

The term "incentive" has both in common and in technical language a rather loose meaning, usually referring to anything that stimulates or motivates somebody to do or to want something. In the economic literature it is often used for the incentives created by the market or by the economic authority; in the context of the economics of a firm, incentives usually refer to ways to promote higher productivity among workers, such as monetary rewards, prizes, longer vacations or even intangible advantages. In its broader sense we may therefore define incentives as "the set of situations that motivate a given action" (Antoñanzas 1989) irrespective of whether or not this situation is the result of purposeful action on the part of one subject who is trying to influence the behaviour of another.

An initial distinction can therefore be made between an *implicit* and an *explicit* incentive according to whether it is the result of a purposeful action of someone intending them to use it as a means to an end.

The simplest conceptual framework of an explicit incentive could be that of a subject, A, who uses means available to him or her to influence a factor which is intended in its turn to influence the behaviour of subject B, thus obtaining certain effects, which are A's objective (see Fig. 1). In the case of an antismoking policy, subject A could be a government using its regulatory powers to restrict accessibility to tobacco products with the aim of inducing the population to reduce its consumption, thus reducing the risk of disease.

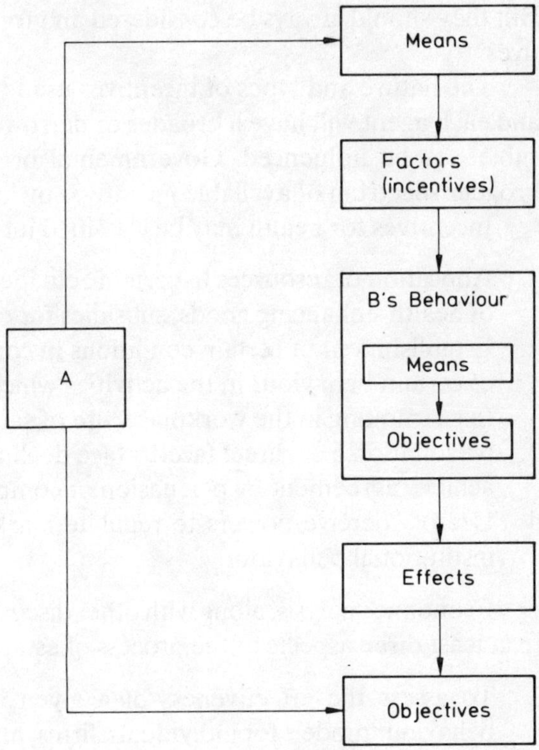

Fig. 1. Model of incentive setting

To establish an incentive, subject A should have:

1. Some explicit objective
2. A model representing the system involved in the chain of causal relationships linking factors which may constitute incentives with the desired effects
3. The means that allow some control over those factors

Incentives may be called effective as long as the effects agree with the objectives. If the incentives generate opposite effects to those intended or undesirable side effects, we may speak of perverse incentives. Again the antismoking policy example will serve as an illustration.

A tax increase on tobacco intended to reduce consumption can be ineffective if demand is very inelastic. Moreover, low-income individuals may reduce the consumption of other essential goods, thus harming their health. Taxes may encourage illegal trade, which may offset, partly at least, the intended effect and also promote criminal behaviour. Smokers may turn from tobacco to other more damaging drugs. And so on. These are of course hypothetical effects. Their existence and importance is an empirical question.

But they should always be considered and foreseen when establishing incentives.

The nature and types of incentives used to promote health are manifold and each agent will have a broader or narrower set available for each type of subject to be influenced. Governmental organizations have in principle a broader spectrum of available incentives owing to their coercive powers.

Incentives for health may be classified into four broad types:

1. Allocation of resources to certain activities: health education, production of health-enhancing goods, subsidies for certain goods or activities.
2. Establishment of certain conditions in contracts: requirement for or ban of certain behaviour in the activities which are the object of the contract (e.g., smoking in the workplace, use of safe materials).
3. Negotiation, i.e., direct face-to-face dealing with other parties in order to achieve agreement by persuasion or compensation of some kind.
4. Use of coercive powers to regulate market conditions or individual or institutional behaviour.

Economic analysis, along with other disciplines, can play an important role in at least three aspects of the process of establishing incentives for health:

1. To assess the effectiveness of a given incentive system by means of behaviour models for individuals, firms, markets, etc. Of course, given the likely complexity of the incentive/effect relationship and the difficulty of controlling all the relevant factors, it may often prove impossible to trace back a given effect to the incentive evaluated. This will be especially true when the measure consists not of the change of a simple element, but of a more radical change of the structure of the system; but economic models may still be useful in assessing partial links in the chain of relationships.
2. To assess the efficiency of a given incentive. Cost-benefit and cost-effectiveness analysis are the traditional tools of economic analysis for this purpose.
3. To discuss the justification of a given incentive. Efficiency can of course be a criterion to justify an incentive, but it is by no means the only legitimate one. Moreover, some people may not agree with the value judgements implied in welfare economics, which form the foundations of the economic evaluation of efficiency. In that case, economics will not be able to provide an answer that satisfies everyone, but it may still help to clarify the terms of the problem, e.g. making explicit alternative technical and value judgements or the implications of taking health or welfare (as defined in welfare economics) as the ultimate objectives of health policy (Culyer 1989).

Incentives for Healthy Consumer Behaviour: An Illustrative Model

In this section I will try to illustrate, with the help of a simple model, the potential contribution of economics to some of the issues raised in the previous section in the particular case of incentives for healthy consumer behaviour.

The growing awareness brought about by the health sciences of the causes and risk factors of ill health has led to the recognition that some of the main factors affecting the health of an individual fall at least partially under his or her control.

This fact has sometimes been put forward by representatives of some ideologies as an argument to justify a withdrawal of the public sector from its responsibilities towards the health of individuals. Their opponents claim, however, that individuals are in fact constrained by social factors – low income, lack of information, etc. – to choose ways of living that damage their health, and that there is no point in blaming individuals for being unhealthy when the social system denies them the resources to make an unconstrained choice. Whichever the ideological perspective might be in relation to public sector responsibility towards health, it would be foolish not to recognize and take advantage of the possibilities of attaining health goals by inducing changes in peoples' life styles and behaviour with the help of suitable incentives.

Table 1 shows the ten leading causes of potential life years lost in Spain in 1978, which amount to 71% of total potential life years lost (PLYL) in this period. PLYL is an index computed as the product of deaths at each age between 1 and 70 years by the number of remaining years to 70 (García et al. 1986). The data highlight the prominent role of behavioural and environmental factors as causes of mortality. According to a recent estimation (González

Table 1. The ten leading causes of potential life years lost in Spain, 1978, by sex (García et al. 1986)

Rank	Cause of death (ICD-8)	Total	Males	Females
1	Malignant neoplasms	12.2	14	10.5
2	Traffic accidents	5.7	8.9	2.6
3	Non traffic accidents	5.2	8.3	2.1
4	Ischaemic heart disease	3.5	5.9	1.2
5	Cerebrovascular disease	3.1	3.6	2.6
6	Cirrhosis	2.3	3.5	1.2
7	Pneumonia and influeza	1.5	1.9	1.1
8	Meningitis	0.94	0.94	0.94
9	Chronic rheumathic heart disease	0.93	0.82	1.04
10	Congenital anomalies	0.90	0.94	0.86

Rates per thousand

et al. 1989), smoking alone accounts for 35% of coronary heart disease, 15% of acute cerebrovascular events, and 68% of cancer deaths. Alcohol is assumed to be responsible for 70% of deaths from cirrhosis, between 40% and 50% of traffic accidents and 15% of deaths from occupational accidents (Freixa et al. 1985).

Three types of incentive will be analysed below:

1. Increasing the price of the harmful goods or making the costs of their consumption higher by other means. Reducing accessibility may be one of these means.
2. Providing information to make individuals aware of the actual negative effects of some goods on consumer health.
3. Trying to persuade consumers to give health a higher priority among their objectives.

Both type 2 and 3 effects are usually sought independently or together in health education programmes.

The model will be based on Lancaster's theory of consumer behaviour. This approach can be summarized as follows (Lancaster 1966):

1. The good, per se, does not give utility to the consumer; it possesses characteristics, and these characteristics give rise to utility.
2. In general, a good will possess more than one characteristic, and many characteristics will be shared by more than one good.
3. Goods in combination may possess characteristics different from those pertaining to the goods separately.

For the sake of simplicity I shall consider that the third assumption does not apply to this case. Further assumptions of the model are:

1. The collection of goods available to the consumer consists of only two goods, X_1 and X_2. X_1 has two characteristics: it gives *satisfaction* (Z_1) to the consumer, but it *reduces his or her health* (Z_2). Z_2 provides satisfaction and has no effects on health. Characteristics are linked to goods by linear transformation functions.[1]
2. The consumer tries to maximize utility subject to a budget constraint. The arguments of the ordinal utility function of the consumer, $U(Z_i)$, are the characteristics Z_1 and Z_2.[2]

[1] The consumer is assumed to know with certainty the negative effects of X_1 on his or her health (stock), in spite of those effects not appearing until some time in the future.

[2] If health is taken as a durable commodity or an asset providing a flow of health services, the decision problem for the consumer should be that of a life time maximizer of an intertemporal utility function (see the seminal work by Grossman (1972); for extensions of the Grossman model see Muurinen (1982), Grossman (1982) and Wagstaff (1986a,b). See also the paper in this volume by Birch and Stoddart. The model that I present is oversimplified but still valid – I hope – for the purposes of my discussion.

3. External effects, uncertainties and addictive properties are assumed to be absent. *U*(*Zi*) is assumed to have the ordinary convex properties of a standard utility function, and the consumer is assumed to spend his or her whole income on the purchase of available goods. The relationship between goods and characteristics is supposed to be a linear one.

A graphic representation of the model is shown in Fig. 2a-f. The utility function, U(Zi), is originally defined in the characteristics space, but the transformation function linking goods to characteristic allows the utility function to be defined alternatively in the goods space, V(Xi). The budget constraint in its turn can be defined either in the goods space as in standard consumer theory or in the characteristics space.

The effects of the three different types of incentives are shown in Fig. 2a,b (price increase), 2c,d (provision of information) and 2e,f (persuasion, i.e., inducing changes in consumer valuation of characteristics). In the initial situation, at points *A* and *A'*, we assume the individual to be consuming positive amounts of both goods. This means that although the consumer is aware of the health-damaging effects of X_1, which reduce his or her utility, the satisfaction he or she gets from its consumption compensates the loss.

An increase in the price of X_1 will change the budget constraint of the consumer; *R* and *R'* will rotate to the left as shown in Fig. 2a,b. The trade-off between satisfaction and health becomes more favorable to health and the consumer will probably move to a new equilibrium like the one represented by points *B* and *B'*, where he or she is consuming less of both goods and is consequently more healthy, but enjoys a lower level of wellbeing, as he or she has been forced to move to a lower indifference curve, from U_0 to U_1.

Consider now that the consumer receives information that persuades him or her that X_1 is more harmful to health than he or she had thought. The budget constraint in the space of goods remains unchanged (as prices and income remain constant) but in the space of characteristics it does change, making satisfaction again more "expensive" in terms of health (Fig. 2c,d). The change in the perception of the transformation function of X_1 will change the derived utility function in the goods space and we could expect a new equilibrium in points such as *D* and *D'* respectively, where the individual will be consuming less of X_1 and more of X_2, and will enjoy a higher level of health. Although he or she is now in a lower indifference curve, it is difficult to state unambiguously that his or her wellbeing is less; he or she may have such a subjective feeling, but can also view the new situation as better than the initial one because the real constraints have not changed and the consumer is now able to make a better informed choice and select the bundle of characteristics *D*, which in the new state is preferred to the bundle he or she was enjoying before.

The third type of incentive considered – any measure that makes the individual increase his or her relative valuation of health – can be represented

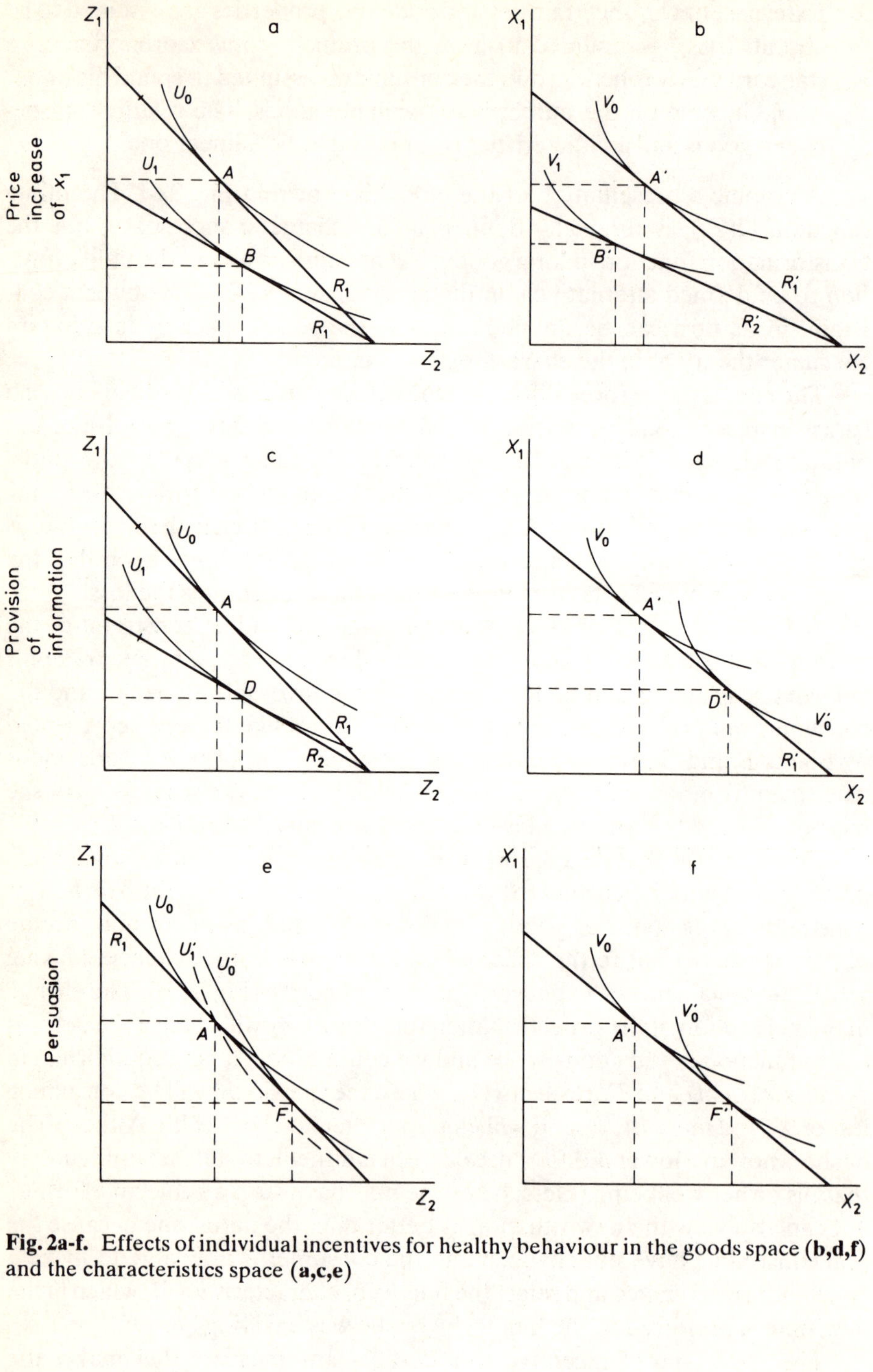

Fig. 2a-f. Effects of individual incentives for healthy behaviour in the goods space (**b,d,f**) and the characteristics space (**a,c,e**)

by a change in the utility function $U(Zi)$, which also implies a change in $V(Xi)$, as shown in Fig. 2e,f. There are no changes in the budget constraint functions and the likely result is an increase in the consumption of X_2, a reduction in X_1 and a higher level of health. In the new utility function the new equilibrium is regarded as superior to A.

The previous analysis has some interesting implications for health policy. The three types of incentive may be effective in terms of improving the individual's health. (Of course, this result is heavily dependent on the assumptions on the utility function. In the case of addictive behaviour, the individual may not reduce consumption of X_1 with any of the three incentives.) The first type of incentive increases health at the expense of reducing wellbeing. Assuming no external factors or information problems, how can such a measure be justified?

Persuading people to assign a higher priority to health may be effective without apparently reducing people's wellbeing. However, the legitimacy of the public powers interfering with or manipulating people's preference orderings is also a debatable issue. The consumer may feel better, but this is hardly an argument, as it would justify any kind of induced changes of values.

Providing information is probably the alternative which is least open to criticism, as long as the information is accurate. It should be noted that erroneous or biased information can have, at least in the short term, the same effect on behaviour as good information, as the consumer will not have the opportunity to judge its validity until a period of time has elapsed. Of course, diffusion of erroneous or contradictory information will undermine in the long run the credibility of its suppliers, which future educational efforts may turn out to be completely incapable of restoring, even when the information supplied is valid.

One of the disadvantages of any type of incentive that reduces consumer utility or wellbeing is that the consumer may try to overcome or bypass the restriction imposed on him or her, e.g., buying the goods in illegal markets at a lower price or substituting alternative products with similar characteristics.

Addictive behaviour could be represented in our model by a utility function generating an indifference map such as the one shown in Fig. 3. Now the consumer is not going to reduce the amount of X_1 consumed below a given minimum as long as he or she can afford to buy it. Price increases will induce him or her to devote a larger share of income to X_1, thus reducing the consumption of the other goods down to zero. Of course this simple static model is not suited for the analysis of the dynamic aspects of addictive behaviour, e.g. the change over time of the minimum level of X_1 needed.

The previous analysis is, as stated initially, only intended to be illustrative. A realistic model would be far more complex and empirical estimations would be required for the model to give accurate and testable predictions. Finally it

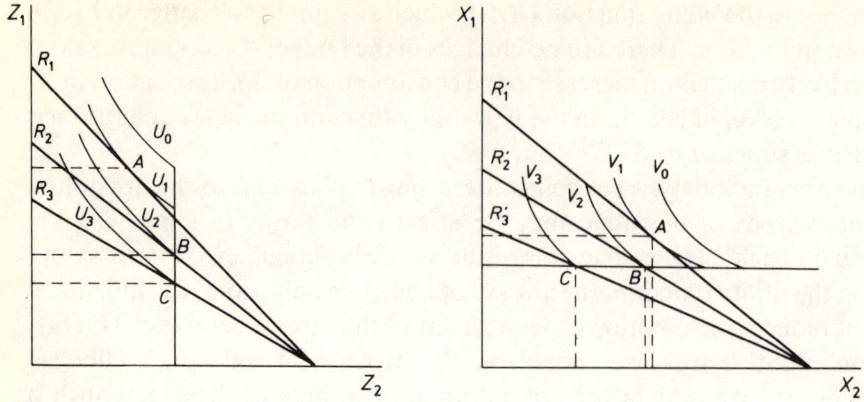

Fig. 3. Effects of incentives on addictive behaviours

should be stressed that economic analysis alone cannot offer the right answer to all questions arising from a policy to provide incentives for healthier behaviour, but it may serve at least to clarify the issues and to help to formulate the relevant questions.[3]

Intersectorial Measures

Intersectorial action (ISA) for health is a health policy approach based on the cooperation of different social sectors in the development of coordinated health strategies to attain given health goals. The justification for ISA derives from the acknowledgement of the limitations of a dominantly disease-oriented and curative health policy and from the assumed superiority of one in which

---

[3] The empirical studies that have tried to estimate the effect of price increases and health education on the consumption of hazardous goods give a wide range of estimates according to the specification of the model and the type of data used. In the case of tobacco consumption, price elasticities range from −0.2 to −1.3 (Lewit and Coate 1982; Maynard and Kennan, undated; Leu 1984; Godfrey 1986; Townsend 1987; Maynard and Jones undated). Price increases reduce cigarette consumption primarily through reductions in the smoking participation rate, while having a much smaller impact on the quantity of cigarettes demanded by smokers (Lewit and Coate 1982). The effects of health education programmes are often difficult to pick out because other factors may be changing at the same time. However, econometric studies of time series data carried out in the United States, the United Kingdom, and Switzerland have provided substantial evidence of the effectiveness of particular campaigns (see Leu 1984; Godfrey 1986 and Townsend 1987). Health education has been introduced as a dummy variable in some of the tobacco demand equations estimated and significant effects have usually been found, although these are small.

the main focus is on prevention of disease, the maintenance and promotion of good health, and the capacity to resist disease (WHO 1986), goals which cannot be realized through the services provided by the health sector alone.

Although many of the ideas behind the ISA approach are by no means new, the rising costs of health care and the perception of the decreasing returns of curative medicine in terms of improved survival and quality of life have stimulated health authorities and governments to pay greater attention to the possibilities of improving health from outside the health sector.

The World Health Organization (WHO) has played a leading role in the process of making governments aware of the capabilities of ISA. In 1981 the WHO initiated a series of studies and research projects designed to gain a better understanding of the interrelationships between development activities and major changes in the health status of the population (Gunatilleke 1984) which have been followed by meetings, technical discussions and recommendations to the member states (WHO 1986; Zöllner 1987). Although much experience has been gained as a result of these efforts, the actual achievements are rather limited and a global conceptual framework for developing ISA is still lacking.[4]

Let us take tobacco as an example: there is widely accepted evidence among policymakers and society on its harmful effects and about the limited effects of health education and incentives to the consumer, while its consumption is strongly promoted from the supply side. However, any policy aimed at reducing consumption conflicts with many parties' goals and is not likely to find any support from them. Farmers, firms, traders, agricultural and trade departments and sometimes even the Treasury perceive antismoking policies as a threat to their interests. What kind of strategy could be developed to make them cooperate in an intersectoral antismoking policy?

In the 1950s and the 1960s the social and political climate favoured economic growth as the main concern. Health, education, and other dimensions of social wellbeing were seen predominantly as instruments to help economic growth. Nowadays, partly as a result of the negative side effects of growth and partly because of the success of growth policies themselves, the perspective is rapidly changing and there is a growing consensus in viewing health and social wellbeing as ends and economic growth as an instrument to attain those ends.

However, this view is not shared unanimously by all members and sectors of society. Even within the power and administrative structures, the division

[4] For some interesting approaches, see ENSP-APES (1987) and Köhler and Martin (1983).

of responsibilities among different organizations results in most of them not sharing the same set of priorities, but each one establishing, to a great extent, its own objectives, often conflicting with those of other organisms.

The main value judgment underlying ISA for health is that health should be a matter of concern for all sectors and not only for the health sector. At present, this statement far from reflects the actual situation. The health sector – authorities, administrative organizations and providers – seem to attach a higher relative priority to health than do the other sectors and, as such, it is likely to be the most interested party in developing ISA for health. This is actually what one would expect, as traditionally legislation and public opinion assigns to the health sector the responsibility to care for people's health.[5]

The health sector will (and probably should) have a leading role in the very first stages of the development of an intersectorial policy, but, because of its proper nature, ISA should be based on participation on a parity basis for all sectors involved. A strong commitment of the higher levels of political power may also be a decisive factor.

So far one cannot speak of global and generally accepted models of ISA. However, there are several elements or steps which seem essential to a rational intersectorial strategy:

1. Establishment of the objectives of the ISA, e.g., elimination or reduction of a given health problem
2. Identification of the epidemiological causes or risk factors of the health problem
3. Identification of the underlying social factors
4. Design of measures or strategies to modify those factors

Intersectorial action implies modifying the behaviour of social agents, which requires: (a) identifying the relevant social agents, (b) identifying which behaviour is required from each agent and (c) setting up the incentives to obtain the required behaviour. All of these steps are quite difficult. The types of agents involved are manifold. Often, for many of them, there will be no reliable models of behaviour available. I shall briefly discuss the problems raised by two types of agents: commercial firms and governmental organizations.

---

[5] However, as most factors causing ill health do not fall under its competence, the health sector has tended often to restrict itself to matters related to health care provision and not to feel responsible for promoting a global health policy. At the most, health sector representatives devote a certain amount of energy to criticisms and blame other sectors for their health-damaging activities, which is not the best way to attain intersectoral collaboration.

Commercial firms have a great influence on the health of the population, especially on the health of their own employees, but also on that of those exposed to the effects of the environment of the firm and of those affected by its economic activities. Commercial firms are basically profit or productivity oriented organizations and these objectives often conflict with health objectives: better safety at the workplace, antipollutant devices or substitution of potentially hazardous materials usually imply higher production costs and hence a loss of competitiveness and profit. It is therefore unlikely that a firm will introduce those kind of measures voluntarily. A firm that did so in a competitive market would place itself in a disadvantageous position in relation to the less health-conscious firms.

To sum up, it is unlikely that "health education" of firms will be effective and incentives will have to rely on coercive regulations or market intervention. However, a competitive market provides some important incentives for firms to be concerned about the health effects of their activities (Economic Report of the President, 1987 pp. 181–182).

A healthier and less risky workplace can induce workers to accept lower salaries than they would earn in similar but riskier firms. The consumers may also be willing to pay a higher price for a healthier product. Moreover, becoming involved in a severe public health incident will probably have a negative impact on profits both because of indemnity payments and through the loss of image, which can affect sales and profits negatively. In some cases, the behaviour of a firm can be modified by providing adequate information. Some polluting industries in Catalonia were induced to install antipollutant devices because the officials of an environmental agency were able to show them that the measure would be self-financing (Rovira 1987).

One advantage for ISA policymakers when dealing with firm behaviour is the availability of a well-established and, to a large extent, reliable body of theory that permits a prediction of the response of the firm to a given incentive.[6] Unfortunately this is not the case when dealing with governmental organizations. In spite of the considerable amount of existing literature on politician and bureaucrat behaviour, the spectrum of public organizations seems to be too broad and heterogeneous to make them amenable to useful modelling of their behaviour.

The literature on ISA usually identifies bureaucratic inertia and diverging objectives as the main obstacles for intersectorial cooperation between governmental organizations. Moreover, intersectorial measures are usually of a preventive kind; the benefits, however important, tend to be diffusely distributed in some future periods, while most costs occur in the present and

---

6 See, for instance, Knesse (1977) for some quantitative economic models which have proven highly useful in the analysis of environmental problems.

are borne by identifiable individuals. These characteristics of ISA make it less than attractive to politicians who are mainly concerned, for electoral reasons, with short-term achievements.

Intersectorial cooperation among governmental organizations should rely fundamentally on negotiation since each organization usually has a high degree of autonomy in its area of competence. Sectorial organizations are usually not able to regulate or exert coercion over other sectorial organizations, and over the entities under their control.

Negotiating means discussing the terms of an agreement. If we assume that a given health prevention policy requires the voluntary agreement of a set of parties, we can assume that the individual parties will give their consent only if they feel that the agreement will make them better off. Those who lose will have to be compensated by the winners, otherwise they will not agree.

Cost-benefit analysis is a widely used approach to decision-making in health care that can be applied to ISA as well. A positive net benefit of some measure would mean that the alternative evaluated increases the wellbeing of society as a whole and therefore should be chosen on efficiency criteria. Some individuals may lose but the potential compensation principle assumes that, as the winners would be able to compensate the losers and still be left better off, the situation is a better one from society's point of view.[7]

However, in a negotiation the losers have to be actually compensated if they are to agree. Therefore, a positive net benefit will not necessarily imply that an ISA measure is feasible. To explore the feasibility of an ISA measure a different approach is needed. Table 2 outlines such an alternative approach, which is nothing but an extension of traditional cost-benefit analysis. In column 1 all the relevant effects of an intersectorial measure to be negotiated among three parties (A, B, C) are listed. The list of effects could be broken down into more specific subcategories of effects. Columns 2 and 3 represent the two standard steps of an economic evaluation, i.e. measurement and

---

[7] For such approaches applied to smoking see Bruce and Schweitzer (1977); Oster et al. (1984) and Hjalte (1984). However, there are several studies that have tried to estimate a broader range of effects of smoking prevention programmes (DHSS 1972; Leu 1981; Harris 1982; Leu and Schaub 1984; Baxter 1986; Stoddart et al. 1986; Rovira and Escribano 1989). Some of the non-intuitive effects found are:

1. The smoking-related health care costs avoided are usually overcompensated, especially in the long run, by the increased utilization due to a longer life expectancy.
2. Smokers are not subsidized by non-smokers, as tobacco taxes provide a surplus to tobacco-related health care consumption even in the short run.
3. The most dramatic effect to be expected from a reduction in smoking is the increase in future social security expenditure related to retirement pensions.

These results do not invalidate the rationale of antismoking campaigns, but they clearly cast some doubts on the validity of some of the arguments often put forward by their supporters.

Table 2. Social and individual valuations of intersectorial measures

Effects	Magnitude	Social Valuation	Individual Valuation		
			A	B	C
Health	M_1	V_1	V_1^A	V_1^B	V_1^C
Resources	M_2	V_2	V_2^A	V_2^B	V_2^C
Intangibles	M_3	V_3	V_3^A	V_3^B	V_3^C
Transfers	M_4	V_4	V_4^A	V_4^B	V_4^C
		$NSB = \Sigma V_i$	$NIB^A = \Sigma V_i^A$	$NIB^B = \Sigma V_i^B$	$NIB^C = \Sigma V_i^C$

NSB, net social; NIB, net individual benefit to X (X = A, B, C)

valuation of all relevant effects, and NSB is the net social benefit. V_4 would normally be zero, unless we wish to value equity or distributional effects along with efficiency. Columns 4–6 show the respective individual valuations of the effects. The same effect can, of course, be valued differently by each party.

It is not easy to make this approach effective, because the parties will probably not be willing to reveal their true valuations, as this would weaken their negotiating position and it may prove impossible to derive these valuations from observed behaviour. But the approach can nevertheless offer an approximate picture of the feasibility of the measure. The net individual benefit (NIB) represents the perceived gain or loss to a negotiating party as a result of implementing the measure. Conceptually, the feasibility of the measure requires the NIB resulting after compensations have been agreed to be positive for each party. Insofar as the structure of priorities of the parties are similar, the differences in the individual valuations of the effects will be small and the negotiation is likely to give a positive outcome. As health improvements will usually be the main positive effect of intersectorial measures, the parties advocating health objectives may be asked by the other parties to lower the level of the objective to be attained, as a means to reducing its own costs.

Allowing non-health sectors to appear explicitly as fundamental contributors to health achievements will increase their net individual valuation of health benefits and hence the feasibility of the measure at no other cost than for the health sector having to share the political and social acknowledgement of those achievements, if this can be termed a cost.

One of the instruments proposed for ISA is the establishment of committees of an advisory or executive nature where the relevant parties and sectors are represented (Gunatilleke 1984). However, the setting up of committees is not a guarantee for effective cooperation, especially if the priorities of each party differ radically and the conflicts of interests are large; committees may delay the decision-making process unnecessarily and still not reach positive results. Informal contacts between sectors may prove to be more effective than formal committees, at least at the beginning of the process of developing ISA, when the commitment of the parties is likely to be low and reciprocal information is lacking. Some authors also point to the convenience of developing ISA at the grass root level, involving the community and its representative organizations. They argue that it is precisely at that level where the needs and constraints of ISA are more evident (Barnard et al. 1987). There are, however, various kinds of problems, e.g. externalities, that may require decision-making at a higher level if they are to be managed efficiently. Some kinds of external effect provide good examples of this statement.

A local authority can feel induced by community pressures to ban the establishment of noisy or polluting industries in its area, which would only mean that the problem is transferred to other areas, which in turn would be induced to take similar measures. In the event that the main local priority were to fight unemployment, the behaviour would be the opposite. The local authority might refrain from fighting pollution, for fear of the industries moving to more permissive areas.

Conclusions

The health of an individual is affected not only by the consumption of health care services but also by the consumption of hazardous goods and by other effects that are dependent upon his or her own behaviour or that of other social agents. Therefore, modifying those behaviours by means of individual incentives and intersectorial measures may be an effective and efficient way to attain health policy goals.

Economics can provide a framework for the positive and also for the normative analysis of incentives. The main contribution of positive economics is probably the models of individual and aggregate behaviour. Welfare theory and especially economic evaluation are the main tools for the normative economic analysis of incentives. The available economic models of behaviour are much better suited to the analysis of the responses to health-promoting incentives of individuals and firms than to those of other types of organization (public, private, non-profit, etc.).

When trying to assess the effects of incentives on health, a multidisciplinary approach including economics, epidemiology, system analysis and other social disciplines and techniques is required. Intersectorial action is one of the areas of health policy where the lack of adequate global and systematic approaches is more evident. Both its complexities and social relevance makes ISA one of the most challenging areas for future research.

References

Antoñanzas F (1989) Los servicios de urgencias. Economía y Salud 4:1 – AES, Bacerlona
Barnard K, Ritsatakis A, Swensson PG (eds) (1987) Equity and intersectoral action for health, NHV-Report 1987:6. The Nordic School of Public Health, Göteborg
Baxter V (1986) Will quitting smoking help medicare solve its financial problems? Inquiry 23:76–82
Birch S, Stoddart G (1989) Incentives to be healthy: an economic model of health related behavior. First European Conference on Health Economics, Barcelona, September 1989
Bruce BR, Schweitzer SO (1977) The economic costs of smoking-induced illness. In Jarvick ME et al. (eds) Research on smoking behavior. Government Printing Office, Washington DC (NIDA research monograph 17
Culyer AJ (1989) Incentives: for what?, for whom?, what kind? First European Conference on Health Economics. Barcelona, September 1989
Department of Health and Social Security (DHSS) (1972) Smoking and Health. HMSO, London
Economic Report of the President (1987). United States Government Printing Office, Washington, DC
ENSP-APES (Escola Nacional de Saúde) Pùblica, Associaçao Portuguesa de Economia da Saùde (1987) Intersectoral action for health: harmonization of economic and health policies. Workshop proceedings, Lisbon, 1987
Freixa F, Melgarejo M, Rovira R (1985) Etiopatogenia: factores sociales y culturales. Jano 656-M:17–23
García LA, Nolasco A, Bolumar F, Alvarez-Dardet C (1986) Los años potenciales de vida perdida: una forma de evaluar las muertes prematuras. Med Clin (Barc) 87:55–57
Godfrey C (1986) Factors influencing the consumption of alcohol and tobacco – review of demand models, Discussion paper 17. Centre for Health Economics, University of York, York
González J, Rodriguez F, Martin J, Banegas JR, Villar F (1989) Muertes atribuibles al consumo de tabaco en España. Med Clin (Barc) 92:15–18
Grossman M (1972) The demand for health: a theoretical and empirical investigation. NBER, New York (occasional paper 119)
Grossman M (1982) The demand for health after a decade. J Health Econ 1:1–3
Gunatilleke G (ed) (1984) Intersectoral linkages and health development. WHO, Geneva
Harris JE (1982) Increasing the federal excise tax on cigarettes. J Health Econ 1:117–120
Hjalte K (1984) Economic benefits of giving up smoking. The Swedish Institute for Health Economics (IHE), Lund
Knesse AV (1977) Economics and the environment. Penguin, Harmondsworth pp 135–150
Köhler L, Martin J (eds) (1983) Intersectoral action for health. Report of an international workshop at the Nordic School of Public Health, Göteborg, Sweden, 30 May – 8 June 1983
Lancaster KV (1966) A new approach to consumer theory. J Polit Econ 74 (2):132–157
Leu RE (1981) Smoking and health care costs: plus or minus? Health Economists Study Group Meeting, 6–8 January 1982, Glasgow
Leu RE (1984) Anti-smoking publicity, taxation, and the demand for cigarettes. J Health Econ 3:101–116
Leu RE, Schaub T (1984) Economic aspects of smoking. Eff Health Care 2 (3):111–122
Lewit EM, Coate D (1982) The potential for using excise taxes to reduce smoking. J Health Econ 1:121–145
Maynard A, Jones A (1982) Economic aspects of addiction control policies. Centre for Health Economics Addiction Research Centre, University of York, York
Maynard A, Kennan P (1981) The economics of addiction. A survey of the literature and a proposed research strategy. Institute of Social and Economic Research, University of York, York

Muurinen JM (1982) Demand for health: a generalised Grossman model. J Health Econ 1:5–28
Oster G, Colditz GA, Kelly NL (1984) The economic costs of smoking and benefits of quitting. Lexington Books, Lexington, Mass.
Roberts JL, Castle PD (eds) (1979) Economic and inter-sector planning for health. Prevention Department, North Western Regional Health Authority, Manchester
Rovira J (1987) Economic argumentation on HFA: the role of economic factors and economic analysis in the development of HFA policies. Meeting on National HFA Policy Formulation and Implementation, Haikko, Finland, 7–11 February 1988
Rovira J, Escribano M (1989) Estimación del impacto económico de una reducción del consumo de tabaco. Ministerio de Sanidad y Consumo, Madrid
Stoddart GL, Labelle RJ, Barer ML, Evans RG (1986) Tobacco taxes and health care costs. Do Canadian smokers pay their way? J Health Econ 5:63–80
Towsend J (1987) Economic and health consequences of smoking. In: Williams A (ed) Health and economics. MacMillan, New York
Wagstaff A (1986a) The demand for health. Some new empirical evidence. J Health Econ 5:195–233
Wagstaff A (1986b) The demand for health: theory and applications. J Epidemiol Community Health 40:1–11
WHO (1986) Thirty-ninth World Health Assembly, Report of the technical discussions on the role of intersectoral cooperation in national strategies for health for all. A 39/Technical Discussions/4.
Zöllner HFK (1987) Intersectoral action in the context of HFA 2000. Workshop of intersectoral action for health: harmonization of economic and health policies, Lisbon, 26–28 November 1987

Reflections on Incentives and Health System Reform

G.L. Stoddart

"Incentives are the essence of economics".
The New Palgrave Dictionary of Economics

"Beware of incentives".
James A. Morone, *Seven Laws of Policy Analysis*

"Just as a war is too important to be left to generals, so are questions of incentives too important to be left to economists".
Bruno Stein, *Incentives and Planning as Social Policy Tools*

Among economists, few tenets would produce more agreement than the statement that people respond to incentives. This is not a tenet of faith, because ample empirical evidence exists for its support. Perhaps this is why it seems such a small step to go from observation of individuals' behaviour in response to incentives to reliance upon them as a major instrument of social as well as economic policy. Although political scientists and policy analysts are often wary of this step (Morone 1986) and can be especially suspect of reliance on financial incentives (Sapolsky 1977), warnings by economists (Stein 1973) are exceedingly rare. Indeed, in the one specific institutional context most familiar to economists – markets – the notion that production and consumption decisions made be individuals in their own self-interest can achieve social interests goes back at least to Adam Smith.

Incentives to firms and individuals, to investors, savers and consumers are regularly used in most countries as a standard tool of macroeconomic policy. Regulatory systems provide other, non-pecuniary but nonetheless direct incentives to the same sets of transactions in the conduct of their daily business. Increasingly, however, incentives of one type or another are being used or advocated for use in the reform of health systems and their health care and health insurance subsystems. It is more accurate, of course, to say that what is becoming more frequent are recommendations for *changes* to incentives, because incentives for particular behaviours – more of this, less of that – have always existed in all health systems. Nevertheless, incentives in general, and reimbursement incentives in particular, are currently receiving unprecedented attention as instruments of health system reform. Perhaps the most frequent single message for health policymakers emanating from health economists is that the structure of incentives facing patients and providers must be changed, in order to align private and social interests. It is a message which I, like many and perhaps most participants at this conference, have myself delivered (Stoddart 1985).

In this paper I want to offer some general observations and reflections about incentives and their role in health system reform. I should point out that I sympathize with the editor of this volume, who states in his chapter, "the problem of achieving the targets of health systems. . . has no universal solution and requires a problem-specific approach", so it may be that little can be concluded from my general rumination. The volume does not have a shortage of problem-specific papers, however. On the contrary, for specific issues in specific contexts, the papers in this volume represent an embarrassment of riches, and no doubt will produce significant ideas and insights.

For my part, I propose to step back somewhat, and begin with a consideration of the multiple and conflicting objectives which may be pursued in health systems and of the daunting task which therefore faces those pursuing reform. Next I comment on the nature of incentives, discussing what they can and cannot do in relation to the common policy agendas in health system reform, including several caveats about their use.

In the final section of the paper I discuss selected aspects of the Canadian experience with incentives, not just for the obvious reason that it is the system with which I am most familiar, but also because it illustrates a main message of the paper: that in such a complex, significant, and highly politicized social system as health, incentives may or may not play an important role in the achievement of policy objectives; however, even if they do they cannot by themselves guarantee achievement of social goals. Something more appears to be necessary.

On the Tasks of Health System Reform

The objectives pursued in health systems, through health systems, and by those acting within health systems are a complex mixture of social good and private satisfaction. They are multiple, frequently conflicting, and usually contested by the parties who influence and decide health policy. Reform is always necessary, at least in someone's mind.

The basic goals of a health system seem obvious: to provide physical and social environments that promote and maintain health; to provide access to effective health care services for the purpose of preventing illness, curing disease, restoring function, and relieving pain; and to seek new knowledge that furthers these activities. That health care is but one determinant of health is well known and accepted, but it has not yet become the primary view shaping health policy and expenditure patterns in developed countries. Thus, the health system is often regarded in practice as coincident with its health care delivery and health insurance (more accurately, sickness care insurance) subsystems. Altering this view is itself one of the tasks of health system reform, though not the primary one I address here. Nevertheless, a broader view of the determinants of health is highly relevant to decisions to be made in the reform of health care insurance and delivery and the role of incentives in these decisions, as will become clearer below.

Most national health systems display a more egalitarian than libertarian character, which is to say that they attempt to provide citizens with access (See Williams (1988) for a thoughtful discussion of the characteristics of egalitarian and libertarian systems) to health services based on need rather than ability and willingness to pay. This is not to say that the systems display *only* egalitarian characteristics for they typically do not; however, ensuring that there exists an adequate supply of health care providers, facilities and technology, and seeing that citizens are protected against the potentially prohibitive financial costs of care, however these missions are accomplished, are common national concerns. Not surprisingly, the cost of this egalitarian approach is another common national concern. Health care expenditure control has become an internationally shared policy objective.

On the surface at least, our first conflict has emerged. The pursuit and achievement of one objective, albeit to varying degrees across countries, has created another, apparently antithetical one. The situation also contains elements of paradox, given the continuing importance which individuals and societies place upon good health. In the Netherlands, for example, van de Ven (1987) notes that during the preceding 20 years the proportion of people who considered good health as the most important thing in their life increased from about one-third to one-half, yet the rising share of GNP accounted for by health care expenditure during the same period was increasingly defined as a problem. In frequent opinion polls conducted over the past decade in Canada, over three-fourths of respondents consistently rate the health system as their most highly valued public expenditure, yet never have provincial authorities placed as much urgency on expenditure control as they currently do.

There are undoubtedly several reasons for a generalized international concern, if not obsession, with health care expenditures. One is the increasing acceptance of the broader view of the determinants of health other than health care and the doubts that it raises about the contribution of health care subsystems. Not on average, for nobody questions that this is large and positive, but at the margin, where the contribution of expenditures on health care relative to other determinants of health, though in all probability positives may be very small. Another reason, the anticipated impact (alone or, worse, combined) of aging populations and expanding medical technology, falls into a category which van Loon (1986) has termed "preventive worry". Recent increases in expenditures, although tolerable by themselves, may just be the trickle of water flowing over the top of the bursting dam.

Yet another reason is the economic and political discomfort that expenditure increases cause for third-party payers, who must raise premiums, accept lower profits, or restrict coverage/benefits in private systems and raise taxes, incur deficits or reduce spending in other sectors in public systems. Perhaps the most important reason, however (in part due to the perception among health policymakers that it is something they can affect *within* the health care system), is the view that better value could be obtained for the money being spent on health care. The findings of clinical and health services researchers repeatedly suggest that current patterns of health care delivery and utilization are frequently ineffective and inefficient. The research has also highlighted the fact that much of what is done routinely in health care systems generally, and the practice of medicine in particular, remains unevaluated. This is not to suggest that current patterns occur for no reason, nor that the underlying reasons are easily dealt with. Diagnosis and knowledge of etiology do not guarantee cure any more in policy than they do in medicine. But a concern for improving efficiency, fuelled by an aversion to other methods of health care expenditure control, appears to be a common motivation in current discussion of health system reform.

Economists and other analysts typically summarize the objectives of health systems in the words "efficiency" and "equity". What does this encompass? Efficiency alone may refer to at least three types (Pauly 1970; Culyer 1989a): (a) "technical", minimizing the amount of inputs for a given output, i.e. being on an isoquant; (b) "cost-effectiveness", minimizing the cost for a given output, i.e. being where an isocost line is tangent to an isoquant; and (c) "allocative" (Culyer (1989a, p. 35) refers to this type as ideal output), producing and consuming cost-effective outputs in socially optimal amounts, i.e. setting marginal rates of transformation in production equal to marginal rates of substitution in consumption.

Imagine for a moment what this means in the health care subsystem. It means that each and every one of the numerous specific health services – from well baby examinations to coronary artery bypasses – is produced in just the right fashion, using just the right amount of each and every input – different types of health professionals, facilities, technologies – and utilized (consumed) in just the right amount such that the population could not be made "better off" through some other allocation of resources.

In the health system as a whole, additional conditions (objectives) apply. Health care services become only one category of inputs in the production of health; technical efficiency and cost-effectiveness require their optimal combination with all other factors which contribute positively to health. Moreover, we may interpret "better-off" as "healthier" at the level of the health care subsystem, but at the level of the health system health is just one of many outputs to which a society's resources can be allocated. Even the one-half of respondents in the Netherlands who said health was the most important thing in their life do not consider it to be the only thing! Allocative efficiency at this level requires the optimal production and consumption of health in relation to other things.

The objectives of health systems and the tasks of health system reform would be complex and difficult enough if efficiency was the only goal. Yet it is not. Equity is as universally accepted a goal as efficiency, and perhaps more so. Its specific meaning can and does vary from one system to another. It may be defined in relation to access to care – by income, geographic location, or other characteristics of citizens/consumers – or to services actually utilized. It may refer to the distribution of health as well as or instead of health services. Equity across individuals or groups may in some cases entail equality, although it need not and usually does not, for example in its application to the distribution of the costs of health systems. Whatever the application, equity connotes "fairness", itself another complex objective of health systems.

Useful though they are as summary statements of health system goals, the terms "efficiency" and "equity" simply do not convey the myriad of specific objectives which must be made operational on a daily basis for their attainment, and to which incentives may be applied. Nor do they seem to capture appropriately other objectives which most of us find important, for example, the desire that services be delivered by willing, kind, cheerful and considerate providers (Enthoven 1987, p. 30).

Both the complexity and difficulty of health system reform are increased by two further dimensions of objectives in health systems. The first is that the objectives of other systems are often pursued through or conflict with those of the health system, thereby restricting the room for policy change. For example, public health insurance systems are well-accepted conduits for the broader social objective of income redistribution (Barer et al. 1979; Enthoven 1987), and agricultural policies sometimes operate against efforts to improve nutrition or reduce smoking. The second is that there is no guarantee that the objectives of the individual actors, whose behaviour constitutes the most important element of health systems, will correspond to the system objectives.

In fact, there is good reason to believe that they will not correspond, or at best that they will only partially coincide. Even altruistic individuals, unless they are saints or martyrs, are concerned about their own welfare and satisfaction as well as others'! The self-interested behaviour may be motivated by income, and often is, but it need not be. The physician who follows an "ethos" which calls for provision of service until the expected marginal benefit is zero, the hospital administrator who is reluctant to downsize his or her facility and lose prestige, and the policymaker who approves a new programme known to be of dubious value in response to intense lobbying from a powerful group are all acting rationally in both the economist's world and their own, whether or not they become richer as a result. Yet their actions all move us farther from an efficient system.

The impact of the objectives of individual actors on health systems does not stem only from the existence in the actors' utility functions of arguments which are absent from the social welfare function. Many arguments of individual utility functions overlap with important social objectives in the care of the ill and the protection of the healthy. They must, or health systems would not perform as well as they do. Even if the utility functions of the individual actors were identical to the collective social welfare function, however, the value (relative weights) placed upon the different arguments would be another source of conflict. In reality, it is precisely this – differences in perceptions of the relative importance of private interests which also serve the social interest – that pose one of the greatest challenges for health system reform.

The best example of this, at least in Canada, is the frequent public statements by health care providers that there is a crisis, and that society will be "worse off" if the health care subsystem does not soon get increased resource commitments. In its extreme form, this lobbying is conducted through public statements by both leaders of professional associations and individual practitioners to the effect that "patients will die" if this or that (the purchase of the latest equipment, a hospital expansion, increased programme budgets, higher incomes to retain workers or boost morale, . . .) is not done. More good *could* probably be done by the health care subsystem if providers received more resources. And the providers themselves would certainly be better off. Whether society would be better off once the opportunity cost of the increased resource commitment to health care was considered is not as clear.

Although examples like this are the most dramatic, the jostling for position by professional associations, major institutions, unions, voluntary organizations, consumer groups, pharmaceutical firms, equipment manufacturers, community support groups, and a variety of other affected interests is a standard feature of everyday life in most health systems. One goal of this activity is purely private gain, but another, not exclusive one is to press for acceptance and adoption of the particular view of the social welfare function held by the lobbying group. To say that lobbying is an attempt to "hijack" the social welfare function may be going too far, although it communicates well the intensity of the environment.

In such an environment, an ordering of priorities is required, and political processes, with all their imperfections, accomplish this task in health as in other areas of human activity and resource allocation. (Not the least of these imperfections is that politicians too face incentives to act in their own interests instead of those of their constituents.) Some jurisdictions do it better than others, but all accomplish it somehow.

Thus, health system reform is complex because the objectives in health systems are themselves complex. This is hardly a profound statement, though it is an important one. Reform may consist of a re-ordering of priorities, as appears to be the case in the United States currently, or changes to the methods through which an existing set of priorities and objectives is pursued, as seems to be the case in Canada and Europe; however, health system reform ultimately involves one of four basic questions:

1. How much to spend on health versus other commodities and characteristics valued by society. (Culyer (1989b) provides a discussion of the importance of characteristics of people for the quality of life as well as the importance of commodities and their characteristics).
2. Which interventions are effective in producing health. (Interventions are not restricted to health care services; they include such things as income maintenance, housing, education, social support and hazardous substances control).
3. How to provide these interventions cost-effectively.
4. Who shall receive the benefits and bear the costs of spending on health.

These are, of course, no more than a variation on the three basic questions any economic system has to answer – what to produce, how to produce, and how to distribute – as presented in standard, introductory economics texts. These same texts normally continue on to present the analysis of markets and the price system, which, in idealized form in theory and for some commodities in practice (albeit with imperfections and distortions), "solves" these problems every day. This is not the case in health systems, however, for reasons which are well known and which have been repeatedly analyzed (Arrow 1963; Evans 1984; Culyer 1989a).

If it were the case, the role of (financial) incentives, in the form of prices for both outputs and inputs, would be clearer and much simpler. For prices simultaneously perform the dual role of eliciting preferences and influencing behaviour. The price system is both a mirror and a tool. It is generally accepted, however, that health and health care are not like other commodities and that their provision through a price system like that which might prevail in non-administered markets would not produce socially optimal outcomes. The glass is thereby broken, though the tool remains.

The emphasis on need as the basis for the distribution of health services, and the rejection of ability and willingness to pay whatever prices might prevail as an alternative basis, are characteristic of an approach to the design and operation of health systems which has been termed "extra-welfarist" by Culyer (1989a). This approach adopts health as the proximate maximand (rather than the utility derived by sovereign, well-informed consumers from their consumption bundles of commodities including information and health care) and stresses the importance of identifying the potential for benefit from health services. It also admits non-utility information, such as the characteristics of people and social relationships, into comparisons of alternative social states. Perhaps most important for our discussion of incentives and health system reform, however, it raises important questions about how and by whom the value and desirability of alternative social states – involving health outcomes, their distribution, and the distribution of their costs – are to be judged. In other words, it creates roles for management.

Williams (1978) has identified several key roles and the parties who (should) play them in health systems. He labels the roles "advertisers", "applicants", "diagnosers", "priority-setters", "treatment-assigners", and "researchers" and outlines rules by which patients and other potential beneficiaries, experts (both medical and other types), politicians and other policymakers, and the electorate at large might be expected to play them. Whether or not one agrees with Williams' allocation of roles to parties (which in general, I do), this practical approach has always struck me as being quite useful in both emphasizing and keeping clear the variety of management tasks in the health system.

In health system reform, two of the most important management tasks are selecting the targets/objectives and choosing the strategies to be employed for their achievement. The first is the source of considerable conflict, mentioned above, as various parties struggle for the critical role of "priority-setter", the most important source of control in health systems. That does not mean, however, that the second task is free of conflict, because this aspect of management inevitably means accomplishing things through other parties (Crusoe has an allocation problem but not a management problem), by the use of incentives and other tools at managers' disposal.

At this point it seems possible and useful to consider more directly the implications of the above discussion of the tasks of health system reform for the role of incentives. A simple fact is immediately obvious; given the variety and complexity of the tasks, incentives alone cannot be expected to accomplish them.

First, if incentives are to be viewed as a policy tool, their type and deployment will depend on the prior selection of policy objectives and priorities, an essentially ideological exercise. Second, because every set of health policy goals will to some extent involve internal trade-offs and conflicts, if incentives are the tool of choice for all or most purposes then they may often be working at odds with one another or competing with one another to influence outcomes, not unlike the stresses in a bridge or the instruments in an orchestra. Their success will be directly proportional to the management skill of the priority-setters and policymakers, the engineers and conductors of the health system.

Third, given the egalitarian nature of national health systems, it seems critical that incentives for efficient behaviour be designed so as not to discourage appropriate use of needed and beneficial services which have already passed the priority-setting test.

Fourth, incentives will need to be carefully and appropriately targeted to specific objectives, specific behaviours and specific roles. An incentive might accomplish more than one task, but seems unlikely to do so well. Its strength and effectiveness lies in its specificity. Also, incentives which encourage selectivity are to be preferred (Fuchs 1986). I take this to mean that incentives should leave management decisions in the hands of those most capable of making them.

Fifth, as a tool for efficiency, especially in health care subsystems, incentives seem best suited to the lower-level objectives of technical efficiency, clinical appropriateness, and cost-effectiveness rather than allocative efficiency, where the complexity of the task increases as social valuations of output must be made.

Finally, if health is the maximand in the exercise of health policy, it would seem that the greatest scope for the use of incentives lies in creating incentives of individuals and populations to be and to remain healthy, rather than in the design of efficient and equitable health insurance and health care subsystems. Unfortunately for policymakers, however, these are likely to be the most difficult incentives to design. (This is the subject of a separate conference paper by Birch and Stoddart 1989).

On the Nature of Incentives

An incentive is an inducement to action, the stimulus in a stimulus-response mechanism. To provide an incentive is to encourage action or behaviour in a particular direction, instead of inaction or behaviour which otherwise would have taken a different direction, by making it in the actor's best interest to behave as desired. As one knowledgeable student of management has simply stated, "Incentives will not serve their intended purposes unless they also serve the purposes of those they are intended to affect" (Ackoff 1986, p. 52). They are clearly intended to affect the actor's perception of whether he is "better" or "worse" off, in material or intangible ways, on some index of satisfaction, comfort, utility or welfare.

In the language of economists, incentives may operate on arguments which already exist in an actor's utility function, or the purpose of incentives may be to change the composition of that function, adding or deleting things that it is in the actor's interest to "care" about. They can be either "positive" or "negative", rewarding (encouraging or enabling) or punishing (discouraging or constraining) behaviour, and can be generated in more ways than economists might normally imagine, e.g. through social norms or the views of peers or friends, as well as through markets, legislation or other institutional arrangements which affect or govern behaviour.

Interpreted this broadly and abstractly, it may seem that almost anything can be (the source of) an incentive because almost anything can (be made to) affect the welfare of individuals or groups. This is not quite true, of course, because behaviour is affected in ways which apparently do not involve incentives, such as education and the removal of opportunity for an action. (If hospital beds do not exist, they cannot be (over-) used, a corollary to Roemer's law that many public planners and managers understand well.) Nevertheless, the scope for the operation of incentives is undoubtedly broad if only because human behaviour is complex. Although economic models purport to distil and abstract from this complexity, to compress it into its key features for predictability even if not for understanding, as with Horatio we economists should stand cautioned that "there are more things in heaven and earth than are dreamt of in (y)our philosophy".

Incentives may be financial or non-financial. The health economics literature is replete with studies of the former – user charges and physician reimbursement methods being the primary examples. Although the elasticities of response to financial incentives may and do vary considerably depending upon the size of the incentive, the behaviour being targeted, and the institutional context, most of us would, I think, agree with the general statement that financial incentives "work", i.e. they change behaviour. (All generalizations may be false, but this does not mean that people do not agree with them!) What is most frequently at issue is not the *existence* of effects caused by incentives, but the *desirability* of the effects.

Although all financial incentives may be economic ones, the converse is not true. Generalizations about the effectiveness of non-financial incentives are precluded by the variety of forms that they may take, but the fact that they can be a powerful influence on behaviour in health systems is well illustrated by the Canadian experience discussed in the following section.

Three other distinctions about incentives are also particularly relevant. The first is that incentives may operate on actors' perceptions of both short-run and long-run welfare. Actions taken or avoided today may be determined not by today's but by tomorrow's reward. The second, and in the Canadian context closely related, is that incentives exist for and can be applied to groups as well as individuals, thereby enlisting the resources and mechanisms of groups to encourage, prescribe, sanction or otherwise control the behaviour of their individual members. One important implication of the view that groups, rather than individuals, are the most important and appropriate unit of analysis in health systems is that "the necessary analysis is political as much as, or more than, economic" (Evans 1987, p. 132) and that much more attention therefore needs to be paid to the "political market for health policy" (Rutten 1987).

The third distinction is that the use of incentives in health systems, even in the form of prices, does not by itself imply anything about the private or public nature of the system, nor its degree of competitiveness or extent of regulation. All administrative processes embody incentives (Evans 1986), a point which should also be clear from extensive work on the private-public mix (McLachlan and Maynard 1982; Culyer and Jonsson 1986; Stoddart and Labelle 1985).

As an instrument, incentives have several characteristics which make them attractive to policymakers and other managers. They allow choice, harness the initiative, judgment and energy of individuals and groups, allow more flexibility than regulatory or command policies, and may be less visible. Yet there are some important functions which incentives cannot perform, and they display other characteristics which render their availability and use a "mixed-blessing" for their designers and managers. Because these can easily be overlooked, and often are, I propose to list briefly a few that I consider to be the more important ones. Incentives may well be the essence of economics, but, "on the other hand"

1. Incentives are ill suited to the tasks of reconciling competing goals and setting priorities, crucial elements in at least two of the four major questions in health system reform noted in the preceding section. This point has already been made above, but its importance warrants repeating. Put somewhat differently, incentives "cannot obviate difficult political choices nor ignore powerful and competing interest groups" (Miller 1973, p. 204).
2. Aside from the example of prices in markets which function perfectly, incentives normally cannot coordinate themselves; thus it is extremely difficult to synchronize behaviour across sectors/programmes of a complex system like health or even a subsystem like health care. Cost-shifting and patient-dumping under prospective reimbursement are illustrations of this problem. In principle, vertical integration of the delivery process across levels, types and settings of care might overcome some of the difficulties; in practice, however, integration on the scale required is all but impossible. (In fairness, incentives are not the only management tool that experiences this difficulty. Incentive compatibility – a characteristic of management systems in which participants in the process would not find it advantageous to violate the rules of the process – eludes other tools as well.)
3. A distinct, though closely related, characteristic is that incentives can and likely will be "gamed" by the subjects whom they are intended to affect, the object of the game being to obtain the reward/avoid the punishment without adopting the desired behaviour. [For a humorous treatment of gaming behaviour in response to the introduction of DRGs, see Neuhauser (1983).]
4. Incentives do not have only one (the desired) effect. They often have unanticipated consequences. Worse, they frequently provide a social illustration of Newton's third law, generating effects (whether or not

equal) that are opposite to those intended, or which may be "wrong" in other ways. For example, capitation payment discourages overservicing, but encourages underservicing; the tort system discourages malpractice but simultaneously encourages defensive medicine, which is at best often unnecessary and, at worst, harmful to health.

5. Incentives are not costless to employ. The likelihood of unanticipated consequences and perverse effects means that some form of monitoring and management (perhaps involving countervailing disincentives to unwanted behaviour) is necessary. Whether incentives are an efficient as well as effective means to an end depends upon the costs of alternative feasible mechanisms and the information required to operate them.
6. The repeated or exclusive use of a particular form of incentive may have "conditioning" effects that may not always be desirable. For example, it is frequently postulated in models of physician behaviour that the objective functions of these professionals include such variables as patient welfare, concern for professional standards, etc. in addition to income and leisure. What message about the importance of these variables is sent by heavy reliance on financial incentives to influence physician behaviour? Most physical materials in this world do not maintain their shape under constant pressure. Can we assume that professional agency and ethics will?

The above list should not be taken to mean that incentives are not or cannot be important and effective instruments of social policy, including health policy. It does suggest, however, that neither are they the simple, all-purpose tools, the "magical wrists guiding the invisible hand" (Miller 1973, p. 200–1), that a naive view of economics might lead one to believe.

On the Canadian Experience

Canada is an interesting study because it has achieved two of the most sought-after objectives in health systems – provision of universal access to needed services irrespective of ability-to-pay, and control of total health expenditure – apparently without extensive reliance on incentives. In fact, with respect to the latter the structure of financial incentives in the Canadian health care system is so perverse that many observers are certain that expenditure control cannot last. The fact that this certainty has existed almost since the completion of the public medical and hospital insurance program 18 years ago only adds interest to the story.

Comprehensive descriptions of the Canadian health care system and statistical reviews of its performance are available in detail elsewhere and are not repeated here (see Andreopoulos 1975; Taylor 1978; Evans 1984, 1988;

Vayda and Deber 1984; Evans and Stoddart 1986, and Culyer 1988. Some salient features for this discussion may be briefly summarized.

Universal public health care insurance for physician and hospital services was introduced in the decade and a half before 1971, engineered by the federal government through cost-sharing arrangements with the provincial governments, who have the constitutional responsibility for and authority over health. Patients receive services free of point-of-service charges, from private practice physicians most of whom are paid through fee-for-service, and from hospitals, owned by communities and other not-for-profit organizations, managed by independent boards of trustees and paid through global budgets. Physicians and hospitals are reimbursed by provincial governments, at rates negotiated annually with those governments, both directly and often indirectly, through frequent public statements by both sides.

Private insurance for physician services is illegal, and for hospital services it is allowed to cover only amenities. Aside from federal transfer payments, which have steadily decreased as a proportion of provincial funding, the provinces finance health care and other health-related programmes from general revenues, raised through taxation. Capital expenditures, including those on new technology, are again negotiated between providers (almost exclusively hospitals) and provincial governments separately from operating funds.

The incentives for expenditure control facing *individual* actors in the system could not be more perverse. Indeed, it would be hard to design a more ostensibly open-ended system than the Canadian system of socialized payment – public payment for private provision. Yet throughout the 1970s total health expenditure as a share of GNP remained a roughly constant 7½% and, although the share jumped to 8½% in 1982 for reasons that had more to do with the denominator than the numerator, it has remained reasonably level since. This contrasts markedly with the experience of the United States, whose share of GNP devoted to health expenditure grew in parallel to that of Canada in the decades prior to 1971 (in 1970 the United States share was 7.5%, the Canadian share 7.3%), but by 1987 had steadily escalated to 11.2% despite the existence in the United States of the most extensive use of powerful financial incentives – including cost-sharing by patients and prospective reimbursement of hospitals by Medicare – among developed countries.

By international standards, the performance of the Canadian health system on other dimensions, including the health status of the population (in so far as the crude measures available allow assessment of this) also appears to be satisfactory. Moreover, Canadians seem genuinely happy with, indeed are proud of, their health insurance and health care subsystems. In a recent public opinion poll of citizens in Canada, the United States and the United Kingdom, over 90% of Canadians indicated that they preferred their own system to either of the other two (Blendon 1989). Again, the contrast between Canada and the United States is dramatic; 61% of Americans said that they would prefer the Canadian system, while but 3% of Canadians chose the American way.

How has Canada achieved this performance and what role did incentives play? The story starts with several features of the introduction of health insurance. The movement towards universal, public insurance enjoyed strong and growing public support for most of the first half of the twentieth century; therefore by the late 1950s there was a solid public constituency for change. It was not political will alone that introduced the Canadian plans. It was, however, political strategy executed by federal "managers" which accomplished it. Federal officials used strong financial incentives as their primary tool, offering to share the cost of a public insurance plan with any province which agreed to operate its plan according to four key principles: comprehensiveness in scope of benefits, universal accessibility on equal terms and conditions, portability across provincial boundaries, and administration by a public agency. These principles, and the regulations subsequently written by provinces to implement them, simultaneously removed barriers to access and laid the foundation for expenditure control.

Political compromise with organized medicine was another key feature of the introduction of public insurance which laid the foundation and set the tone for future management of health care. Medical associations had opposed the introduction of the public insurance plans, especially medical insurance, preferring instead a system of private insurance with public subsidy; however, in an unwritten and tacit compromise sometimes referred to by health policy commentators as the "medicare pact", the opposition was dropped on the understanding that provincial governments would not interfere with the clinical freedom of physicians in dealing with individual patients. On the whole, the deal has been kept by provincial governments (although accusations by medical associations to the contrary fly frequently both in public and in private), who until very recently adopted a "pay the bills" philosophy. The exercise of clinical judgement by Canadian physicians is relatively unhindered, and certainly so by comparison with their American counterparts (Evans et al. 1989). The preservation of this freedom continues to be of paramount importance to Canadian physicians, which in turn gives them as a group a powerful long-run incentive, primarily though not exclusively a non-financial incentive, to cooperate with provincial governments in managing the health care system.

For their part, the provincial governments have used their leverage a sole-source financers and purchasing agents on behalf of consumers, and the overwhelming public support for the existing system, to control total outlays on health services. This has been accomplished largely without direct financial incentives, through limitations on institutional capacity, budgets, and technology acquisition, and through tough bargaining over physician fee schedules.

Whether it is called "the Canadian way" or "muddling through" (contrary to popular belief, this may be a purposeful strategy; Lindblom 1959), this pragmatic, give-and-take process of incremental adjustments made through explicit political processes has served Canadians well. There has been much "sound and fury" – which itself plays an important function (Tuohy 1986) – and the external perception is one of continual crisis and confrontation, but in the end the channelling of this conflict into political institutions focuses and resolves it, unlike market processes which may diffuse it and leave it unresolved as appears to be the case in the United States (Evans et al. 1989).

This does not mean that the Canadian health system has no blemishes or deficiencies, as critics both within and outside the system are quick to point out. The most frequently heard charges are that the system is underfinanced, that waiting times are lengthening, that quality of care is deteriorating due to both low morale among providers and limits on the diffusion of the latest technology, and that the spectre of rationing of care is fast approaching.

To deal with each of these in turn and in depth would require a separate paper or papers, some of which have already been written (e.g. Culyer 1988; Evans 1988), and which space here precludes. By and large they are levelled by providers as expressions of dissatisfaction with the outcomes of the political resolution to the questions of how much to spend and how to distribute the costs and benefits of that spending. There may be a factual basis for some of them (waiting times for certain procedures have increased recently), but in general they are difficult to investigate or verify empirically. The underfinancing and rationing arguments also imply a rejection of the fundamental economic notions of scarcity and choice, a rejection which arises more from strategic than naive behaviour on the part of critics.

It does not appear that these views command strong public support, although this too is difficult to ascertain with precision. At least they are not what appears to be driving health system adjustments – reform may be too strong a word – in Canada. But there are real weaknesses and specific problems in the Canadian system which provincial governments (and the task forces commissioned by them recently in almost every province) have identified.

Increases in nominal spending on health care are starting to outstrip the perceived ability, and certainly the willingness, of provincial treasuries to raise taxes. Past investments in and overreliance upon acute care hospitals have created an imbalanced institutional sector, with the distribution of facilities and programmes heavily skewed in favour of capital-intensive ones instead of being more evenly distributed among long-term care, community-based care and home care. Increases in the physician supply, which have exceeded population growth for the past 20 years and continue to do so with no end in sight, have been associated with steady increases in servicing intensity, which in addition to putting pressure on expenditure control reinforces a medical view of health and its determinants. The clinical appropriateness and cost-effectiveness of the utilization of many services leaves much to be desired, as does the unequal distribution of health itself across socioeconomic groups and geographic areas within the provinces. Finally, innovation in the organization and delivery of health services and implementation of measures to reallocate resources across sectors of the health system have become very difficult, falling victim, ironically, to the general public satisfaction with the existing system.

As the Canadian system emerges from its adolescence, issues such as these are increasingly difficult to ignore, as they have often been in the past. Yet the provincial governments at this point appear firm in their resolve to hold the line on health care spending in particular, and overall spending on health in general. Any characterization of recent responses or current developments on a national level inevitability runs the risk of masking substantial interprovincial variation in both priorities and approach; nevertheless, I shall briefly sketch what I see as some of the more interesting and common lines of response in current Canadian health policy. They encompass a blend of incentives (both financial and non-financial) and other mechanisms.

Within the health insurance and health care subsystems there have not been, and seem unlikely to be, any attempts to use financial incentives in the form of user charges to control or moderate utilization growth, although consumer expectations and "demand" are accepted as one of the contributing factors to recent utilization increases. First-dollar insurance coverage is one of the most highly valued characteristics of the public plan, and policy-makers who would alter it do so at their own peril. Moreover, it is not at all clear that user charges will contribute to the objectives of health systems, unless one of those objectives is to raise revenue (Barer et al. 1979) and they may impose significant barriers to access (Stoddart and Woodward 1980). They also fail to discriminate between necessary and unnecessary services (Lohr et al. 1986). The most significant change in the health insurance system in recent years has in fact been intended to remove financial disincentives to patients. In 1984 the federal government passed the Canada Health Act, which established severe financial penalties for provinces who did not eliminate the practice of "extra-billing" (billing patients privately for amounts beyond those reimbursed by the public plan), a privilege physicians had previously enjoyed and were increasingly using. The provinces responded to the (dis)incentive. Within the 3-year limit imposed by the federal legislation all provinces had negotiated or legislated an end to the practice.

An alternative strategy for introducing financial incentives to patients, termed "publicly-financed competition", has been proposed by Stoddart and

Seldon (1984), but it does not appear likely to be tried. Based on the ideas of Enthoven (1980) and McClure (1982), the proposal would establish competition between competing delivery modalities defined by method of physician payment (fee-for-service, capitation and salary) *within* the existing structure of the public plan. One of the roles of public managers would be to establish an annual surcharge to patients based on the performance and relative cost of the modalities in which they were enrolled. The proposal is premised on the assumption that incentives to consumers can assist in the achievement of cost-effective delivery patterns, but will only do so if the incentives simultaneously affect the welfare of providers. Although the proposal has helped to stimulate enthusiasm for alternative delivery modalities, it has stalled, largely because of a general reluctance to charge patients in any way and because of unanswered questions of legislative and operational feasibility. Also, initial estimates of the marginal savings attributable to competition *per se* (beyond simply encouraging greater use of capitated delivery organizations) are small (Muldoon and Stoddart 1989).

Although policymakers have avoided the use of traditional forms of user charges and have not embraced the concept of publicly financed competition, this does not mean that they have not focused on the "lower-level", related goals of technical efficiency, clinical appropriateness and cost-effectiveness. Quite the opposite is in fact the case. The reconciliation of patterns of utilization of health services with both population-based information on health needs and clinical epidemiology studies of the efficacy and effectiveness of specific services has become a top priority of provincial ministries of health, in the name of quality as well as expenditure control. It has taken a long time and a large accumulation of evaluative studies for the policy climate to change from a "pay-the-bills" mentality to a management mentality; nevertheless a definite change seems to have occurred. The null hypothesis now appears to be that a considerable amount of health service utilization is ineffective, inefficient, or unevaluated and suspect. The burden of proof of effectiveness seems to be shifting, transferred to providers who seek to continue existing patterns of delivery and utilization (Rachlis and Kushner 1989; Evans 1986).

The new emphasis on appropriate utilization requires delicate handling, so as not to undermine public confidence in the health care system and its dedicated professionals. Policymakers, both government officials and health professionals, are employing a number of strategies. Perhaps more so that at any time in the past, consideration is being given to altering the financial incentives faced by providers. For example, a few major Canadian hospitals are experimenting with clinical budgeting, and the province of Ontario is actively encouraging fee-for-service physicians to switch to capitation payment or participate in globally budgeted or capitated and vertically integrated organizations called Comprehensive Health Organizations. Ontario has also recently unveiled a cautious plan to introduce prospective, case-based reimbursement into new hospital financing in a limited way. It is far too early to tell if these tentative steps signal a general trend in Canadian management of health care, much less whether they will make a difference, but they do represent a departure from the historical policies in Ontario.

Providers are reacting to the new climate with their own calls for better management of utilization – controlled by providers (Linton and Peachey 1989). This reaction seems motivated in equal parts by the belief that health professionals are the best qualified experts to play the role of "effectiveness assessors" and the fear that if they do not accept and execute this responsibility they will lose clinical freedom along with it. The combined effects of provincial government initiatives and provider reaction have produced an unprecedented flurry of interest and activity in the promulgation of clinical guidelines and consensus statements, sometimes even issued as joint statements by provincial ministries of health and medical associations (Ontario 1989).

Meanwhile, provincial governments continue to exert pressure for change within the health care system from the top down by firm control of overall budgets for health care spending, backed by specific actions – sometimes real, sometimes strategic posturing. Alberta, British Columbia and Quebec have endured nurses' strikes in an attempt to hold expenditure. Ontario recently cancelled a promised hospital capital expansion programme of almost one billion dollars (although it is likely to be reallocated within the health care system) and imposed a fee schedule increase on physicians that was well below its own mediator's recommendation. British Columbia recently proposed and then withdrew an explicit plan for capping expenditures on physician services. Moreover, across Canada, provinces now view fee schedule negotiations with medical associations as negotiations about income and total expenditures rather than fees alone. Fee schedule increases are increasingly being made conditional upon utilization rates remaining within "acceptable" levels (Lomas et al. 1989). The message is clear.

It is also carefully delivered, however. Continued emphasis primarily on overall expenditure control intentionally leaves the selective adjustments to be made at more micro levels, by individuals practitioners and administrators in their own practices and organizations, where differences in local needs and individual patients can be respected. Front-line providers, and their professional organizations, are given a strong incentive to find and apply knowledge about the effectiveness of interventions and the cost-effectiveness of alternative delivery methods. Evidence of the response to this incentive is mixed but it is still early in the management era, and the call for a new clinical ethos is just beginning to be heard.

The management of health care in Canada has been characterized as respecting "competing sources of legitimacy": the "politically legitimate authority of the state" and the "professionally legitimate authority of the providers of care" (Evans 1984, 1988). Much of the current real dialogue between the two sources, rather than the symbolic sound and fury to satisfy vocal constituents on both sides, seems aimed towards the creation of more explicit processes for shared management which match tasks and roles to the source of the legitimacy. This may be too optimistic an assessment, but it does seem to be reflected in the calls for cooperative approaches to management that are becoming increasingly frequent (Ford 1986; Ontario 1987; Sutherland 1989).

This discussion of the Canadian experience has concentrated on the health insurance and health care subsystems, as discussions of health systems frequently do. One reason for this is that these subsystems account for the bulk of what are typically labelled *health* expenditures. They are where attention naturally focuses when the subject of health system reform arises and where policymakers feel that they must – and can – begin if they are to release resources for other social programmes with the potential to contribute as much or more to health.

Canada has not been silent on the broader issues of health system reform. A number of examples of public and private policies can be found that illustrate attempts to increase individuals' awareness of healthy life-styles, or to restrict unhealthy behaviour such as smoking, or to improve physical and natural environments. On the whole, however, it seems fair to say that Canada has not met the high expectations in this domain that were raised by the 1974 *White Paper on the Health of Canadians* known as the Lalonde Report (Canada 1974). The reasons for this are both political and economic (Hancock 1986; Evans 1982). Furthermore, the information base required for the use of incentive strategies in particular in this area is more extensive than is commonly believed (Barer et al. 1985).

Conclusion

Success in health system reform depends on many things, including clear priorities, well-defined roles for key actors, sound research evidence, political will, a public constituency for change, and good management skills. Picking the right tool for the task at hand is one of those skills. Incentives, in a variety of shapes and sizes, can be and often are that tool. Both economists and non-economists should be cautious, however, when reaching into the toolbox. As Mark Twain said, "If your only tool is a hammer, all your problems look like nails".

Acknowledgements. I wish to thank Roberta Labelle and Robert Evans for their helpful discussions during the preparation of this paper, although the views expressed herein, and any errors or omissions, are solely the author's responsibility.

References

Ackoff RL (1986) Management in small doses. Wiley, New York
Andreopoulos S (ed) (1975) National health insurance: can we learn from Canada? Wiley, New York
Arrow K (1963) Uncertainty and the welfare economics of medical care. Am Econ Rev 53:941–973
Barer ML, Evans RG, Stoddart GL (1979) Controlling health care costs by direct charges to patients: share or delusion? Ontario Economic Council, Toronto
Barer ML, Evans RG et al. (1985) Lifestyles, linkages and liabilities: theory and evidence justifying economic incentives for healthier lifestyles. QSEP Research Report No. 112, Program for quantitative studies in economics and population. McMaster University, Hamilton
Birch S, Stoddart GL (1989) Incentives to be healthy: an economic model of health-related behaviour. Incentives in health systems. 1st European conference on health economics. Barcelona, September 19–21, 1989
Blendon RJ (1989) Three systems: a comparative survey. Health Management Q 11:2–9
Canada (1974) A new perspective on the health of Canadians (Lalonde Report). Government of Canada, Ottawa
Culyer AJ (1988) Health care expenditures in Canada: myth and reality: past and future. Canadian Tax Foundation, Toronto
Culyer AJ (1989a) The normative economics of health care finance and provision. Oxford Rev Econ Policy 5:34–58
Culyer AJ (1989b) Commodities, characteristics of commodities, characteristics of people, utilities and the quality of life. In: Baldwin S, Godfrey C, Propper C (eds). The quality of life: perspectives and policies. Routledge, London
Culyer AJ, Jonsson B (eds) (1986) Public and private health services. Blackwell, Oxford
Enthoven AC (1980) Health plan: the only practical solution to the soaring costs of medical care, Addison-Wesley, Reading
Enthoven AC (1987) Theory and practice of managed competition in health care finance. Prof. Dr. F. de Vries Lectures in Economics, Erasmus University, Rotterdam
Evans RG (1982) A retrospective on the 'new perspective'. J Health Polit Policy Law 7:325–344
Evans RG (1984) Strained mercy: the economics of Canadian health care. Butterworth, Toronto
Evans RG (1986) Finding the leaves, finding the courage: lessons from cost containment in North America. J Health Polit Policy Law 11:585–615
Evans RG (1987) Public health insurance: the collective purchase of individual care. Health Policy 7:115–134
Evans RG (1988) 'We'll take care of it for you': health care in the Canadian community. Daedalus 117:155–159
Evans RG, Lomas J, Barer ML et al. (1989) Controlling health expenditures – the canadian reality. N Engl J Med 320:571–577
Evans RG, Stoddart GL (eds) (1986) Medicare at maturity: achievements, lessons and challenges. University of Calgary Press, Calgary
Ford DK (1986) Cost control in the health care industry: can there be a Canadian way?. Can Med Assoc J 135:593–595
Fuchs VR (1986) Has cost containment gone too far?. Milbank Q 64:479–488
Hancock T (1986) Lalonde and beyond: looking back at 'a new perspective on the health of Canadians. Health Promotion 1:93–100
Lindblom CE (1959) The science of 'muddling through'. Public Admin Rev 19:79–88
Linton AL, Peachey DK (1989) Utilization management: a medical responsibility. Can Med Assoc J 141:283–285
Lohr KN, Brook RH et al. (1986) Use of medical care in the Rand Health Insurance experiment: diagnosis and service – specific analysis in a randomized controlled trial. Med Care 24 [Suppl]

Lomas J, Fooks C, Rice T, Labelle RJ (1989) Paying physicians in Canada. Health Aff 8:80–102

McClure W (1982) Implementing a competitive medical care system through public policy. J Health Polit Policy Law 7:2–43

McLachlan G, Maynard A (eds) (1982) The public/private mix for health. Nuffield Provincial Hospitals Trust, London

Miller SM (1973) On not abusing incentives. In: Stein B, Miller SM (eds) Incentives and planning in social policy. Aldine, Chicago, pp 199–204

Morone JA (1986) Seven laws of policy analysis. J Policy Analysis Management 5:817–819

Muldoon JM, Stoddart GL (1989) Publicly-financed competition in health care delivery: a canadian simulation model. J Health Econ 8:313–338

Neuhauser DG (1983) DRG's in Jersey. Eff Health Care 1:153–154

Ontario (1987) Toward a shared direction for health in Ontario, Report of the Ontario Health Review Panel. The Panel, Toronto

Ontario (1989) Recommendations to physicians for detection and management of asymptomatic hypercholesterolemia in adults, Ontario Medical Association/Ontario Ministry of Health Task Force on the Use and Provision of Medical Services, Toronto

Pauly MV (1970) Efficiency, incentives and reimbursement of Health Care. Inquiry 7:114–131

Rachlis M, Kushner C (1989) Second opinion: what's wrong with Canada's health-care system and how to fix it. Collins, Toronto

Rutten FFH (1987) Market strategies for publicly financed health care systems. Health Policy 7:135–148

Sapolsky HM (1977) America's socialized medicine: the allocation of resources within the veterans' health care system. Public Policy 25:359–382

Stein B (1973) Incentives and planning as social policy tools. In: Stein B, Miller SM (eds) Incentives and planning in social policy. Aldine, Chicago, pp 3–10

Stoddart GL (1985) Rationalizing the health care system. In: Courchene TJ, Conklin DW, Cook GC (eds) Ottawa and the Provinces: the distribution of money and power. Ontario Economic Council, Toronto, pp 3–39

Stoddart GL, Geldon JR (1984) Publicly financed competition in Canadian health care delivery: a proposed alternative of increased regulation? In: Boan JA (ed) Proceedings of the second Canadian conference on health economics. University of Regina, Regina, pp 121–143

Stoddart GL, Labelle RJ (1985) Privatization in the Canadian health care system: assertions, evidence, ideology and options. Health and Welfare Canada, Ottawa

Stoddart GL, Woodward CA (1980) The effect of physician extrabilling on patients' access to care and attitudes toward the Ontario health care system department of clinical epidemiology and biostratistics, McMaster University, Hamilton

Sutherland RW (1989) Utilization management must be shared. Can Med Assoc J 141:287

Taylor M (1978) Health insurance and public policy. McGill-Queen's University Press, Montreal

Tuohy C (1986) Conflict and accommodation in the Canadian health care system. In: Evans RG, Stoddart GL (eds) Medicare at maturity: achievements, lessons and challenges. University of Calgary Press, Calgary, pp 393–434

Van de Ven WPMM (1987) The key role of health insurance in a cost-effective health care system: towards regulated competition in the Dutch medical market. Health Policy 7:253–272

Van Loon R (1986) Learning from our experience. In: Evans RG, Stoddart GL (eds) Medicare at maturity: achievements, lessons and challenges. University of Calgary Press, Calgary

Vayda E, Deber RB (1984) The Canadian health care system: an overview. Soc Sci Med 18:191–197

Williams A (1978) 'Needs' – an economic exegesis. In: Culyer AJ, Wright KG (eds) Economics aspects of health services. Robertson, London

Williams A (1988) Priority setting in public and private health care. J Health Econ 7:173–183

Part II
Research on Health System Incentives

Theoretical Developments

Fee-for-Service and Quantity Rationing in the Physician Services Market

W. Neudeck

Introduction

Recent work on economic theory has focused on the consequences of asymmetrical information for the performance of private markets. An important insight of this literature is that we cannot always rely on the price mechanism to equilibrate supply and demand. Quantity (i.e. non-price) rationing may be a recurrent phenomenon (see Stiglitz 1987). Since problems of incentives and asymmetrical information play a prominent role in health economics, it is tempting to apply these results to the health care market. This paper shows that the rational response of social insurance funds to physician behaviour in a fee-for-service system may entail quantity rationing of both physicians and patients. The ambulatory care sector in Austria seems to provide a good illustration of this phenomenon. The Austrian institutional setup is sketched and the empirical "paradox" is described. This is followed by a statement of the main argument, which is then presented in a simple model.

Quantity Rationing in Austria

Just 100 years ago Austria followed the German example and adopted Bismarck's "Social Insurance Model" of compulsory universal health insurance financed by employers' and individual contributions to (mainly regional) social insurance funds (SIFs). SIFs are self-governing political bodies with a central umbrella organization (Hauptverband der Sozialversicherungstraeger) as their main agent in the health care market. The finance of ambulatory care by the SIFs in Austria is thus highly centralized and politically determined.

The providers of ambulatory care, on the other hand, are individual doctors in their private offices. The SIF offers them standard contracts specifying reimbursement. Patients freely select a "contract-doctor" (general practitioner or specialist) and receive treatment from him or her. The physician is then directly reimbursed by the SIF according to the terms of the standard contract. These terms (i.e. payment levels and types of services covered) are negotiated between the central SIF and the Doctors' Association (or Chamber of Doctors, as it is called in Austria). However, the law prescribes payment on a fee-to-service basis.

We are thus confronted with two different "markets": first, the market for contracts with the SIF offering contracts and individual physicians demanding them; and, secondly, the interaction between doctors and patients, where patients demand and doctors supply ambulatory care services.

Somewhat surprisingly, quantity rationing seems to occur in both these markets. Some doctors who want to acquire a contract find it difficult to get one. There are waiting lists in most regions. On the other hand, we observe an excess demand for doctors by patients. In a recent opinion survey, "too few doctors", "overworked doctors" and long waiting lists were found to be the main problems of ambulatory care in Austria (IMAS 1987). It seems paradoxical to have an excess supply of doctors willing to accept the given contract and an excess demand for doctors by patients at the same time. Why does the SIF not reduce the fees and offer more contracts to eliminate this "double rationing"?

One possible explanation stresses the bargaining power of the Doctors' Association. The Association is seen as a classic monopoly union enforcing higher fees for its members even though this may mean that some doctors do not get contracts at all. (We should not forget, however, that in Austria doctors without a contract are also members of the Association.)

Moral Hazard

I would like to propose a somewhat different explanation. Double-rationing of this kind may be the optimal answer of the SIFs to moral hazard by patients and doctors in a fee-for-service system even if we ignore the bargaining power of the Doctors' Association. Let us first look at patients' moral hazard, a phenomenon mentioned in Arrow's classic article of 1963 and extensively discussed ever since (see Arrow 1963 and Pauly 1968). If insurance coverage is complete, patients have no incentive to restrain their demand for health services in case of illness. This may lead to an excessive use of resources in health care.

In view of this problem many authors advocated the introduction of coinsurance and deductibles in order to restore incentives (Zeckhauser 1970; Shavell 1979). These proposals are disliked by most policymakers because of their distributional consequences. Furthermore, demand for physician services is hardly determined by the autonomous decisions of patients-consumers. Patients' ignorance of medical technology compels them to rely on the advice of their doctors. Providers of ambulatory care thus exert considerable influence on the demand for their own services.

Most national insurance systems have therefore tried to cope with moral hazard problems by directly rationing the quantities supplied instead of using price incentives on the demand side. These supply restrictions provide a straightforward explanation of the excess demand for doctors observed in Austria: SIFs rely on quantity rationing of patients in order to avoid excessive use of medical services. [Buchanan (1965) saw this as the main characteristic of the British National Health Service many years ago.] As a first step, SIFs usually set a limit to aggregate funds available for ambulatory care. Individual rationing decisions must of course be left to doctors. This is why the direct contractual relationship between SIFs and doctors is so important in Austria. In a fee-for-service system, the SIF can restrict supply by two different methods:

We have seen that in Austria the SIF has set a limit on the number of contracts offered to doctors. The contract doctors therefore face an excess demand for their services and have to decide how to ration their patients. Since they care about health outcomes, they will usually ration in an efficient manner. Doctors clearly have no incentive to create artificial demand in this situation (a problem otherwise encountered in fee-for-service systems). To some extent demand is reduced automatically by search and waiting costs.

A different and apparently more efficient way to use doctors as "rationing agents" is suggested by Pauly's analysis of the fee-for-service system (Pauly 1980, 57 ff.). The SIF can simply reduce fee levels! This will remove quantity constraints in the contract market, since the SIF will be able to offer more contracts and fewer doctors will be inclined to accept the offer. If individual physicians face increasing marginal costs – including the money value of sacrificed leisure – in the "production" of their services (i.e. if their individual supply curve is upward sloping), they will also provide fewer services. With low enough fees an expansion of services is not profitable and doctors will ration their patients: Again they have no incentive to give in to inflated demands and even less incentive to "create" demand themselves.

The SIF can thus use the price mechanism to clear the contract market *and* to provide the right incentives for quantity rationing in the market for ambulatory services. Why then do we observe quantity rationing in both markets? Why does the SIF not enforce lower fee levels? In the remainder of this paper we shall try to answer these questions.

Fee Levels and the Quality of Care

Health outcomes depend not only on the quantity but also on the quality of medical care. SIFs find it difficult or impossible to monitor the quality of physician services. If the quality of services increases as the fees paid to doctors increase, it may be optimal for the SIF *not* to lower fees to their market-clearing level. High fees may just be the best way to maintain quality standards. Similar arguments have been used to explain involuntary unemployment in the labour market. (For a good survey of these "efficiency wage models", see Yellen 1984.) There are indeed several reasons for a positive relationship between fees and the quality of services. In the following we shall discuss four of them in turn.

Target Income

Our first explanation of the fee-quality-nexus uses the target income model of physician behaviour by Evans. This model assumes "... that physicians have rough targets with respect to income and workload, based on their training, expectations and previous experience. Discrepancies between these targets and actual experience lead to adjustment behaviour." (Evans 1974, p. 167). In this model doctors react to a reduction in fee levels by increasing the quantity of services in order to achieve their income targets. As we have seen, patients are quantity constrained and therefore willing to accept the additional services. Given their "target workload", doctors will only be able to expand the quantity of their services by spending less time for each service activity. Obviously this will reduce the quality of ambulatory services. This first negative effect of lower fees on quality is not easily removed. Even if the SIF limits the total amount paid per contract doctor (a kind of rationing occasionally attempted in Austria), doctors will reduce the intensity (time) of services and try to sell additional health care (not covered by social insurance) in the private market to reach their target. Homeopathy or dental hygiene come to mind.

Adverse Selection

If – indistinguishable to the SIF – physicians differ in their ability and high-ability doctors will only accept contracts which offer higher fees, a lowering of fee levels will reduce the proportion of "good doctors" working for the SIF and thus the quality of service (for a labour market analogue, see Weiss 1980). Since better-qualified doctors have good reason to believe that they have better chances for earning higher incomes outside the social insurance system, it is not implausible to assume that their "reservation fees" are higher.

More than 20% of ambulatory care practitioners in Austria hold no contract – some of them, of course, involuntarily. A large number of these doctors are well-known specialists (or even GPs) who expect higher fees from their private (and often privately insured) patients than they would receive under a SIF contract. A cut in SIF fees would drive the most successful doctors into the private patients market (or the pharmaceutical industry and private hospitals) or, indeed, abroad. Naturally this trend would be partially offset by a decline in fees in the private market.

In the very long run, we could argue that only high fees will attract the brightest students to medical studies.

A strong argument against adverse selection models in the labour market stresses the fact that firms will find out less productive employees over time and fire them. There is little "danger" of this happening in the physician contract market: Contract doctors lose their contract only in cases of obvious malpractice.

Gift Exchange and Medical Ethics

Akerlof (1982) has provided a sociological explanation of the efficiency wage hypothesis. Following his argument we could say that the relationship between doctors and SIFs is characterized by an "exchange of gifts": The SIF (on behalf of patients) gives physicians a gift of higher-than-market-clearing fees. In return, doctors develop a special professional "ethos" of "caring" for their patients and provide service quality above the minimum standard. Contract partners want to share gifts because they develop "sentiment" for one another. Feelings of that sort cannot be incorporated in pure market exchange.

If this is true for "cash posters" (Akerlof's example), it appears even more plausible in the provision of ambulatory care. Indeed, an ethical bond between the doctor and patient lies at the heart of the much-discussed agency relationship. Direct gifts of patients to doctors are not uncommon either. Even sentiment towards institutions is often observed (vide British doctors' present concern about "their" NHS).

A reduction in fee levels might impair this special relationship and induce doctors to reduce their effort and provide only the minimum quality of care.

Shirking

Finally, the shirking model of the labour market (e.g., Shapiro and Stiglitz 1982) can be applied to ambulatory care. As we have seen, the SIF can terminate a contract if a case of malpractice (or fraud in collecting fees) comes to its notice. Doctors know that they may lose their contract if they provide their services in a careless way (even though the risk of being "caught" is rather low). To induce them to fulfil their obligation of providing good-quality care, the penalty of losing the contract must be substantial. This may be an additional reason why SIFs offer fees above the market-clearing level in the contract market. For average doctors, holding a contract must be preferable to earning an income in the private health sector. Only then will the threat of losing the contract reduce "shirking" (i.e. low effort) by doctors.

A Simple Model

In this section we shall present a simple model that captures the main idea of the paper. Again, the model is similar to efficiency wage models of the labour market.

Let

$$H = H\,[e(f) \cdot M(f) \cdot A];\ H' > 0,\ e' > 0,\ e(0) = 0 \qquad (1)$$

be a health production function where H is health output [output measurement is evidently no easy task; for a recent survey see Drummond (1989)]; A is the number of contract physicians in ambulatory care; f is the fee level specified in the contract; $M(f)$ is the quantity of services provided by each doctor. Higher fees may either increase M [$M' > 0$, as in Pauly (1980)] or reduce it ($M' < 0$, as in the target income model). $e(f)$ is productivity (efficiency) per service provided and an indicator of service quality. H', e', and M' denote the (first) derivatives of the functions H, e, and M.

For the reasons outlined in the last section, quality and thus productivity will be higher at higher fee levels, i.e., $e' > 0$. The "efficiency" of services is zero if no fees are paid ($e(0) = 0$, a technical assumption). Furthermore we shall assume that the function $e(f)$ has the shape shown in Fig. 1: At low fee levels, increasing fees may have a substantial and growing influence on quality, while this influence will be diminished at higher fees when doctors do their best anyway.

In Eq. 1 health outcome depends on the input of physician services measured in efficiency units (i.e. taking account of service quality). An increase in the quantity or quality of services will increase health ($H' > 0$). All other factors influencing health are assumed constant.

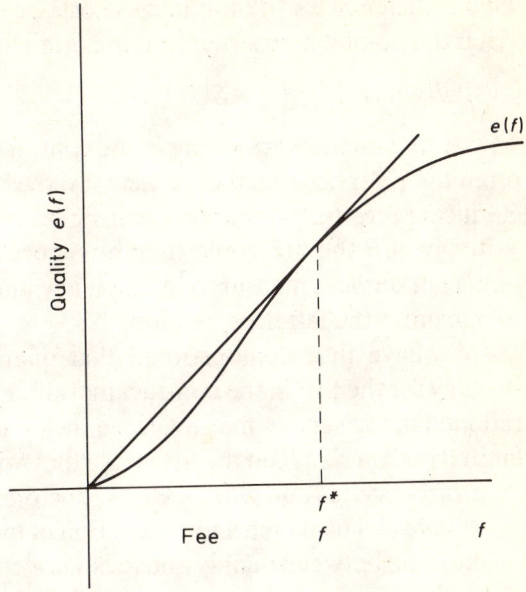

Fig. 1. Effect of fee levels on quality

For simplicity let us assume that the SIF has decided to spend the amount B on ambulatory care; B is exogenously fixed.

$$B = f \cdot M(f) \cdot A \tag{2}$$

It can therefore buy B/f services and offer $B/f \cdot M(f)$ contracts. Given B, the SIF will choose f to maximize health under the condition that there are enough doctors prepared to accept its contracts:

$$\max_f H\,[e(f) \cdot M(f) \cdot A] = H\,[e(f) \cdot \{B/f\}] \quad s.t.\ B/[M(f) \cdot f] \leq AS \tag{3}$$

where $AS(f)$ is the number of doctors willing to accept a contract with fee level f.

In our formulation maximizing health is equivalent to maximizing physician services measured in efficiency units. The SIF will not necessarily choose the smallest f compatible with Eq. 3: Lower fees enable it to pay for more services, but at the same time they will lower the effectiveness e of these services! There is thus a trade-off between quantity and quality of services. If Eq. 3 is not binding, SIFs will in fact offer a fee f^*, which satisfies the "Solow condition" that the elasticity of service productivity with respect to fee levels equals one:

$$e' \cdot (f/e) = 1 \tag{4}$$

This "efficiency fee" f^* minimizes costs per efficiency unit of service. In Fig. 1, it is the point where a ray from the origin becomes tangent to the $e(f)$ curve.

$$\text{If } B/[M(f^*) \cdot f^*] < AS(f^*) \tag{5}$$

we observe quantity rationing in the contract market: Some doctors willing to offer their services at the "efficiency fee" f^* are unable to get contracts. Reducing fees to the market-clearing level would be irrational for the SIF. With given B the SIF could then buy more physician services B/f, but fewer physician services measured in efficiency units $e(f) \cdot B/f$, because f^* is defined to maximize the latter expression.

We have thus demonstrated that quantity rationing can be a rational strategy for the SIF in the contract market. Evidently the patients, too, will be rationed in the service market, since owing to moral hazard on their side and limited budget size B on the SIF's side they will in all probability demand more than B/f^* services and $B/[f^* \cdot M(f^*)]$ doctors.

Finally, let us sketch a formalization of two of our arguments for a positive relationship between quality and fees, i.e. $e' > 0$. Starting with the simplest form of *target income model*, we assume that doctors are characterized by their target income YT and their target workload WT. Service quality e depends positively on time t which doctors spend on each activity. As indicated in Eq. 1:

$$H = H\,[e(t) \cdot M \cdot A];\ e' > 0,\ H' > 0$$

Doctors select t and M in order to achieve their targets.

$$YT = f \cdot M \text{ and} \tag{6}$$
$$WT = t \cdot M \tag{7}$$

If fees are lowered, doctors have to increase M to reach their income target (Eq. 6), but increasing M necessitates a reduction in t in order to attain the workload target (Eq. 7). Hence we observe a positive relationship between fees and time spent per service activity (i.e. quality of service):

$$e(t) = e[f \cdot (WT/YT)] \tag{8}$$

For a simple illustration of the *adverse selection* argument, we assume that a proportion G of all doctors are highly qualified "good" doctors with productivity e_g and "reservation fee" f_g. A proportion $(1–G)$ of all doctors are "bad" doctors with productivity e_b and acceptance fee f_b. For the reasons mentioned in the last section (alternative income options):

$$e_g > e_b \text{ and } f_g > f_b \tag{9}$$

For simplicity, we take f_g and f_b as given, i.e. not dependent on the number of doctors actually "employed" by the SIF. (This implies a very big "outside" market.) The SIF cannot identify "good" and "bad" doctors. If

$$[e_g \cdot G + e_b \cdot (1-G)]/f_g > e_b/f_b \tag{10}$$

the SIF will never reduce fees below f_g even if there is an excess demand for contracts at that fee level and some doctors would accept contracts at lower fees. f_g is the lowest fee where the SIF gets both types of doctors and efficiency e equals $e_g \cdot G + e_b \cdot (1-G)$. Cost per efficiency unit is the inverse of the expression on the left-hand side of the inequality sign in Eq. 10. At fees below f_g (but above f_b), the SIF gets only bad doctors, efficiency is e_b and "efficiency" cost is at least f_b/e_b. Lower fees result in lower quality (efficiency). If Eq. 10 holds, a reduction in fees would therefore be irrational because it increases unit costs.

In order to illustrate our main argument in the simplest possible way, the model chosen was highly restrictive. We have treated ambulatory care as one service (even though the right mixture of services is a well-known weak spot of the fee-for-service system) and we have ignored the effects of ambulatory care on other parts of the health care sector (hospitals, prescriptions, etc.). The production function was very specific (quality is seen similar to quantity) and the assumptions about SIF's and doctor's behaviour were very crude. Perhaps most importantly, we have been rather vague about the fate of those doctors who do not get a contract. In the spirit of our model it is best to assume that they either wait and are unemployed or that they leave the market to do something else (study economics, drive a taxi, work for the pharmaceutical industry). In fact, many of these doctors remain in the market and provide ambulatory services to private patients. In Austria, patients with social insurance coverage have to pay private doctors' fees directly but get a partial refund from the SIF. The SIF therefore cannot really ignore its influence on private health production outside the "contract" system.

Nevertheless the forces we have stressed should be present in a more refined model too.

Conclusion

In this paper we have shown that it may be rational for the SIF in a fee-for-service system to ration doctors in the contract market and patients in the services market for ambulatory care. SIFs find it difficult to establish the quality of physicians' services and there are many reasons for a positive relationship between fees and quality of services. In order to ration patients' (and doctors') consumption of medical care, it may therefore prove necessary to ration the supply of contracts. This explanation of quantity rationing may be relevant for other parts of the health care sector governed by payment-for-service (e.g. the rationing of beds in hospitals instead of adjusting prices).

Finally, we should probably think about alternative renumeration methods that avoid the rationing consequences of the fee-for-service system.

References

Akerlof G (1982) Labour contracts as partial gift exchange. Q J Econ 97:543–569

Arrow K (1963) Uncertainty and the welfare economics of medical care. Am Econ Rev 53:941–973

Buchanan J (1965) The inconsistencies of the National Health Service; Institute of Economic Affairs, London

Drummond M (1989) Output measurement for resource allocation decisions in health care. Oxford Rev Econ Policy 5:59–74

Evans R (1974) Supplier-induced demand: some empirical evidence and implications. In: Perlman M (ed) The economics of health and medical care. MacMillan, London, pp 162–173

IMAS – Institut für Markt- und Sozialanalysen (1987) Wie human ist die Medizin? IMAS Linz (IMAS-Report 17)

Pauly M (1968) The economics of moral hazard. Am Econ Rev 58:531–557

Pauly M (1980) Doctors and their workshops: economic models of physician behaviour. University of Chicago Press, Chicago

Shapiro C, Stiglitz J (1984) Equilibrium unemployment as a worker discipline device. Am Econ Rev 74:433–444

Shavell S (1979) Risk sharing and incentives in the principal and agent relationship. Bell J Econ 10:55–73

Stiglitz J (1987) The causes and consequences of the dependence of quality on price. J Econ Lit 25:1–48

Weiss A (1980) Job queues and layoffs in labour markets with flexible wages. J Polit Econ 88:526–538

Yellen J (1984) Efficiency wage models of unemployment. Am Econ Rev 74:200–205

Zeckhauser R (1970) Medical Insurance: a case-study of the trade-off between risk-spreading and appropriate incentives. J Econ Theory 2:10–26

Coexistence of Private and Public Health Care: Some Implications for Demand and Resource Allocation

A. E. Risa

Introduction

The coexistence of a private and a public health care system influences the total allocation of resources to health care in an economy. The present analysis focuses on the impact of an exogenous public supply policy on individual agents' demand for private health care. Structurally the analysis is very simple, and it is embedded in a quite standard moral hazard model[1] where individual agents maximize the expected utility of treatment within a stochastic medical technology. The strength of this approach is that the model is tractable, and it generates strong, and empirically testable, restrictions on the coefficients of the reduced forms. Furthermore, the analysis provides a framework that supports intuition on the relationship between a public and a private health care system.

One result from the analysis is that the comparative static impact on demand for private health care from a change in public supply policy can be precisely expressed in terms of a modified income effect. Similarly, the impact from a change in the probability of getting sick in the population can also be expressed in terms of income effects. Another result is that the analysis suggests that the total resources allocated to health care are larger in a mixed system, as compared with a pure public or private system.

[1]The approach is in the vein of Erlich and Becker (1972), and it has been applied in health economics by Hey and Patel (1983) and de Meza (1983).

A Model of Individual Demand for Health

Measuring Ill Health

Consider an individual with a utility function V, over health (h), and consumption (k). In a given state of the world the individual has a health level h, and an income Y, that is fully consumed. This individual's utility function can be formulated as

$$V = V(Y,h)$$

Health is measured as a scalar index over the interval [0,1], where increasing h denotes better health.

For the purposes of the present analysis we will define ill health by a monetary equivalent (m). This measure will be derived in the following simple manner: An individual with health index h will be asked how much income he or she would be willing to forgo if he or she could be guaranteed perfect health. The monetary equivalent of ill health can thus be found by equating:

$$V(Y,h) = V(Y - m, 1)$$

This defines:

$$m = m(Y,h) \tag{1}$$

Obviously $m(Y,1) = 0$ in this formulation, since the individual will have no loss with perfect health. By differentiating through Eq. 1 it is easy to see how a change in income or health status affects the monetary equivalent m:

$$V_k(Y,h)dY + V_h(Y,h)dh = V_k(Y - m,1)dY - V_k(Y - m,1)dm \tag{2}$$

where subscripts k and h represent partial derivatives of the utility function with respect to consumption and health status, respectively. From Eq. 2 we get the following expressions for the partial derivations of the function in Eq. 1:

$$m_Y = \frac{V_k(Y-m,1)-V_k(Y,h)}{V_k(Y-m,1)} \tag{3}$$

$$m_h = -\frac{V_h(Y,h)}{V_k(Y-m,1)} < 0 \tag{4}$$

Theoretically the sign of m_Y is ambiguous. We will hypothesize that health is a normal good, and in the remaining analysis it will be assumed that $m_Y > 0$.

We can now rewrite the utility function $V(Y - m,1)$ in a way where the argument for health is suppressed as:

$$V(Y - m,1) = U[Y - m(Y,h)] \tag{5}$$

The utility function U will be used for the remainder of the analysis. The argument in the U function is health-adjusted income $y = Y - m(Y,h)$. It will be assumed that the U function is concave, indicating that the individual is risk averse with respect to health-adjusted income.

In a paper on job hazards, Viscusi (1978) also applies utility functions with income as the only argument, but he argues against our approach to modelling the disutility of ill health. His point is that the functional form of the utility function should be allowed to differ between the healthy and unhealthy state. To ensure interior solutions to his problem, he makes the "plausible" assumption that the marginal utility of consumption is higher in the healthy state than in the injured state. In the notation of the present paper Viscusi's empirical assumption is the following:

$$V_k(Y,1) - V_k(Y,h) > 0 \tag{6}$$

Our empirical assumption of the monetary equivalent of ill health being an increasing function in income can be formulated as follows, using Eq. 3:

$$m_Y > 0 \Leftrightarrow V_k(Y - m,1) > V_k(Y,h)$$

This inequality easily transforms to:

$$V_k(Y - m,1) - V_k(Y,1) > V_k(Y,h) - V_k(Y,1) \tag{7}$$

Given our (and Viscusi's) assumption of utility being concave in income, the left-hand side of the inequality is positive. It follows directly from Viscusi's empirical assumption that the right-hand side of the inequality is negative.

It is also interesting to note that de Meza (1983) models utility the same way as Viscusi (1978). But to solve his model, de Meza makes a "plausible" empirical assumption on the marginal utility of income according to health status that is exactly opposite from Viscusi. In our notation:

$$V_k(Y,1) < V_k(Y,h)$$

This shows that our empirical assumption on the utility implications of ill health is always satisfied if Viscusi's (1978) is, and it may or may not be satisfied if de Meza's (1983) is. It also shows that even if the approach chosen by the two other authors may be technically more flexible, it is empirically more restrictive than the present approach.

The Production of Health

It will be assumed that an individual with a health level h can get treatment through a public health system free of charge, and additional private treatment at a private cost. The medical technology will be represented as follows: Using public and private health care resources will leave the patient with a probability (p) that the treatment does not work, and the patient remains at health level h. Increased use of resources publicly or privately will reduce the probability of failure to cure the problem. The probability of failure to get well will be a function of public costs (x) and private costs (c). The medical technology can thus be summed up in a prevention function:

$$p = p(c,x) \quad p_c < 0, p_{cc} > 0$$

$$p_x < 0, p_{xx} > 0 \tag{8}$$

Again, subscripts denote partial derivatives, and p is defined over the interval [0,1].

Individual Demand for Private Health Services with an Exogenous Public Health Care System

We will now derive the individual's demand for private health care services given an exogenous public system that will provide a certain amount of services free of charge to the individual. The analysis will not consider possibilities of private insurance. Justifications for this admittedly drastic simplification can be of two types: technical and empirical. In a recent paper Arnott and Stiglitz (1988) have shown that, even in the simplest model of moral hazard in insurance markets, predictions become intractable.[2] The empirical justification for assuming away private insurance might be more satisfactory in some situations. If we consider the Scandinavian countries and some other western European countries with a large public health sector, private health insurance is not a prevalent feature in the economy. In spite of this it is possible to buy privately provided health services. This is a possible environment for application of the present model. Another such empirical environment could be the case of compulsory company insurance systems. It seems improbable that a worker who participates in such an insurance system would choose to take extra private insurance in addition to the company insurance. In this case, what we label the public health system must be interpreted as the company insurance.

It will be assumed that an individual with health level h wishes to maximize expected utility with respect to private costs for health care. The maximization is carried out given the prevention function (Eq. 8). The health-adjusted income, with health expenditures c, if the individual gets well is $y^1 = Y - c$, and

[2]They predict that equilibria in insurance markets "will be characterized by exclusive contracts entailing quantity rationing, when these are enforcable." (p. 412)

if he does not get well it is $y^0 = Y - c - m(Y,h)$. The objective function for the individual to be maximized becomes:

$$\max_c U^* = [1 - p(c,x)]U(Y - c) + p(c,x)U[Y\text{-}c\text{-}m(Y,h)] \tag{9}$$

This general optimization problem is primarily known from the moral-hazard literature. The first-order condition for a maximum becomes:

$$U^*_c = -p_c(U^1 - U^0) - (1 - p)\, U^1_y - pU^0_y = 0 \tag{10}$$

where subscripts denote partial derivatives, and superscripts 1 and 0 denote utility evaluated in the favourable and the unfavourable state of the world, respectively. The second-order sufficient condition for a maximum becomes:

$$U^*_{cc} - p_{cc}(U^1 - U^0) + 2p_c\,(U^1_y - U^0_y) + (1 - p)\, U^1_{yy} + pU^0_{yy} < 0 \tag{11}$$

Given that Eq. 11 is satisfied, Eq. 10 defines the optimal level of private costs:

$$c^* = c\,(x,Y,h) \tag{12}$$

Equation 11 is, however, not generally satisfied. In Risa (1989a) it is shown that, when health is a normal good, a sufficient condition for Eq. 11 to hold is that $-El_c\, p_c \geq -El_c\, p$. In the following we will assume that Eq. 11 holds.

To facilitate the interpretation of the results we will define:

$$-\frac{U^1_y - U^0_y}{U^1 - U^0} = R \tag{13}$$

as the average absolute measure of risk aversion over the relevant part of the utility function. Observe that the following restriction on attitudes towards risk holds at an interior optimum:

$$R < -\frac{p_c}{p} \tag{14}$$

To find the optimal response in c^* to a change in exogenous variables, differentiate Eq. 10 with respect to c,h,Y and x:

$$\begin{aligned} &Ddc^* + [-p_c\,(U^1_y - U^0_y) - p_c\, U^0_y\, m_y - (1 - p)U^1_{yy} - pU^0_{yy} + pU^0_{yy}m_y]dY \\ &+ [-p_c U^0_y m_h + pU^0_{yy} m_h]dh \\ &+ [-p_{cx}(U^1 - U^0) + p_x U^1_y - p_x U^0_y]dx = 0 \end{aligned} \tag{15}$$

where D equals U^*_{cc} in Eq. 11. This gives rise to the following comparative static results for the demand function for private health services (Eq. 12):

$$c^*_h = \frac{1}{D}\left[pU^0_y\, m_h \left(\frac{p_c}{p} + R^0\right)\right] \tag{16}$$

$$c_Y^* = \frac{1}{D}\left[p_c(U_y^1 - U_y^0) + (1-p)U_{yy}^1 + pU_{yy}^0 + pU_y^0 m_y\left(\frac{p_c}{p} + R^0\right)\right] \tag{17}$$

$$c_x^* = \frac{1}{D}\left[p_{cx}(U^1 - U^0) - p_x(U_y^1 - U_y^0)\right] \tag{18}$$

In Eqs. 16 and 17 $R^0 = -\frac{U_{yy}^0}{U_y^0}$, i.e. the measure of absolute risk aversion in the unfavourable state of the world.

From Eq. 16 we can see that the sign of c_h* is ambiguous. Intuitively one would expect c_h* to be negative, that is individuals would spend more to fight severe illnesses than milder ones. The condition for this expected result to emerge is that:

$$R^0 < -\frac{p_c}{p} \tag{19}$$

From Eq. 14 we know that the *average* measure of absolute risk aversion is less than $-p_c/p$ in optimum. The only case where the condition (Eq. 19) does not hold is for a Decreasing Absolute Risk Aversion (DARA) utility function with sufficiently high risk aversion in the unfavourable state of the world. The intuitive explanation of this seemingly paradoxical result is that individuals with a comparatively high risk aversion for unfavourable states of the world might save on preventive activity to make these situations better should they emerge. The individual might therefore accept a higher probability of experiencing this state as long as the resources available are somewhat higher. In our terms it would be a question of keeping some extra money that will be needed if the individual should continue to be sick after the treatment.

From Eq. 17 we can see that the effect from a change in income on the level of private health expenditures can be split into two parts: There is a direct effect measuring the immediate impact of a changed Y on the willingness to bear health costs, c. Then there is an indirect effect that looks much like the effect on demand from a change in health status. This effect stems from the fact that a change in Y will change to monetary equivalent of ill health, m, and thereby the health-adjusted income in the unfavourable state of the world. To illustrate this point by substitutions from Eqs. 10 and 16, in optimum Eq. 17 can be reformulated as:

$$c_Y^* = \frac{1}{D}\left[p_c(U_y^1 - U_y^0) + (1-p)\,U_{yy}^1 + pU_{yy}^0\right] + \frac{m_Y}{m_h} \cdot c_h^* \tag{20}$$

Given our assumptions the sign of the indirect effect will be opposite from the sign of c_h*. It is therefore reasonable to expect that this contributes to a positive sign of c_Y*. Theoretically the sign of the direct income effect is ambiguous.

Empirically one would expect that the demand for private health services will increase with increased exogenous income. If health service is a normal good in this sense, the direct effect will be positive.

A slight reformulation of Eq. 18 shows that:

$$\text{sign}(c_X^*) = \text{sign}(p_{cx}/p_X + R)$$

It is straightforward to show (using Eq. 14) that a sufficient condition for an increase in the public health system to have a negative impact on demand for private health services (i.e. $c_X^* < 0$) is:

$$-El_c\, p_X > -El_c\, p$$

The primary aim of the present analysis is to focus clearly on the impact of interaction between a public and a private health system on demand for private health services. To achieve this task, we will introduce a final simplification to the model: We will assume that the medical technology in the public and private health care sector is additive. This yields the following health technology:

$$p = p(c + x) \tag{21}$$

The interpretation of Eq. 21 can be the following: Individuals can demand health services from a private system, but a fixed amount of the costs (x) will be refunded from the public sector. In this way there are no technological differences between the public and the private sector. The effect of the coexistence between the two financial sectors on private demand can therefore be highlighted.

A technical implication of the simplification made in Eq. 21 is that the partial derivatives of the p function with respect to c and x will be identical. From Eq. 20 we get the following expression for the direct income effect on the demand for private health services:

$$(\overset{*}{c}_Y)_{dir} = \frac{1}{D}\left[p_c\,(U_y^1 - U_y^0) + (1 - p)U_{yy}^1 + pU_{yy}^1\right] \tag{22}$$

By some simple manipulation, and using Eqs. 18 and 21, this can be formulated as:

$$(\overset{*}{c}_Y)_{\text{dir}} = 1 + c_X^* \tag{23}$$

From Eq. 22 we can draw some new conclusions: Firstly, the only way it is possible for c_X^* to become positive is when the direct income effect on the demand for health services is greater than one. That is to say that an exogenous increase in income will lead to an increase in demand for health services that is greater than the total income increase. Empirically this seems quite unlikely. Secondly, given that c_X^* is negative, it is interesting to see what will happen to total health expenditures if the public sector expands. If the total health expenditures are to increase when the public sector expands, the reduction in private spending must be less than the increase in public spending. This is to say that $c_X^* > -1$. Comparing this condition with Eq. 22 yields the following sufficient condition for total health care resources to increase when public spending increases:

$$c_X^* > -1 \rightarrow (c_Y^*)_{\mathrm{dir}} - 1 > -1 \rightarrow (c_Y^*)_{\mathrm{dir}} > 0 \tag{24}$$

We can conclude that a positive direct income effect on the private demand for health will secure increases total health spending in response to an expanding public system.

Individual Demand with Private Contributions to the Public System

In the preceding section the analysis took no account of the necessity to fund the public health system. One important result of this analysis was that the effect of the public system on private and total demand is closely related to the sign of the direct income effect of the demand for health. In the present section we will investigate to what extent these results can withstand a reformulation of the model where the public system has to be funded by the individuals in the economy.

As in the preceding section we will assume that the government has decided on an exogenous cost level x, to be provided to an individual who has a health problem corresponding to health level h. The economy has a population of a individuals, of which b are expected to get the health problem. The probability of becoming sick is therefore $q = b/a$. All members of society have to contribute to the public health system. When a sick person has expenditure paid for by the public health care system equal to x, the total revenue which it is necessary to raise in the system equals bx. Payment per capita then becomes $(bx)/a$, which can be expressed as qx.

We can now formulate an individual's optimization problem determining demand for private health services in addition to the public service:

$$\begin{aligned} \max_c U^* = (1-q)U(Y-qx) + q[(1-p)U(Y-qx-c) \\ + pU\{Y-qx-c-m(Y-qx,h)\}] \end{aligned} \tag{25}$$

The analytical framework formulated in Eq. 25 is quite flexible. It can be used to analyse public health systems or private insurance systems. It can also be used for analyses of the implications between lifestyles and health. Endogenous or exogenous changes in q can be interpreted as a change in lifestyle. Alternatively such changes can be given an interpretation of population aging.

In the present section we will limit ourselves to a brief discussion of the comparative static properties of the problem in Eq. 25 given the very simple additive medical technology defined in Eq. 21.

The qualitative comparative static results for Y and h in correspond exactly to the ones obtained in Eqs. 16 and 17 in the preceding section. The effect from a change in q on the demand for private health services is the following:

$$c_q{}^* = -\frac{x}{D}\left[p_c\,(U_y^0 - U_y^1) + (1-p)U_{yy}^1 + pU_{yy}^0 + pU_y^0 m_Y\,(p_c/p + R^0)\right] \quad (26)$$

Using Eq. 22, Eq. 26 can be reformulated as:

$$c_q{}^* = -x c_Y^* \quad (27)$$

The interpretation is straightforward: An increase in the probability of getting sick will decrease the ex post profitability of the public health care system to the individuals that have become sick, and therefore demand health services. This can be regarded as a negative income effect for the individuals concerned.

The comparative static effect from a change in the public service on private demand can be expressed as follows:

$$c_x{}^* = (1-q)\,c_Y^* - 1 - pU^0 m_y\,(p_c/p + R^0) \quad (28)$$

Here we can see that the effect of a change in the public system on private demand is slightly different in Eq. 28 as compared with Eq. 23 in the previous section. By the previous analysis, we expect the last term in Eq. 28 to be non-negative. In that case, a positive income effect on private demand is a sufficient condition to ensure that an increase in the public system will lead to a total increase in health care costs.

Pauly (1983) has pointed out that the influence of income effects on total demand in models like this depends on the formulation of no health care being demanded in the healthy state. In the case where some private health care in demanded even in the healthy state, the presence of a public system that has to be funded will represent a negative income effect in the healthy state.

The simplicity of the present model places strong restrictions on the empirical predictions that are generated. In other circumstances it might be a severe handicap of the model that substitution effects are disregarded altogether. It might happen, however, that this is different in the particular case of health care demand. In many cases it seems reasonable to expect that the question of total cost as opposed to relative prices is dominating the actual choices people make regarding different health services. If this is true, the present model provides a good framework for empirical testing. An advantage in this respect is that the model predicts both the theoretical signs of coefficients of the reduced form, and in addition structural relationships between these coefficients (as defined in Eqs. 27 and 28.[3]

We can conclude the analysis thus far by asserting that, given a positive income effect of health demand, an increase in public health services will increase total resources spent on health care, provided individuals can freely demand private health services. This relationship is illustrated in Fig. 1.

In the figure we measure total health expenditures on the vertical axis, and the proportion of private expenditures to total on the horizontal axis. Point *A* illustrates one individual's demand for private health care in the case where there is no public health system. If the public sector offers some health services, the proportion of private to total health expenditures will decrease from 1. The total health expenditures for this individual will increase on the schedule *AB* provided the income effect on health expenditures is positive. Point *B* on the schedule indicates that the public sector provides a quantity of health services that totally satisfies this particular individual's demand.

In spite of the argument above, recent Organization for Economic Cooperation and Development (OECD) data reveal that the public sector's share in total health costs runs as high as 98.4% even in western OECD countries. It seems reasonable to conjecture that this empirical fact is not an indication of large overspending on health services, but rather an indication of rationing in the market for private health services. In Fig. 1 point *D* represents a public health care system with full rationing in the private market. Given a public supply like *D*, individuals would like to demand extra private

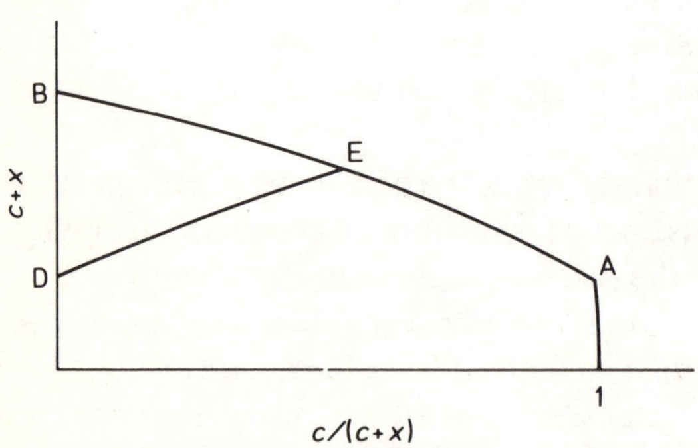

Fig. 1. Total health expenditure and the proportion of private to total expenditure. *c*, Private health care expenditure; *x*, public health care expenditure

[3]The original paper by Risa (1989b) contained an empirical "test" of these restrictions on an aggregate OECD data set. In this "test" all the coefficients were significant, and of the right sign, but the restrictions on the relative magnitudes of the coefficients were refuted.

services to reach the point E. With partial regulation of the private market, the level of total expenditures may be characterized by moving from D to E as the stringency of regulation decreases. It is interesting to note that a mixed system produces higher total health care costs regardless of the point of departure being A or D.

This paper has characterized the AB schedule within a simple framework. A characterization, and empirical implementation, of the DE schedule for economies where rationing constraints bind remains the subject for future study.

Acknowledgement. I am grateful to Tor Iversen, Aina Uhde and Gunnar Bramness for helpful comments on an earlier draft of this paper. The paper was also presented at the 9th annual meeting for Norwegian economists, Oslo, January 1989, and ESEM '89 in Munich, September 1989. I wish to thank participants of the conferences for comments and discussions. Financial support from the Norwegian Research Council for Science and the Humanities (NAVF – Ruhrgas scholarship scheme) and the Bank of Norway is gratefully acknowledged.

References

Arnott RJ, Stiglitz JE (1988) The basic analytics of moral hazard. Scand J Econ 90:383–413

de Meza D (1983) Health insurance and the demand for medical care. J Health Econ 2:47–54

Erlich I, Becker G (1972) Market insurance, self insurance and self protection. J Polit Econ 80:623–648

Hey JD, Patel M (1983) Prevention and cure? or: is an ounce of prevention worth a pound of cure? J Health Econ 2:119–138

Pauly M (1983) More on moral hazard. J Health Econ 2:81–85

Risa AE (1989a) Public regulation of private accident risk: the moral hazard of technological improvements. Institute of Economics, Bergen

Risa AE (1989b) Individual demand for private and public health care. Institute of Economics, Bergen

Viscusi WK (1978) Wealth effects and earnings premiums for job hazards. Rev Econ Stat 60:408–416

Distribution Effects of Coinsurance Options in Social Health Insurance Systems

F. Breyer

Introduction

During the debate on the so-called cost explosion in the social health insurance system in the Federal Republic of Germany in the 1970s, the introduction of coinsurance options for sickness fund members was proposed as a means of inducing more efficiency in health care utilization by some authors (e.g. Schmidt 1976) and sharply refused by others (e.g. Griesewell 1976; Standfest 1976). In spite of the lack of response on the part of health policymakers, similar proposals have been made in connection with the recent health insurance reform in Germany (Schneider 1986; Schulenburg 1987; Wissenschaftliche Arbeitsgruppe "Krankenversicherung" 1987).

From an allocative point of view, this proposal is easy to justify. Since illness costs are ex ante uncertain for the individual, the risk spreading accomplished by a health insurance contract increases welfare, but, on the other hand, insurance coverage distorts relative prices and induces the individual to overconsume health services relative to other goods ("moral hazard"). This unavoidable dilemma between risk spreading and incentives (see Zeckhauser 1970) is resolved one sidedly in favour of risk spreading in a system with compulsory full coverage of all health care expenditures (as is the case with very minor exceptions in Germany).

For the individual household, the optimal compromise between both targets and therefore the *optimal* extent of insurance coverage depends upon their preferences for health care, their degree of risk aversion and the probability distribution of health costs they are confronted with (see, e.g. Breyer 1984). Since the members of a society differ in these characteristics, a choice between a variety of insurance plans with different copayment rules appears to be necessary from the allocative point of view.

Ideally, and in the absence of adverse selection, the plans with higher copayment levels would then be chosen predominantly by those insured who are convinced that they have a noticeable influence on their health care costs, whereas those who expect to be unable to control their need for health services in case of illness – e.g. when the illness is likely to be critical – should be interested in full coverage. Therefore, the offer of different copayment options would lead to some degree of risk selection within the social health insurance system.

If adverse selection is taken into account, the division of risks would look somewhat different: the high copayment plans will be attractive for people with low expected health care expenditures ("good risks") and unattractive for people with high expected expenditures ("bad risks"). There is, however, some plausibility that these two criteria are positively correlated: people probably have more influence on the probability and costs in the case of illnesses which are trivial and inexpensive to treat than in the case of serious and high-cost illnesses.

Through this mechanism, the introduction of copayment options can have distributive effects in that it changes the so-called solidarity compensation (*Solidarausgleich*), which is inherent in the German health insurance rules. Since in this system the contributions of an insured person (or family) depend only on their income and not on their risk structure – as would be the case in private health insurance contracts – a threefold redistribution of income is implied:

— From high-income to low-income members
— From childless to large families
— From good risks to bad risks

The normative justification for the third component of income redistribution could be based on the assumption that the susceptibility to illness is only to a small extent caused by one's own behaviour, and is mostly inherited. Under the "veil of ignorance" (Rawls 1971) of a fictional initial situation, in which nobody knows their future identity, a representative risk-averse individual would in this case prefer to live in a society in which the health insurance premiums are not differentiated by risk classes but are uniform so that everyone is ex ante insured even against the *susceptibility* of illness.

Lest this health-risk related redistribution is destroyed through complete risk selection, when copayment options, are offered, several authors (e.g. Griesewell 1976; Henke and Metze 1979; Pfaff et al. 1980; Männer 1989) have demanded assurances that the "bad risks" who stay in the full coverage plans should not suffer from the migration of the "good risks" to the copayment plans. It is obvious that this require cross-subsidization of premiums among different plans that are offered by the respective sickness funds (see Neipp 1988).

Such a cross-subsidization, however, is not viable if, as has recently been proposed more and more (e.g. by the Wissenschaftliche Arbeitsgruppe "Krankenversicherung" 1987), competition among sickness funds is intensified through the introduction of a free choice of fund by the insured. For the less a particular fund increases the contributions in the copayment plans to subsidize the full coverage plan, the more attractive it becomes for the "good risks". If a fund abandoned the cross-subsidization altogether, it would force the others to do likewise if they wished to keep *some* good risks in their membership. This effect could be circumvented only by introducing compensation payments across sickness funds, which would lead to serious allocative disadvantages, e.g. the attenuation of incentives to health-conscious behaviour.

Therefore the following analysis will be based on the assumption that, while not every insured person will be required to pay contributions equivalent to his or her expected health care costs, each insurance *plan* must be supported by a contribution rate sufficient to cover its costs. For sake of simplicity, administrative costs will be ignored.

It is the goal of this analysis to examine under what conditions the introduction of optional copayment plans can improve the welfare *even* of those people who are "bad risks" and choose to remain in the full coverage plan. Since there is no doubt that the welfare of the "good risks" is improved through the additional options, we thus ask under what circumstances the introduction of optional copayment plans leads to a Pareto improvement within the group of all sickness fund members.[1]

This analysis will be performed in a theoretical model[2], which exhibits a number of drastic simplifications. Since our concern is with the redistribution among different risk classes, we do not consider the redistribution among income classes by assuming that each insured person has the same gross income. In doing this, we also avoid possible correlations between income and the risk of illness. The same holds analogously for redistribution according to family size.

Likewise we do not consider a gap between public and private information on the health risk ("adverse selection") so that a further standard justification for compulsory (and uniform) insurance coverage (see Spence 1978; Dahlby 1981) does not apply. Finally, the relative prices of health services are assumed as exogenously given. This implies that we avoid consideration of a possible

---

[1] We shall not be content with a *potential* Pareto improvement, e.g. according to the Kaldor-Hicks criterion (see, e.g. Friedman 1984, Chap. 5), since the compensation payments demanded in this criterion are seldom actually paid in practice.

[2] Empirical studies of the distributional effects of (mandatory) copayment rules are found, e.g. in Pfaff and Pfaff (1986) and Schulenburg (1987), Chap. VII.

downward pressure on health care prices – and thus on the actuarial premium in the full coverage plan – which increased competition among the health care providers as a consequence of copayment rules could generate (see Henke and Metze 1979, p. 38).

The Model

We consider a static world in which there are only two goods: a homogeneous health good ("medical care") and general consumption ("bread"). Since the relative price of medical care in units of bread will be assumed as constant, we can set it without loss of generality to be equal to 1 so that the *quantities* of the respective goods that a household (or, synonymously,an individual) consumes can be replaced by the *expenditures* for medical care, x, and for bread, y. If the individual has health insurance coverage, then $g(x)$ denotes his or her copayment as a function of his or her health care costs x and P denotes the premium. If w denotes his or her gross income, his or her budget restriction implies that:

$$y = w - P - g(x) \tag{1}$$

For every consumer there are but two possible states of the world, and at the beginning of the period the consumer does not know which one will be realized: He or she will be "ill" with the (publicly known) probability π and "healthy" with the probability 1-π. In the case of illness, his or her ex-post utility function is given by $u(x,y)$, and in the case of good health by $v(y)$. We assume that both conditional utility functions are strictly increasing and strictly concave with respect to bread, i.e. $u_y, v_y > 0$ and $u_{yy}, v_{yy} < 0$. Ex ante, expected utility of an insured person with a contract $[g(x), P]$ is given by:

$$U = \pi \cdot u[x, w - P - g(x)] + (1 - \pi) \cdot v[w - P] \tag{2}$$

The population is divided into two homogeneous risk groups, the fraction μ belonging to the "good risks" (denoted by the superscript g) and the fraction 1-μ to the "bad risks" (superscript b). The groups differ from each other both in the probability of getting ill:

$$\pi^g < \pi^b \tag{3}$$

and in the urgency of getting treatment once ill. For a "bad risk" the consumption of x^* units of medical care is vitally necessary in this case:

$$\begin{aligned} u^b[x,y] &= v^b[y] && \text{if } x \geq x^* \\ u^b[x,y] &= -\infty && \text{otherwise} \end{aligned} \tag{4}$$

where the value "minus infinity" denotes death. Equation 4 thus states that in the case of illness the individual reaches the same utility level as in the case of health if and only if his or her expenditures for health care are at least equal to x^*. This implies that the sick person has no choice but to consume x^* units of medical care to survive, but a larger quantity is neither required nor useful.

In contrast, the welfare of a type g individual ("good risk") rises continuously with the consumption of medical care until an upper limit of x^{**} units, i.e.

$$\begin{aligned} u_x^g &> 0 \quad \text{if } x < x^{**} \\ u_x^g &= 0 \quad \text{otherwise} \end{aligned} \tag{5}$$

This dependence implies, as shall be demonstrated below, that in the case of illness the consumer will demand less medical care, the weaker his or her health insurance coverage is, i.e. the more bread he or she is forced to give up for an additional unit of medical care. Thus g persons are in a situation of "moral hazard of type 2" (see Breyer 1984, p. 300 ff.).

Therefore, our model mimics exactly the conditions described above under which the introduction of copayment options in a social health insurance system is considered desirable from an allocational but problematic from a distributional point of view: Those people who in the case of illness have a genuine choice on the utilization of health care are at the same time the "good risks" who will be attracted by the copayment plans.

Optimal Demand for Health Care and Optimal Proportional Coinsurance

If the individual consumer can freely choose his or her insurance coverage, he or she is confronted with a two-stage optimization problem (see, e.g. Zeckhauser 1970): In the second stage (ex post), given that the consumer has become sick, he or she has to find the utility-maximizing consumption bundle (x,y) under the budget constraint (Eq. 1) and with given reimbursement function $g(x)$. In the first stage (ex ante) he or she has to find among the alternative reimbursement functions (and the corresponding premium levels) the one which maximizes his or her expected utility (Eq. 2), taking account of his ex-post behaviour determined above. To avoid unnecessary complications we assume that only insurance plans with proportional coinsurance are available:[3]

$$g(x) = c \cdot x \ (0 \leq c \leq 1) \tag{6}$$

[3] Without this restriction, the optimal copayment function is in general non-linear (see Spence and Zeckhauser 1971, p. 387).

We start with the optimal demand for medical care in the case of sickness (ex post optimization): A type b consumer obviously chooses $x^b = x^*$ in view of Eq. 4. In contrast, a type g consumer maximizes the function

$$u(x^g, w - P^g - c \cdot x^g) \tag{7}$$

Setting the first derivative with respect to x^g zero yields

$$u_x(x^g, w - P^g - c \cdot x^g) = c \cdot u_Y(\chi^g, w - P^g - c \cdot x^g) \tag{8}$$

from which the demand for medical care can be determined as a function of the coinsurance rate c,

$$x^g = x^g(c) \text{ with } x^g(0) = x^{**} \tag{9}$$

Supposing that this function is continuously differentiable, one obtains by partially differentiating Eq. 8 with respect to c:

$$u_{xx} - x_c{}^g - u_{xy} \cdot (x^g + cx_c{}^g) = u_y + c \cdot u_{xy} \cdot x_c{}^g - c \cdot u_{yy} \cdot (x^g + cx_c{}^g) \tag{10}$$

or

$$x_c^g(u_{xx} - 2_c \cdot u_{xy} + c \cdot u_{yy}) = u_y + u_{xy} \cdot x^g - c \cdot u_{yy} \cdot x^g \tag{11}$$

Under the usual assumptions on the utility function ($u_{xx}, u_{yy} < 0, u_{xy} > 0$) the term in parentheses is negative, the right-hand side of Eq. 11 positive and hence $\partial x^g/\partial c$ smaller than zero. It makes sense to make the additional assumption that

$$x^g(0) = x^{**} \leq x^* \tag{12}$$

i.e. that even with full coverage a "good risk" does not demand more medical care than a "bad risk".

As the next step, we determine the optimal insurance coverage for bad risks: By inserting Eq. 4 into Eq. 2 and using the strict concavity of the function v, one obtains the result that expected utility is maximized at full coverage ($c = 0$), given the premium function is "marginally fair" (see, e.g. Mossin 1968, p. 556 ff.), i.e. with a linear premium function the premium for full coverage must not be higher than the expected insurance payment $\pi^s \cdot x^*$. This condition is fulfilled in our model due to the absence of administrative costs.

A type g consumer maximizes ex ante the expected utility

$$U^g(c) = \pi^g \cdot u[x^g(c), w - P^g(c) - c \cdot x^g(c)] + (1 - \pi^g) \cdot v[w - P^g(c)] \tag{13}$$

by choosing the appropriate coinsurance rate c. In order to solve this problem one not only needs to know the demand function for health care (Eq. 9), but the premium function $P^g(c)$ also has to be precisely specified. The calculation of the premium, however, depends upon whether the same plan is also chosen by type b consumers. If this is not the case, i.e. if the risk segregation is perfect, then the premium function is given by

$$P^g(c) = \pi^g \cdot (1-c) \cdot x^g(c) \tag{14}$$

with

$$P_c^g = \pi^g \cdot (1-c) \cdot \chi_c^g - \pi^g \cdot x^g \tag{15}$$

By setting the first derivative of Eq. 13 with respect to c equal to zero one obtains the following implicit condition for the optimal coinsurance rate c^o:

$$\pi^g \cdot u_x \cdot x_c^g - \pi^g \cdot u_y \cdot (P_c^g + x^g + cx_c^g) - (1-\pi^g) \cdot v_y \cdot P_c^g = 0 \tag{16}$$

or, by using Eqs. 8 and 15

$$(1-c^o) \cdot x_c^g = x^g \cdot \left(1 - \frac{u_y}{\pi^g \cdot u_y + (1-\pi^g) \cdot v_y}\right) \tag{17}$$

In the following we shall show that full coverage cannot be optimal for good risks, i.e. that the optimal c^o from Eq. 17 cannot be zero. We only have to assume that – given the level of bread consumption – marginal utility of bread in the state of good health is not less than in the state of sickness if the satiation level x^{**} of medical care is reached, i.e.

$$u_y(x^{**}, y) \leq v_y(y) \tag{18}$$

We now evaluate the derivative of expected utility $U^g(c)$ at $c = 0$:

$$\begin{aligned} U_c^g(0) &= \pi^g \cdot u_x \cdot x_c^g(0) - \pi^g \cdot u_y \cdot [P_c^g(0) + x^{**}] \\ &\quad - (1-\pi^g) \cdot v_y \cdot P_c^g(0) \\ &= - P_c^g(0) \cdot [\pi^g \cdot u_y(x^{**}, y) + (1-\pi^g) \cdot v_y(y)] - \pi^g \cdot u_y(x^{**}, y) \cdot x^{**} \end{aligned} \tag{19}$$

since from Eq. 8 and $c = 0$ the first term on the right-hand side of Eq. 19 is zero. Noting that with full coverage of medical costs bread consumption is the same in both health states, we can insert Eq. 18 into Eq. 19. Using this and Eq. 15 we obtain

$$\begin{aligned} U_c^g(0) &\geq - u_y(x^{**}, y) \cdot [P_c^g(0) + \pi^g \cdot x^{**}] \\ &= - u_y(x^{**}, y) \cdot [\pi^g \cdot x_c^g(0) - \pi^g \cdot x^{**} + \pi^g \cdot x^{**}] \\ &= - u_y(x^{**}, y) \cdot \pi^g \cdot x_c^g(0) > 0 \end{aligned} \tag{20}$$

due to $u_y > 0$, and $x_c^g < 0$. This demonstrates that expected utility rises with an increase of the coinsurance rate from $c = 0$ so that an optimum requires strictly positive c^o.

If the probability of illness, π^g, rises, so does the denominator on the right-hand side of Eq. 17 due to $u_y > v_y$, and the absolute value of the term in parentheses falls. Ceteris paribus this implies that $(1-c^o)$ falls, and the optimal coinsurance rate increases. The same effect results if the price elasticity of the demand for medical care is increased by a rotation of the demand curve around the optimal point: x^g remains constant, $x^g{}_c$ rises in absolute value and hence $(1 - c^o)$ falls.

As the demand for health care was assumed to be bounded from above (by x^{**}), it cannot be proved that the optimal coinsurance rate c^o is always positive. In the following, however, we shall assume that this is the case because otherwise the discussion on the effects of optional copayment plans would be irrelevant.

Welfare Effects of a Free Choice of Coinsurance Rates

To assess the welfare effects of alternative institutional designs of social health insurance, we calculate for each regime the level of expected utility of a (representative) member of each of the two groups of consumers, assuming optimal behaviour given the choices they have in the respective situation. In comparing two regimes (characterized by different subscripts), the Pareto criterion can be applied only if both individuals attain higher expected utility in the same situation, i.e. if, e.g.

$$U_1^g > U_0^g \text{ and } U_1^b > U_0^g \tag{21}$$

As a first step we compare the regimes, 0: compulsory full coverage for everybody, and 1: free choice of proportional coinsurance. In the first alternative, the status quo, both risk groups are members of the same plan in the proportion $\mu:(1-\mu)$. In the other case, we know from the analysis in the previous section that a complete separation of risks occurs since all type g consumers choose the coinsurance rate $c = c^o$, which solves Eq. 17, whereas all type b consumers choose $c = 0$.

For "bad risks" the welfare comparison is easy to perform since they are in both cases fully insured against the costs of medical care and thus their expected utility,

$$U_j^b = \pi^b \cdot v^b(y_j) + (1-\pi^b) \cdot v^b(y_j) = v^b(y_j) = v^b(w - P_j^b) \quad j = 0{,}1 \tag{22}$$

is uniquely determined by their premium level P^b. In regime 0 the premium (for *both* types of consumers) is given by:

$$P_0^b = P_0^g = \mu \cdot \pi^g \cdot x^g(0) + (1-\mu) \cdot \pi^b \cdot x^* \tag{23}$$

in regime 1 a type b insured consumer pays

$$P_1^b = \pi^b \cdot x^* \tag{24}$$

and from Eqs. 3 and 10 it follows immediately that

$$P_1^b > P_0^b \tag{25}$$

so that, as could be expected, the utility level of "bad risks" falls with certainty when copayment options are introduced.

For "good risks", however, we have in regime 1:

$$P_1{}^g = \pi^g \cdot x^g\,(c^o) < \pi^g \cdot x^g\,(0) < P_0{}^g \tag{26}$$

Therefore they prefer regime 1 to regime 0 for two reasons: First, their optimal coinsurance rate is c^o, which equates to the statement that in choosing between the options $c = c^o$ and $c = 0$, where each is combined with the fair premium $P^g{}_1$ and $\pi^g \cdot x^g$ (0), respectively, they prefer the first one. In addition, regime 0 differs from the second option through a higher premium level due to Eq. 26.

Thus the Pareto criterion is silent on the effect of the introduction of a free choice of proportional coinsurance. The effects that do result have a distributive nature in that "good risks" are better off and "bad risks" are worse off than in the initial situation of compulsory full coverage for all.

Welfare Effects of Mandatory Copayment with Supplementary Insurance Options

The disadvantage of a free choice of coinsurance rates for type *b* consumers has two reasons: First they do not benefit from the savings induced by the copayment feature in the health insurance plan chosen by the good risks, and secondly the latter can avoid contributing to the coverage of "bad risks" by opting for their own plan. For both effects, the perfect separation of risks is responsible. Therefore, if coinsurance aims at a Pareto improvement, the mixing of risks has to be maintained as far as possible. In this vein we propose the following regime 2:

2: There is compulsory health insurance with a positive coinsurance rate c^*. Each insured is allowed to buy supplementary insurance at a fair premium to pass on the copayment.

In the following we compare regimes 0 (compulsory full coverage) and 2 with respect to their welfare effects.

Obviously, all type *g* consumers prefer regime 2 because here the risk-related redistribution is limited to the fraction $(1 - c^*)$ of health care costs and thus at given insurance coverage the premium for them is lower than in the case of a complete mix of risk groups. In addition, they benefit from the relaxation of the compulsion to "overinsure", the more so the higher c^* is set. This is true also for $c^* > c^o$, for then they can buy supplementary coverage for the fraction $(c^* - c^o)$ of their health care costs at a fair premium.

Members of group *b* again obtain complete coverage by buying supplementary insurance for fraction c^* of their health care costs. Hence the calculation of the effect on their welfare again (as in the previous section) boils down to a comparison of the respective premium levels. In regime 2 the sum of the premiums for the compulsory and the supplementary insurance for a type *b* individual is given by

$$P_2^{\,b} = (1 - c^*) \cdot \{\mu \cdot \pi^g \cdot x^g\,(c^g) + (1 - \mu) \cdot \pi^b \cdot x^*\} + c^*\,\pi^b \cdot x^* \tag{27}$$

where

$$c^g = \min\,[c^*, c^o] \tag{28}$$

is the coinsurance rate realized by the "good risks".[4] In Eq. 27 the first term denotes the premium for the compulsory insurance, the second term the fair premium for the supplementary insurance.

So, using Eq. 23, the change in total premium for a type *b* consumer implied by a transition from regime 0 to regime 2 is

$$\begin{aligned}\Delta P^b = P_2^{\,b} - P_0^{\,b} &= \mu \cdot \{c^* \cdot \pi^b \cdot x^* - \pi^g \cdot x^g\,(0) + \pi^g \cdot (1 - c^*) \cdot x^g\,(c^g)\} \\ &= \mu \cdot \{c^* \cdot [\pi^b \cdot x^* - \pi^g \cdot x^g\,(0)] - \pi^g \cdot (1 - c^*) \\ &\quad \cdot [x^g\,(0) - x^g\,(c^g)]\}\end{aligned} \tag{29}$$

On the right-hand side of Eq. 29, the first term in the braces corresponds to the reduction of the risk-related redistribution brought about by the fall in the compulsory coverage level from 1 to $1 - c^*$: It is always positive and thus tends to raise the premium. The second term contains the fall in health care demand by the type *g* insureds, which always reduces the premium. The sign of the change in the premium as a whole now depends upon the relative strengths of these two counteracting effects. One observes that the relative sizes of the two risk groups, i.e. the parameter μ, does *not* affect the sign of the net effect.

A Pareto improvement through the introduction of regime 2 now requires that the mandatory coinsurance rate c^* is set at a value for which the premium differential ΔP^b is smaller or equal to zero. Assume for simplicity that ΔP^b is a continuously differentiable function of the parameter c^*. Obviously we have

$$\Delta P^b\,(0) = 0 \text{ and } \Delta P^b\,(1) = \mu \cdot [\pi^b \cdot x^* - \pi^g \cdot x^g\,(0)] > 0 \tag{30}$$

The answer to our problem depends upon the behaviour of this function in the neighbourhood of the origin: If the first derivative of ΔP^b at $c^* = 0$ is non-positive, then ΔP^b itself is zero or negative for sufficiently small positive values of c^*. Therefore we evaluate

---

[4] We do not consider the possibility that the income effect implied by the change from regime 0 to regime 2 affects the choice of the optimal coinsurance rate by a type *g* individual.

$$\partial(\Delta P^b)/\partial c^* = \mu \cdot \{\pi^b \cdot x^* - \pi^g x^g(0) + \pi^g \cdot [x^g(0) - x^g(c^g)] + \pi^g \cdot (1 - c^*) \cdot \partial x^g(c^g)/\partial c\} \quad (31)$$

at $c^* = 0$ using Eq. 28 and obtain

$$\text{at } c^* = 0, \frac{\partial(\Delta P^b)}{\partial c^*} = \mu \cdot \{\pi^b \cdot x^* - \pi^g \cdot x^g(0) - \pi^g \cdot \partial x^g(0)/\partial c\}$$
$$\leq 0 \text{ if } |\partial x^g(0)/\partial c| \geq [\pi^b \cdot x^* - \pi^g \cdot x^g(0)]/\pi^g \quad (32)$$

So a fall in the total premium for type b individuals as the outcome of the introduction of a (marginal) coinsurance for everybody is more likely:

1. The larger $|\partial x^g(0)/\partial c|$ is, i.e. the more price elastic the health care demand of type g individuals at point $c = 0$
2. The smaller $[\pi^b \cdot x^* - \pi^g \cdot x^g(0)]$ is, i.e. the smaller the amount of risk-related redistribution involved in compulsory full coverage
3. The larger π^g is, i.e. the probability of illness for type g individuals

To illustrate these results let us consider the following example: Let the health care demand function of a type g consumer be linear with:

$$x^g(c) = x^* \cdot (1 - c) \quad (33)$$

i.e. at full coverage ($c = 0$) the utilization of medical care is equal to that of a type b individual, and without insurance ($c = 1$) it is zero so that:

$$\partial x^g(c)/\partial c = -x^* \quad (34)$$

In this case Eq. 32 is reduced to:

$$\pi^b \leq 2 \cdot \pi^g \quad (35)$$

i.e. in this example "bad risks" benefit from the introduction of (at least a marginal) coinsurance clause and of optional supplementary insurance if their own probability of illness is no more than twice as high as the one of a "good risk".

Now assume that Eq. 32 – the condition for regime 2 being favourable to "bad risks" – is fulfilled as strict inequality. The premium change ΔP^b involved in the transition from the "status quo" (regime 0) to regime 2 can be shown graphically as a function of the coinsurance rate in the compulsory insurance, c^* (see Fig. 1). Here c denotes the value of c^* at which ΔP^b is a minimum and c'' denotes the limit above which ΔP^b is positive.

What kind of policy must be pursued in setting the coinsurance rate c^* in the compulsory insurance in order to make sure that regime 2 leads to a Pareto improvement over regime 0, and what are the corresponding distribution effects?

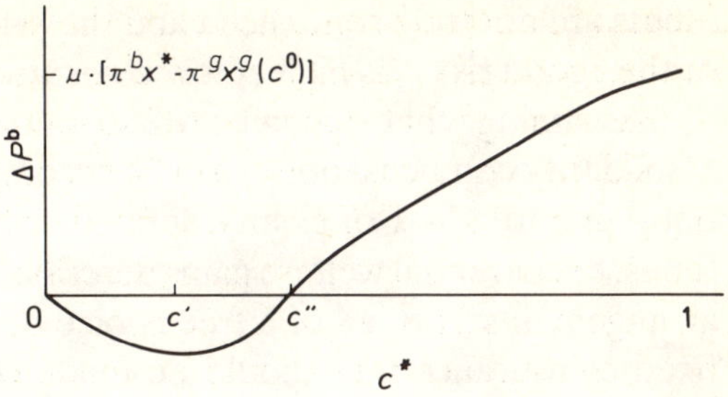

Fig. 1. Premium variation (ΔP) and compulsory coinsurance rate (C^*) for "bad risk" consumers (b)

It was derived above that the "good risks" are better off, the higher c^* is fixed. Figure 1 shows that the same is true for "bad risks" as long as c^* lies in the interval $[0, c']$. A Pareto improvement over regime 0 – which, by the way can be viewed as a special case of regime 2 with $c^* = 0$ – is still possible with a c^* in the interval $[c', c'']$. Once c^* exceeds c', however, a conflict of interest between the two risk groups emerges: Here a further increase in c^* implies a redistribution from the "bad" to the "good" risks. Only when c^* exceeds c'' does the result confirm the suspicion mentioned in the introduction that the "bad risks" are worse off than under compulsory full coverage.

Hence a health insurance design which is both Pareto optimal and improves the welfare of *both* risk groups as compared with the status quo requires that the coinsurance rate is fixed between c' and c''. However, we do not want to underestimate the difficulty of empirically determining the shape of the P^b function in order to find these crucial values even in the simplified case of only two risk groups.

Conclusions

Within a highly stylized model with only two health states and two risk groups we showed that the introduction of optional copayment in social health insurance systems may under certain circumstances improve the welfare even of those individuals who are "bad health risks" and wish to retain full insurance coverage.

This result can appear if the reduction in risk-related redistribution due to the copayment feature is compensated by the fall in the premium brought about by the more cost-conscious behaviour of the "good risks". The second effect outweighs the first and thus the combined effect on the welfare level of the "bad risks" is positive if the differences in the probability and the costs of illness are not too pronounced and the price elasticity of health care demand of the "good risks" is high at low coinsurance rates.

Assuming that income redistribution among different risk groups ("solidarity compensation") can be accomplished only *within* insurance plans but – due to a lack of clearly defined criteria – not across plans or sickness funds, the potential welfare gains described above require certain institutional arrangements: Instead of a free choice of copayment plans for everybody, a fixed coinsurance rate should be made compulsory for *all* individuals, and supplementary insurance should be offered. To maintain a sufficient degree of risk-related redistribution in favour of the "bad risks" requires that the coinsurance rate in the compulsory part not be set too high.

Finally one has to be careful not to allow perfect risk separation through the choice of sickness fund. As most people who are interested in supplementary insurance will try to get this from the same company as the compulsory part, either *all* statutory sickness funds must be obliged to offer supplementary plans at fair premiums, or the supplementary part must be completely excluded and assigned to private health insurance companies. In the second case, however, there remains the problem that private insurers may want to discriminate with respect to risk groups *within* the set of demanders of supplementary coverage.

We do not want to repeat here all the simplifying and restrictive assumptions under which the results presented in this paper were derived. The most crucial is perhaps the assumption that administrative costs are zero. The transition from a system of direct third-party payment to one of cost reimbursement which would accompany the introduction of copayment features would probably lead to a sizeable increase in administrative costs which could exhaust the welfare gains at least at low levels of coinsurance rates.

Despite the last-mentioned qualification we can summarize that the widespread presumption, that optional copayment in social health insurance systems necessarily makes high-risk people worse off, is invalid at least in this crude version.

Acknowledgement. The author is grateful to Peter F. Clever, J. Neipp and participants at a workshop in Wuppertal for helpful comments on an earlier version of this paper.

References

Breyer F (1984) Moral Hazard und der optimale Krankenversicherungsvertrag. Eine Übersicht. Z gesamte Staatswissensch 140:288–307

Dahlby BG (1981) Adverse selection and Pareto improvements through compulsory insurance. Public Choice 37:547–558

Friedman LS (1984) Microeconomic policy analysis. McGraw-Hill, New York

Griesewell G (1976) Wahltarife in der gesetzlichen Krankenversicherung – Überlegungen zur Praktikabilität des FDP-Modells. Krankenversicherung 28:221–224

Henke K-D, Metze I (1979) Selbstbeteiligung und Kostenentwicklung. Med Mensch Ges 4:34–39

Männer L (1989) Einführung von Wahltarifen und deren Auswirkungen auf den Solidarusgleich in der GKV: empirische Ergebnisse. In: Gäfgen G, Oberender P (eds) Verteilungsziele und Verteilungswirkungen im Gesundheitswesen. Nomos, Buden-Buden

Mossin J (1968) Aspects of rational insurance purchasing. J Polit Econ 76:553–568

Neipp J (1988) Die Rolle ökonomischer Anreize bei pluralistischer Organisations- und Vertragsstruktur des Krankenversicherungssystems. In: Schulenburg J-M, Hauser H (eds) Health maintenance organizations. Eine Reformkonzeption für die gesetzliche Krankenversicherung in der Bundesrepublik Deutschland? Bleicher, Gerlingen

Pfaff A, Pfaff M (1986) Distributive effects of alternative health-care financing mechanisms: cost-sharing and risk-equivalent contributions. Institut für Volkswirtschaftslehre der Universität Augsburg, Augsburg Volkswirtschaftliche Diskussionsreihe No 27

Pfaff M, Schneider M, Kerschreiter M, Stumpf M (1980) Wahltarife in der Krankenversicherung. Forschungsbericht/Gesundheitsforschung no 42 Der Bundesminister für Arbeit und Sozialordnung, Bonn

Rawls J (1971) A theory of justice. Harvard Univesity Press, Cambridge, Mass; Clarendon, Oxford

Schaper K (1981) Selbstbeteiligung in der GKV? Zur wissenschaftlichen Auseinandersetzung und sozialpolitishcen Problematik. Soziale Sicherheit 30:141–146

Schmidt H (1976) Wahltarif in der GKV – ein Lösungsvorschlag. Soziale Sicherheit 25:5–6

Schneider M (1986) Sozial tragbare und kostendämpfende Selbstbeteiligung. Sozialer Fortschr 35:29–34

Schulenburg J-M (1987) Selbstbeteiligung. Mohr (Siebeck), Tübingen

Spence AM (1978) Product differentiation and performance in insurance markets. J Public Econ 10:427–447

Spence AM, Zeckhauser RJ (1971) Insurance, information, and individual action. Am Econ Rev 61:380–387

Standfest E (1976) Wahltarif in der GKV – ein Lösungsvorschlag wofür? Soziale Sicherheit 25:70–73

Wissenschaftliche Arbeitsgruppe "Krankenversicherung" (1987) Vorschläge zur Strukturreform der Gesetzlichen Krankenversicherung Bayreuth

Zeckhauser RJ (1970) Medical insurance: a case study of the tradeoff between risk spreading and appropriate incentives. J Econ Theory 2:10–26

Health Insurance Reforms and Incentives in the Netherlands

W.P.M.M. van de Ven

Introduction

Health insurance reform is quite a hot issue in the Netherlands today. For several decades the forming of a national health insurance system has been a major item on the political agenda. However, so far the Netherlands is the only European country in which more than one-third of the population has no compulsory insurance which covers the costs of acute health care such as hospital care, physician services and medicines. In addition to the health insurance reform, the issue of cost containment has become more and more important during the past 20 years. Since the early 1970s the Dutch government have tried to contain health care costs by direct control over prices and productive capacity. As the results of this policy have been disappointing, several proposals were formulated for a structural reform based on a market-oriented approach (see van de Ven 1987). In march 1987 a government-appointed committee presided by Dr. W. Dekker, former president of the Philips company, published its report entitled "*Willingness to change*". Two major issues proposed by this Dekker committee were the introduction of a *national health insurance* ("basic insurance") and *regulated competition* between insurers and between providers. After a year of intensive discussion and numerous seminars and conferences, the Dutch government and parliament decided to adopt the main details of the Dekker proposals. Health insurance incentives to consumers as well as to providers play a crucial role in the governmental proposals for reform. Compared with the past 15 years this can be seen as an about turn in health care policy with respect to health care cost containment. Because of the revolutionary character of the proposals one can really speak of a *Perestrojka* in the Dutch health care system.

In this paper we will focus on health insurance reforms and incentives, concentrating first of all on the key role of health insurance in a cost-effective health care system, followed by discussion of the health insurance reforms as proposed by the Dutch government. These proposals are interesting for a wider audience because the proposals leave ample room for health insurance incentives and because they can be adopted by other countries.

Health Insurance Incentives

In most developed countries the percentage of gross national product spent on health care has been growing quite steadily during recent decades. In the Netherlands, for instance, there was an increase from 4.3% in 1963 to 8.3% in 1986. It is generally felt that the high health care expenditures could be considerably reduced if the efficiency in health care was improved. However, in the present Dutch health care system – and probably also in many other countries – there are very few financial incentives for efficiency on the part of providers, consumers and insurers.

The Dekker Commission and current government actions both start from the premise that there is a non-negligible degree of inefficiency in the Dutch health care system. Unfortunately, this assumption is warranted. For instance, an examination of financial reports from the 40 Dutch sickness funds reveals a large variation in the per capita expenses ranging from 1249 to 2106 guilders (1985), i.e. a difference of 69% (Ziekenfondsraad 1986). Correction for differences in age and sex composition explains roughly one-third of this difference, suggesting that there is ample room for improving efficiency. A recent literature review of the numerous demonstration efforts related to the improvement of efficiency in the Dutch health care system concluded that the estimated inefficiency in the Dutch health care system, expressed as potential savings, was about 15% of total health care expenditures (Van de Ven 1988). The review also concluded that many of the demonstrations appeared to have simultaneously improved quality and reduced costs, even though many of the reviewed projects were intended to have only one of these goals. It appears that in the Netherlands – at the present level of quality and cost – in medical care quality and efficiency usually go hand in hand.

This brings us to the question: what can be the contribution of health insurance towards improving efficiency in health care? An essential difference between buying health care and buying other goods is in the function of prices. In buying cars or buying holiday trips market prices function as signals to both the producer and the consumer, resulting in an efficient production process and an allocation of those goods according to consumer preferences. In the health care sector, however, this market mechanism does not work, partially because most consumers have comprehensive health insurance. The lack of price sensitive consumer behaviour together with many cost-increasing provider incentives and the passive role of the insurer creates a health care system in which there is ample opportunity for waste and inefficiency.

Although incentive reimbursement, which rewards the providers for delivering medical care in a cost-effective way, can be an important step towards a cost-effective health care system, it is not sufficient. If the insured consumers are completely insured and if the insurance premium is independent of the consumer's choice of provider, it is simply rational consumer behaviour to "demand" the most expensive and specialized care. As long as the insured consumers have both comprehensive health insurance coverage and freedom of choice of provider, providers will have great difficulty in resisting consumers' demand for more and more costly medical care and politicians or other decision makers will have great difficulty in restricting capacity and in preventing overcapacity. Fear of losing patients or voters might be a dominant factor. Therefore, the fundamental way in which health insurance can contribute to a cost-effective health care system can be described as "*rewarding the insured consumers for choosing cost-effective providers*". Essentially there are two ways of doing this and these two ways follow directly from those two aspects of health insurance that are widely held to be responsible for the health care cost-inflation, i.e. comprehensive insurance coverage and free choice of provider. So the key elements in discussing the contribution from health insurance to improving efficiency in health care are "cost sharing" and "limited provider plans".

Cost Sharing and Limited Provider Plan

Cost sharing can be described as a mode of health insurance whereby insured consumers are required to pay some portion of their covered medical expenses out of their own pocket. In the case of *limited provider plans* it is advantageous for the insured consumers to receive their care from or through referral from a limited group of specified providers. Limited provider plans can broadly be divided into two categories, health maintenance organization (HMOs) and preferred provider organizations (PPOs), as they are referred to in the United States. HMOs are the most "extreme" form of limited provider plan because in the HMO system the consumer, who pays a fixed amount per period to the HMO, agrees to receive *all* care from or through referral from the physicians participating in the HMO. In general, HMOs do not have large deductible schemes as is usual in traditional health insurance in the United States. In order to stimulate patients to make efficient use of health care, HMOs use minor copayments (e.g. per physician visit, per medicine or for the use of the emergency room). Apart from some exceptions, all out-of-plan use has to be paid for by the consumer.

In the PPO system the providers agree to deliver medical care to the PPO subscribers at reduced fees, and the PPO subscribers are encouraged to choose the preferred providers by lower out-of-pocket payments for services rendered by the preferred providers. The distinction between cost sharing and PPOs, therefore, is not always clear cut. Variations on the theme are indemnity insurance (Kaplan and Lare 1971), variable cost insurance (Newhouse and Taylor 1971), health care alliances (Ellwood and McClure 1976) and many other alternatives.

An essential difference between HMOs and PPOs is that HMOs accept the responsibility of providing or otherwise assuring the delivery of an agreed upon set of health services to its subscribers, while PPOs do not take this responsibility. Another difference is that generally HMO providers are at financial risk, i.e., they somehow share in the financial result of the organization, while PPO providers do not.

Effectiveness

What can be said about the effectiveness of the different ways of making the consumers, and through them also the providers, cost conscious? As little is known about the performance of PPOs and the many variations on the theme, I will limit myself to the effects of cost-sharing and HMOs. From many empirical studies we may conclude that there is little doubt that increased cost sharing would reduce the demand for the medical care in question (Newhouse 1978; Van de Ven 1983). Results from the Rand Health Insurance Experiment indicated that families required to pay 25% of their bills up to a maximum out-of-pocket amount spent 19% less on services than those with full coverage; in the case of an income-related deductible scheme, which was at most $1000 per family per year, total health care expenditures were 31% lower than in the case of full insurance (Manning et al. 1987). It appeared that, with some minor exceptions, in general the provision of free care did not improve the health status of the participants (Brook et al. 1983).

In discussing the results of the HMOs, I will consider only the prepaid group practice (PGP), the dominant HMO type. (In interpreting the results one should realize that they are based on the classic HMOs (say before 1980). We know of no evidence on the recent performance of HMOs in the 1980s.) The well-known results of Luft (1978, 1981) indicate that total health care costs for PGP subscribers are 10%–40% lower than those for similar people in the traditional health care system. On the basis of a number of non-experimental studies the quality of care in PGPs appears to be at least similar to that in the traditional health care system (Cunningham and Williamson 1980; Wolinsky 1980; Wyszewiansky et al. 1982; Roemer 1982). Results from the Rand Health Insurance Experiment indicated that the expenditures for PGP subscribers are 28% below those of similar people with full coverage or 25% coinsurance in the traditional fee-for-services system (Manning et al. 1984). For the vast majority of experimental participants, the medical care delivered through the PGP produced health outcomes similar to, and in some cases better than, the traditional fee-for-services system. However, poor PGP patients who entered the experiment with medical problems seemed to experience worse health than similar people who entered the experiment through several conventional insurance plans in the fee-for-service system (Ware et al. 1986).

In most cases PGP subscribers have nearly full insurance coverage for all medical costs, i.e. with little cost sharing, while most traditionally insured people in the United States are confronted with considerable cost sharing. Based on the effects of cost sharing alone, one would expect higher costs for PGP-insured than for traditionally insured people. In reality, however, we see on average some 25% *lower* costs per person in the PGPs compared with the traditional, non-PGP system. Clearly *the cost sharing effect is more than compensated for by the effects resulting from the organizational and financial characteristics of the PGP structure*, such as the closed panel, utilization review, quality assurance, broad benefit package (which prevents the substitution of cheap uninsured care by expensive insured care), peer review and the providers being at financial risk.

In interpreting this finding, one should realize that the above-mentioned experimental cost-sharing effects are *partial* price-effects, i.e. when other relevant factors are kept constant. However, in real practice, especially when the physicians are reimbursed on a fee-for-service basis, the overall cost-reducing effect of cost sharing may be adversely influenced by supplier-induced moral hazard and by other forms of supplier-induced demand or overdemand. The PGP structure clearly offers an effective means of coping with these phenomena.

If the consumers have a choice between several health plans such that the premiums or the out-of-pocket payments reflect the cost-effectiveness of the provider chosen, this will give the providers incentives for cost-effective behaviour or it will sustain such incentives when they already exist. As a result, competition may arise between different providers, between provider groups or between provider-insurer organizations. Increasing cost sharing as a means of stimulating competition between providers, however, may lead to the undesirable situation that a poorly informed consumer has to shop around for the cheapest provider while he or she is ill. Furthermore, as we saw above, the effects resulting from the specific characteristics of the PGP structure appear to be superior to the cost-sharing effect in improving efficiency. [For a thorough discussion of the limited possibilities of using direct charges as a strategy for cost containment or efficiency enhancement, see Barer et al. (1979), and Enthoven (1980).] Therefore, rather than increasing cost sharing, stimulating competition between all kinds of alternative delivery systems like HMOs and PPOs should be preferred.

In the next section we will see that this conclusion appears to be one of the guiding principles of the proposals for health insurance reforms in the Netherlands.

Health Insurance Reforms in the Netherlands

In discussing the health insurance reforms as proposed by the Dutch government we will first explain the necessity for changes in the Dutch health care system, followed by a summary of the main details of the governmental proposals and a discussion of consequences for the various parties involved.

Necessity for Changes

In a letter to parliament, the Dutch government (1988) gave the following reasons for changes to the health care system:

1. The uncoordinated financing structure
2. Lack of incentives for efficiency
3. Unworkable detailed government regulation on volume and price
4. Several problems with the present health insurance system

Besides these problems in the present system the government drew attention to important developments like the rapidly increasing medical technology, the aging population and changes in the nature of health problems. These developments would lead to a growing demand for care. In order to maintain a system of high-quality care that is accessible for everyone, the government thinks it necessary to change the organizational and financing structure of the present health care system.

Below we will successively discuss each of the above-mentioned reasons for change.

Uncoordinated Financing Structure

The uncoordinated financing structure for health care and social welfare work (old people's homes, family assistance programmes and social work) impedes efficiency and desired substitution of care and stimulates an undesired process of shifting off. Interrelated forms of care which are substitutes for each other are now often financed in different ways. For instance:

1. Hospital care and care by general practitioners is paid for by the sickness funds or private health insurers.
2. Financing of home care delivered by cross organizations is based on the AWBZ (Exceptional Medical Expense Act).
3. Family assistance programmes are paid for by private payments and out of the national budget.
4. Social work is paid for by private payments and out of the municipal budget.
5. Financing of nursing home care is based on the AWBZ.
6. Old people's homes are paid for out of the national budget.

Besides this uncoordinated financing structure there are also strong regulations about the nature of the care, the institution that should deliver the care, the place where the care should be delivered and other conditions. Furthermore the financing system is strongly oriented towards institutions and is less function oriented (e.g. rehabilitation services versus rehabilitation institutes). In summary, one may conclude that as a result of the multiform financing system and the complex regulations efficient substitution is often impeded.

Lack of Incentives for Efficiency

In the present Dutch health care system there are very few financial incentives for efficiency on the part of providers, consumers or insurers. The financing system is such that in many cases economic and efficient actions are financially punished, while non-economic actions are financially rewarded. For instance:

1. The hospital financing system makes an expensive 3-day admission much more attractive than lower-cost day surgery.
2. The fee-for-service payment system (primarily for specialists) rewards the physician for unnecessary and unnecessarily expensive medical treatments.
3. The capitation system (for general practitioner care provided to sickness fund patients) stimulates the physician to refer the patient to specialists for conditions which could be treated by the general practitioner.
4. Most consumers are nearly fully insured for all health care costs, mostly independent of the choice of provider: this implies that an individual consumer generally is not interested in an efficient use of health care resources.

5. For private insurers it is more attractive to select good health risks than to improve efficiency in health care, given the existing premium structure.
6. Finally, all sickness funds receive full payment from the General Fund for all medical expenses incurred by their members: if an individual sickness fund succeeds in improving efficiency, it receives less revenue from the General Fund, and so an individual sickness fund has little financial incentive for efficiency.

In summary, one may conclude that changing the present financing system is a *necessary* condition for improving efficiency in health care.

Unworkable Detailed Government Regulations on Volume and Price

According to the letter to parliament (1988), many problems in the present health care system are a consequence of the present complex legislation and detailed regulation:

1. Up to now the very detailed regulations on volume planning in health care appeared to be unworkable. This is caused by the complexity of the planning process, the many parties involved, their conflicting interests and the lack of clarity of the regulation (many rapid changes and inconsistency with other forms of regulation).
2. A major problem appears to be the relationship between planning and financing. A crucial question is whether planning should lead to financing or whether the planning should follow the willingness to finance. In the present system planning and financing are separated, which poses many problems.
3. The complex tariff regulations impede flexibility and efficient allocation.

Besides the above-mentioned problems there is – not only within the health care sector – a political and ideological movement in favour of "less state and more market".

Problems with the Present Health Insurance System

In the present Dutch health insurance system all employees (and their families) with an annual wage below 50 000 guilders (which equals about U.S. 25 000) are compulsorily insured with 1 of the 40 regional sickness funds. This. also continues after retirement. The rest (about 39%) of the population, consisting of mainly self-employed and higher income groups, can voluntarily buy private health insurance at 1 of the 70 competing health insurance companies operating in the Netherlands. Besides this there is compulsory insurance for the whole population which provides cover against exceptional medical expenses, such as hospital care for longer than 1 year, nursing home care and care for mentally and physically handicapped persons.

Many problems exist in the present Dutch health insurance system. Without going into details the following can be mentioned:

1. An unbalanced distribution of premium payments, which is frequently experienced as "unfair".
2. No freedom of choice for sickness fund insured persons with respect to insurance arrangements.
3. Complete freedom for one-third of the population to decide whether or not to buy health insurance, which can lead to a free rider problem, i.e. people receiving benefit without being charged.
4. The insufficient functioning of the market for private health insurance.
5. Several problems with respect to the transition of members of the sickness fund insurance to private health insurance, and vice versa.

The introduction of a national health insurance which can solve these problems has already been discussed for decades, but still does not exist.

Government Proposals for a New Health Care System Structure

In formulating its proposals for a new structure of the health care system, the Dutch government started from the following three points:

1. Health care and social welfare work are so much interrelated so that their financing system should become more and more integrated.
2. The flexibility, efficiency and substitution of care must be improved. Measures to do so should be addressed to the producers of care, the insurers and the consumers.
3. As a third starting point the government formulated a shift from government regulation to market and self-regulation. Although the government recognizes that the special character of health care and social welfare work provides the government with special responsibilities, it is asserted that this does not always imply direct government control on volume and prices and that it does not exclude market and self-regulation. According to the governmental letter (1988), the governmental responsibility especially relates to ensuring the appropriateness of the following elements of care and the process of providing care: (a) quality of care; (b) financial and geographical accessibility to care; (c) sufficient supply of care, according to the needs of the population; (d) solidarity between several groups; (e) cost development in health care; (f) allocation of responsibility back to

consumers, providers and insurers; and (g) effectiveness and efficiency of care.

According to the present Dutch government, these governmental responsibilities do not exclude the option that the parties involved in the health care "market" do play a prominent part. Under conditions set by government and stimulated by the right incentives, market and self-regulation could help achieve society's goal and respect to health care.

Two key elements in the note governmental letter (1988) are "*basic insurance*" and "*regulated competition*". The basic insurance should be a kind of "national care insurance", i.e. a compulsory insurance for the whole population with for the greater part an income-related premium and a benefits package which roughly includes all AWBZ benefits, the greater part of all benefits in the present sickness fund insurance and health care related social welfare work. The basic insurance will be executed by insurers who observe certain rules concerning, e.g. open enrolment and premium setting. The insurers will compete with each other for patients and they are allowed selectively to contract with providers of care.

In fact the insurers, who are supposed to become a powerful party on behalf of their insureds and who have a lot of information about the providers' behaviour at their disposal, and expected to function as an intermediary between the consumers and the providers of care. To a high degree the insurers and the providers will be free to negotiate about the conditions of the contracts. As a result of these negotiations limited provider plans may emerge. The consumer will be free to choose from the different insurers the insurance policy he or she likes the most. The premium the consumer pays then reflects the efficiency and cost-generating behaviour of the contracted physicians. In this way it is expected that a situation will arise in which: (a) the insureds are being rewarded for choosing efficient insurers and choosing efficient providers of care; (b) the providers are being rewarded for effective and efficient provision of care; and (c) the insurers are stimulated to contract efficient providers and to do market research into the consumers' preferences.

The government aims to introduce the new structure in 1992. For several reasons the new structure will gradually be introduced step-by-step. Firstly, gradual year-to-year changes will mitigate the redistributive income effects. Secondly, there is time needed for new legislation. Thirdly, there is time needed for the development of a system of risk-adjusted premium-replacing payments from the Central Fund to the insurers. And finally a step-by-step approach offers the opportunity to learn from the new experiences and to adjust future changes.

It is clear that the governmental proposals for a competitive health care system imply radical changes in the relations between consumers, insurers and providers of care. In the next subsections we will successively discuss each of these relations.

Relation Insurer-Insured

One of the major points in the governmental proposals is the introduction of a compulsory basic insurance. This basic insurance as proposed covers about 85% of all medical costs (in total about 36 billion guilders) and health care related social welfare costs (old people's homes, family assistance programmes and social work; in total about 6 billion guilders). The composition of the proposed benefits package for the basic insurance is based on the following two criteria:

1. All health care provisions that are uninsurable or constitute a financial risk that an individual person cannot carry are included in the basic insurance.
2. The basic insurance covers all health care provisions, which to a high degree substitute for each other.

The premium for the basic insurance will be the greater part be income related. A small part of the premium (about 10%) will consist of a flat premium to be directly paid by the insured to the insurer. The benefits package will not be described in terms of institutions like hospitals, nursing homes or old people's homes, but rather in terms of functions of care.

Anybody meeting certain quality standards is allowed to provide these functions of care. This will largely increase the flexibility and substitution of care. Besides the compulsory basic insurance there will be a voluntary supplementary insurance, which covers all extramural medicine, physical therapy and dental care for all people 18 years and over.

The basic and supplementary insurance will be executed by both sickness funds and private health insurers. Ultimately the differences (in rights and duties) between these organizations will disappear. This situation should gradually be reached in 1992. According to the governmental proposals all income-related premiums will be collected in a Central Fund. All insurers who execute the basic insurance and who observe the procompetitive regulation will receive a risk-adjusted premium-replacing payment per insured from this Central Fund. This amount of money is risk adjusted, i.e. it depends on the actuarial group (e.g. age, sex, health status) the insured belongs to. The remaining part of the premium will be paid directly to the insurer by the insured. On average, this will be about 10% of the total premium, but it can be considerably lower if the person chooses an efficient insurer or an insurer who contracts efficient providers of care. The consumer will be free to buy the basic insurance from any insurer who observes the procompetitive regulation.

This regulation requires, among others, that all insureds at the same insurer pay the same premium. This holds both for the basic insurance (besides the income-related premium) and for the supplementary insurance. Furthermore the regulation requires open enrolment, i.e. the insurer cannot refuse to insure some persons, e.g. because they have a bad health status. As a compensation for this open enrolment the premium-replacing payment that the insurer receives out the Central Fund will be risk adjusted. This implies, e.g. that for a 80-year-old person the insurer will receive on average an amount that is about tenfold the payments for a 20-year-old person. The key function of the Central Fund therefore is that it combines solidarity and efficiency: income-related payments from the insureds to the Central Fund guarantee any desired solidarity between high- and low-income groups, between healthy and unhealthy people and between young and old persons; risk-adjusted premium-replacing payments from the Central Fund to the insurers take away from the insurers the incentives for preferred risk selection (i.e. to select healthy insureds) and provides them, because of the competitive environment and the fixed-price premiums between insurers and insureds, with the incentives for efficiency.

As proposed the open enrolment requirement with respect to the supplementary insurance will be restricted only to those people who were previously insured at another insurer and to "the first time" that someone buys supplementary insurance as a self-supporting person. Furthermore the basic insurance and the supplementary insurance have to be bought at the same insurer. The premium for each insurance may be reduced if the insured chooses a low-option plan (i.e. with some forms of cost sharing). Finally it is important that in the new insurance structure limited provider plans will be explicitly allowed. This means that in principle all kind of constructions like health maintenance organizations (HMO) and preferred provider organizations (PPO) are possible. This may have far-reaching consequences for the new health care system and for the relations between insurers and providers.

Relations Between Insurers and Providers

A major change in the relations between the insurers and the providers of care will be that they may voluntarily enter into a contract with each other about the medical care to be provided. The contents of the contracts may differ from each other, so that insurers and providers can negotiate on the terms, e.g. with respect to volume, price and quality. As an intermediary between consumers and providers the insurers will get more room for manoeuvre than in the present system. The sickness funds will no longer be obliged to enter into a contract with each physician in the community who expresses the wish to do so. By selective contracting the insurers will be able to contract only with qualitatively good and efficient providers. The Health Services Act (WVG), which regulates or was intended to regulate the volume of health services, will be withdrawn.

Major reasons for the failure of this act are the distinction between the planning authorities (local and provincial authorities) and the payers (insurers) and the division of the planning authority over provinces (inpatient care) and municipalities (outpatient care). The Hospital Provision Act (WZV) will be deregulated: specialist outpatient facilities will no longer be covered by this act; it will cover only large-scale inpatient facilities. Tariffs and fees will no longer bet set by the Central Health Charges Board (COTG) subject to detailed government regulation based on the Health Care Charges Act (WTG). It is the government's intention to make the insurers and the providers of care as much responsible as possible for all financial aspects associated with the contracts they enter into. The government will make conditions with respect to minimum quality and minimum supply of facilities that should be fulfilled. Furthermore the government will take measures to counteract undesired monopolies and cartels of insurers as well as providers of care.

With respect to the training of new health care personnel, the government will stay responsible for the capacity and the entry requirements of initial full-time schooling programmes. A major guideline in assessing the capacity of these programmes will be the demand for the care in question. Insurers and providers of care will be jointly responsible for the capacity of in-service training programmes, refresher courses and updating courses.

Relations Between Providers and Insureds

An important aspect of the relations between the insureds (patients, consumers) and the providers of care is the quality of care. The government sets a high value upon the common responsibility of the insurers and providers of care for a good quality of health care. One possibility would be the establishment of private certification institutes. According to certain standards these institutions could control several aspects of the quality of health care (just like the quality control of, e.g. electronic articles). Providers of care who fail to get approval from the certification institute will have a rough time getting a contract with an insurer. Insured consumers probably will have a preference not to make use of non-certified providers and therefore insurers preferably will contract with certified providers.

The government will set minimum requirements with respect to a qualitatively acceptable level of care and will stimulate the provision of independent consumer information. A powerful instrument for the consumer to strengthen his position is "voting with his feet". If the consumer is not content, he may ultimately choose another insurer, another insurance policy or another provider of care.

Consequences for the Various Parties Involved

The above-mentioned proposed changes will have far-reaching consequences for the various parties involved in health care. In this section some major consequences for the various parties will be discussed.

Insurers

It is to be expected that the role of the insurers – both sickness funds and private health insurance companies – will dramatically change. They are supposed to act more as cost-conscious purchasers of care on behalf of their insureds than as administrative offices or as pure indemnity insurance companies. Their new position can be sketched as being an intermediary between consumers and providers of care.

A major change for the *sickness funds* is that their incomes will be budgeted so that they will have a restricted amount of money to finance the care provided to their insureds. Furthermore most of them will lose their regional monopoly and will have to compete with other insurers. They will have to develop new activities like premium calculation, cost containment strategies and marketing. Their obligation to enter into a contract with each physician in the community who expresses the wish to do so will be abolished.

Private health insurance companies will be confronted with new procompetitive regulations like open enrolment and premium setting. Preferred risk selection will no longer be attractive because of the risk-adjusted premium-replacing payments from the Central Fund. Therefore they will have to compete on quality of care, service and price. It will become necessary for them to be increasingly engaged in the process of delivering medical care: What is good quality? Which criteria to use? How to determine inefficiency and waste? How to stimulate good-quality and efficient provider behaviour?

Providers of Care

In the new system the providers of care will have to negotiate with the insurers about the volume, price and quality of the care to be delivered. Probably the insurers, who function as cost-conscious purchasers of care on behalf of their insureds, will be well-motivated and well-informed negotiators. Providers of care who can make plausible that they deliver good-quality care, prevent inefficiencies and have good procedures for patients' complaints will be in a better position than those who cannot.

Physicians will be confronted with the situation that the present, fixed fees are no longer guaranteed and that they will no longer automatically get a (new) contract with the insurers. In my view *hospitals* are among the providers the ones who will be mostly threatened by the new system. At present the overcapacity of hospital beds is about 25%. I expect that the strong decrease in number of hospital days per capita that took place during past few years will continue unabated in the next few years. Competition in health care and incentives for efficiency can even accelerate and intensify this development. The possibility exists that in the next few years the number of hospital days per patient will be reduced by 25% or more, which will lead to a huge overcapacity of hospital beds.

Consumers

Hopefully it is the *consumer* who ultimately will benefit the most from the proposed new developments. Regulated competition is expected to lead to an efficient health care system that closely matches the consumer preferences. As regards quality concerns, one often hears the argument that price competition may lead to an unwarranted reduction in the quality of care. However, there are many strong counterarguments in favour of the opposite. First, a strong argument for the expectation of good-quality medical care in a competitive health care system is competition itself. If the consumer is not satisfied, he or she will choose some other provider organization. Even one well-documented case of clearly poor quality care can lead to a bad image and thereby to a dramatic drop in the number of consumers. Therefore it is to be expected that insurers, who selectively contract providers will primarily be interested in good quality. Of course, *given* a certain level of sufficient quality, they will be interested in the lowest costs.

Secondly, competition may lead to the introduction of a system of certification. This kind of market and self-regulation – eventually supported by government regulation – may improve the quality of care.

Thirdly, in a competitive health care system more information on quality might become available than in a non-competitive system. Insurers will demand for information on quality or they will collect it themselves in order selectively to contract high-quality providers. Also consumer organizations will provide the consumer with clear information in order to make the right choices. The availability of public information on quality will stimulate the providers of care to improve quality.

Fourthly, the experience with the competing health maintenance organizations (HMOs) in the United States does not support the statement that competition leads to lower quality. On the contrary, the quality of care in HMOs appears to be at least similar to that in the conventional United States health care system (Dutch government 1988).

Fifthly, moral and ethical considerations and peer pressure will answer for quality.

Sixthly, good-quality care in the short term may prevent high health care expenditures in the future.

Finally it is a great misunderstanding to think that "more care is better care" or "higher costs imply better quality". As Enthoven states: "The first and most important way to control cost while maintaining quality is to control quality. That is, to do it right the first time. The right diagnosis made promptly and the appropriate procedure done by a person who is proficient and experienced and good at it produces both the best-quality result and the most economical result. In medical care quality and economy usually go hand in hand" (Enthoven 1987). As mentioned in the introduction, this last statement has been supported by study of the literature, reviewing studies related to the improvement of efficiency in the Dutch health care system. The purpose of many of the reported studies was either "improving efficiency" or "improving quality". However, the result of many of these studies appeared to be improving both efficiency and quality (Van de Ven 1988).

Government

With respect to the role of the government in a competitive health care system it is a misunderstanding to think that there is a contradistinction between "competition" and "regulation". The opposite of "competition" is "monopoly", while the opposite of "regulation" is "no regulation" or "free market". It is clear that an unregulated or free health care market will yield several undesirable outcomes. Therefore it is important to realize that in the governmental letter (1988) proposals are made for *"regulated competition"* in health care. Government regulation will surely not fade away, but its accent will dramatically change. Instead of direct government control on volume and prices, the government will have to create the necessary conditions in order to let the market achieve society's goal with respect to health care. The emphasis of government regulation will therefore be primarily on mandatory health insurance for everyone, anti-cartel, quality control and information disclosure.

Conclusions

My personal view is that the governmental proposals for a restructuring of the Dutch health care system as presented in their letter (1988) form a promising alternative for the health care policy of the past 15 years. The proposed structure of the health care system creates a situation in which:

1. The insured consumers will be rewarded for choosing efficient insurers and choosing cost-effective providers.
2. The providers will be rewarded for providing effective and efficient health care.
3. The insurers, who function as an intermediary between the insured consumers and the contracted providers, are stimulated to contract efficient providers and to do market research into the consumers' preferences.

However, several necessary conditions have to be fulfilled before a successful implementation of the proposals can take place. Major issues to be dealt with are: how to develop the right formula to budgeting the insurers? How to abolish all the existing differences between sickness fund insurance and private health insurance? And how to develop and enforce an effective anti-cartel policy in health care? Although there are technical solutions for each of these issues (Schut and Van de Ven 1989), it is necessary that policymakers should pay ample attention to these and other issues, each of which can be a hindrance for successful implementation of the proposed health care reforms. With respect to the implementation of the governmental proposals one can also point to the severe steering problem: *How to come from here to there?* We now have legislation for government control on volume and price, but there is little legislation for government regulation on quality control, cartels and information disclosure in health care. Experience has shown that it can take many years to enact new legislation. This leaves us with the odd situation that government announces a complete new health care policy, but does not want to abolish the old instruments for cost containment as long as the new ones are not available. At the same time new initiatives in the health care field emerge that anticipate the new situation, but are blocked by the present legislation. A way to give these initiatives a fair chance would be to give them experimental status.

What developments are to be expected in the Netherlands in the next few years? Because government has severely committed itself to the new health care policy (Governmental letter 1988), I expect all new developments in the coming years to be steps in the new direction. But the crucial question is: How far and how fast? Probably 1992 is too optimistic. I expect that the degree of competition in health care will strongly depend on the degree that there is sufficient legislation to effectively counteract existing cartels. Given the rather competitive market for private health insurance and given the long-standing, government-supported cartels of providers of care (fixed tariffs, licence to start practice and a strong national organization of providers with much experience in bilateral negotiations), I expect that at short notice there will be more perspective for competition between insurers than for competition between providers. Competing insurers will then try to enter into a favourable contract with providers and they will try to stimulate efficiency-improving measures, e.g. pre-admission screening, concurrent review, discharge planning, quality assurance and second opinions. Some providers will agree with these measures, while others – presumably an overwhelming majority – will not. The established providers, who fear all the new developments, might boycott their colleagues who cooperate with the insurers in improving efficiency in health care. Looking at the experiences in the United States it is to be expected that there will be several anti-cartel lawsuits, based on either national laws or European laws, the outcomes of which will largely determine the degree of future competition in the Dutch health care system.

References

Barer ML, Evans RG, Stoddart GL (1979) Controlling health care costs by direct charges to patients: snare or delusion? Ontario Economic Council, Toronto (occasional paper 10)

Brook RH, Ware JE, Rogers WH, Keeler EB, Davies AR, Donald CA, Goldberg GA, Lohr KN, Mastay PC, Newhouse JP (1983) Does free care improve adults health? N Engl J Med 309:1426–1434

Commissie Structuur en Financiering Gezondheidszorg (1987) Bereidheit tot verandering (Willingness to change). Staatsuitgeverij, The Hague

Cunningham FC, Williamson JW (1980) How does the quality of health care in HMOs compare to that in other settings? Group Health J 1:4–25

Dutch government (1988) Verandering verzekerd (Changes assured). Governmental letter to Parliament, March 7, 1988 ("third Dekker letter")

Ellwood PM, McClure W (1976) Health delivery reform. InterStudy Excelsior, MN (mimeographed)

Enthoven AC (1980) Health plan: the only practical solution to the soaring cost of medical care. Addison-Wesley, Reading, MA, pp 32–37

Enthoven AC (1987) Lecture, 17 September 1987. In: Schut FT, van de Ven WPMM (eds) Proceedings of the conference on regulated competition in the Dutch health care system. Available from: Erasmus Universiteit Rotterdam, Studierichting Beleid en Management Gezondheidszorg, Postbus 1738, 3000 DR Rotterdam

Kaplan RS, Lave LB (1971) Patient incentives and hospital insurance. Health Serv Res 6:288–300

Luft HS (1978) How do health maintenance organizations achieve their savings? N Engl J Med 298:1336–1343

Luft HS (1981) Health maintenance organizations: dimension of performance. Wiley, New York

Manning WG, Leibowitz A, Goldberg GA, Rogers WH, Newhouse JP (1984) A controlled trial of the effect of a prepaid group practice on use of services. N Engl J Med 310:1505–1510

Manning WG, Newhouse JP, Duan N, Keeler EB, Leibowitz A, Marquis MS (1987) Health insurance and the demand for medical care: evidence from a randomized experiment. Am Econ Rev 77:251–277

Newhouse JP (1978) Insurance benefits, out-of pocket payments and the demand for medical care: a review of the literature, Rand Corporation, Santa Monica, CA, P-6134

Newhouse JP, Taylor V (1971) A new type of hospital insurance. J Risk Insurance 38:604–612

Roemer MI (1982) Sickness absenteesm in members of health maintenance organizations and open-market health insurance plans. Med Care 20:1140–1146

Schut FT, van de Ven WPMM (1989) Op weg naar een nieuwe stelsel van gezondheidszorg: overstappen op de Dubbel-Dekker? Openbare Uitgaven, August 1989

Van de Ven WPMM (1983) Effects of cost-sharing in health care. Eff Health Care 1:47–58

Van de Ven WPMM (1987) The key role of health insurance in a cost-effective health care system; towards regulated competition in the Dutch medical market. Health Policy 7:253–272

Van de Ven WPMM, Winkens CGF, Wohrmann LJE (1988) Doelmatigheid gezondheidszorg: een miljardenkwestie. Ned Tijdschr Geneeskde 132:1623–1627

Ware JE, Brook RH, Rogers WH, Keeler EB, Davies AR, Scherbourne CD, Goldberg GA, Camp P, Newhouse JP (1986) Comparison of health outcomes at a health maintenance organization with those of fee-for-service care. Lancet i:1017–1022

Wolinsky FD (1980) The performance of health maintenance organizations: an analytic review. Milbank Mem Fund Q/Health Soc 58/4:537–587

Wyszewiansky L, Wheeler JRC, Donabedian A (1982) Market-oriented cost containment strategies and quality of care. Milbank Mem Fund Q/Health Soc 60/4:518–550

Ziekenfondsraad (1986) Jaarverslag Ziekenfondsraad 1985: Financieel Deel. Ziekenfondsradd, Amstelveen

Equity in the Finance of Health Care: Effects of the Dutch Health Insurance Reform

E. van Doorslaer, R. Janssen, A. Wagstaff, J. van Emmerik, and F. Rutten

Introduction

Under the auspices of the European Community (EC), researchers of ten countries have recently begun collaborating on a comparative study of equity in the finance and delivery of health care. The project's initial aim is to facilitate comparisons of the distributional consequences of alternative health care financing and delivery systems. The methodological framework and some tentative results have already been published by Wagstaff et al. (1989). In a second phase it is planned to examine the distributional consequences of specific health care finance reforms and/or cost-containment measures. This paper presents the first attempt with respect to the latter aim. The focus of attention is limited to only one country, the Netherlands, and to only one type of equity, namely vertical equity on the finance side of the health care system, as measured by the degree of progressivity of health care payments with respect to income. By means of a simulation exercise we have tried to establish how the progressivity of the Dutch health care financing system would have been affected if the proposed Health Insurance Reform had already been introduced in 1985. The progressivity of the simulated distributions under various assumptions is then compared with the progressivity of the actual distribution of health care payments across income deciles in 1985.

Definition and Measurement of Equity in the Finance of Health Care

Vertical Equity

Egalitarians typically define equity on the finance side in terms of requirement that payments for health care be directly related to ability to pay. This is a statement about *vertical equity* – the requirement that unequals (defined here in terms of "ability of pay") be treated unequally. It directly raises the question of how "ability to pay" is to be measured and whether unequal means just proportional or progressive, and if so how progressive? Typically policy statements fail to address questions such as these. We use pre-tax household income (per adult-equivalent) as a proxy for ability to pay and have adopted the strategy of merely describing the degree of progressivity.

In contrast to previous work on equity in the finance of health care (cf. Hurst 1985; Gottschalk et al. 1986; Wagstaff et al. 1989), we have employed several indices taken from the tax literature to measure the progressivity of health care payments. The indices we have used are those of Kakwani (1977), Reynolds and Smolensky (1977), Suits (1977) and Pfähler (1983). The review of the indices below is based on Lambert (1985) an is explained in terms of health care payments rather than taxes.

Kakwani's index is based on the extent to which a payment system departs from proportionality and can best be illustrated using Fig. 1. The curve labelled g^{pre} gives the Lorenz curve for prepayment income. The second curve – labelled g^{pay} – gives the *payment concentration curve*, which plots the cumulative proportions of the population (ranked according to prepayment in-

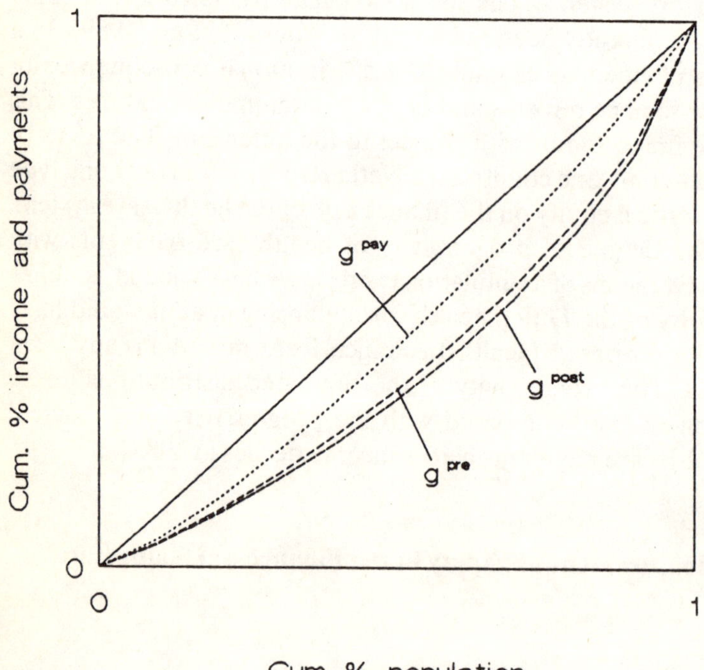

Fig. 1. Lorenz curves for pre- and postpayment income and payments concentration curve (based on data in Table 1)

come as with g^{pre}) against the cumulative proportion of health care payments.

If payments were levied strictly in proportion to income, the payment concentration curve and the Lorenz curve for prepayment income would coincide. If the average payment rate rises with income (so that the payment system is progressive), the payment concentration curve lies outside the Lorenz curve for prepayment income. The opposite is true if payments are regressive. The degree of progressivity can therefore be assessed by looking at the size of the area between g^{pre} and g^{pay}. If G^{inc} is the Gini coefficient for prepayment income and C^{pay} is the concentration index for health care payments, Kakwani's index of progressivity, π^{K}, is defined as

$$\pi^{K} = C^{pay} - G^{inc} \tag{1}$$

which is twice the area between g^{pay} and g^{pre}. If the system is regressive so that g^{pay} lies above g^{pre}, π^{K} is negative. The value of π^{K} ranges from –2.0 (when all prepayment income is concentrated in the hands of the richest person and the entire payment burden falls on the poorest person) to 1.0 (when prepayment income is distributed equally and the entire payment burden falls on the richest person).

The index proposed by Reynolds and Smolensky is based not on the extent to which a payment system departs for proportionality but on the extent to which it is redistributive. It, too, can be illustrated using Fig. 1. The curve labelled g^{post} is the concentration curve for afterpayment income. This plots the cumulative proportions of the population (ranked according to prepayment income as with g^{inc}) against the cumulative proportion of afterpayment income received. If payments are levied strictly in proportion to income, g^{post} and g^{pre} coincide. If the payment system is progressive, g^{post} lies above g^{pre}. The opposite is true if payments are regressive. If C^{post} is the concentration index for postpayment income, the Reynolds-Smolensky index of progressivity, π^{RS}, is defined as

$$\pi^{RS} = G^{pre} - C^{post} \tag{2}$$

which is twice the area between g^{post} and g^{pre}. If the system is regressive so that g^{post} lies below g^{pre}, π^{RS} is negative. The value of π^{RS} ranges from –1.0 (when prepayment income is distributed equally but all postpayment income is concentrated in the hands of one person) to 1.0 (when all prepayment income is concentrated in the hands of the richest person and postpayment income is distributed equally).

The Reynolds-Smolensky and Kakwani indices are related: it can be shown that

$$\pi^{RS} = [t/(1-t)]\,\pi^{K} \tag{3}$$

where t is the average payment rate. Equation 3 shows that one can break down differences in the redistributive effect of progressive payment systems into (a) differences in the average payment rate and (b) differences in the departure from proportionality.

The indices of Kakwani and Reynolds and Smolensky are based on standard Lorenz and concentration curves. The indices of Suits and Pfähler, by contrast, are based on what Lambert and Pfähler (1988) call *relative* concentration curves. The Suits and Pfähler indices are illustrated in Fig. 2. The curve labelled h^{pre} is the relative concentration curve for prepayment income. This plots the cumulative proportion of prepayment income (starting at the bottom of the distribution) against the cumulative proportion of prepayment income. Thus h^{pre} coincides with the 45° line and serves as the benchmark against which to assess progressivity. The curve labelled h^{pay} plots the cumulative proportion of prepayment income (starting, as before, at the bottom of the distribution) against the cumulative proportion of health care payments borne by the households in the relevant part of the income distribution.

If payments are levied in proportion to income, h^{pre} and h^{pay} coincide, so that, for example, the bottom 10% of prepayment income pays 10% of health

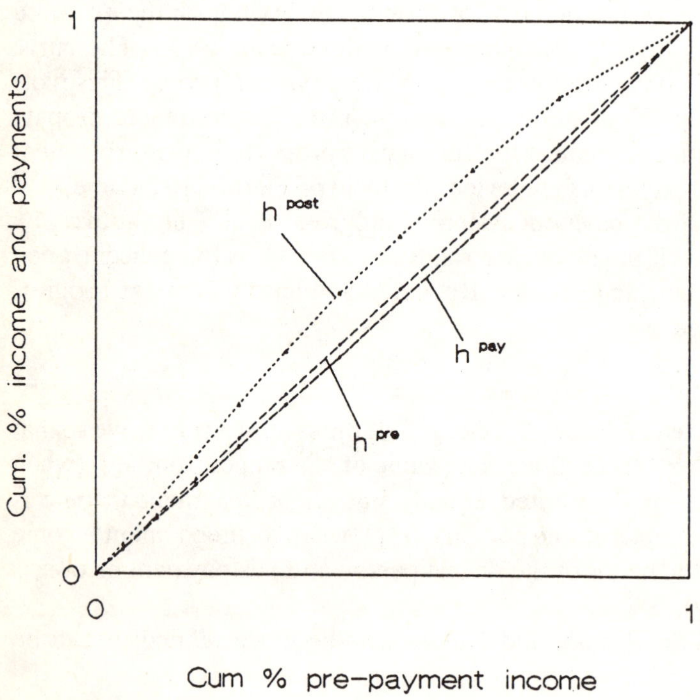

Fig. 2. Relative concentration curves of payments and postpayment income (based on data in Table 1)

care payments. If the payment system is progressive, h^{pay} lies below the diagonal (the case illustrated). The opposite is true if payments are regressive. The degree of progressivity can therefore be assessed by looking at the size of the area between h^{pre} and h^{pay}. If H^{pay} is the relative concentration index for health care payments, Suits' index of progressivity, π^S, is defined as

$$\pi^S = H^{pay} \tag{4}$$

which is twice the area between h^{pay} and h^{pre}. If the payment system is regressive so that h^{pay} lies above h^{pre}, π^S is negative. The value of π^S ranges from –1.0 (when the entire payment burden falls on the poorest person) to 1.0 (when the entire payment burden falls on the richest person).

Pfähler's index differs from Suit's index in the same way as the Reynolds-Smolensky index differs from Kakwani's. The curve labelled h^{post} is the relative concentration curve for postpayment income. It plots the cumulative proportion of prepayment income (starting, as before, at the bottom of the distribution) against the cumulative proportion of postpayment income received by the households in the relevant part of the income distribution. If payments are levied strictly in proportion to income, h^{post} and h^{pre} coincide. If the payment system is progressive, h^{post} lies above h^{pre}, so that the bottom 10% of prepayment income translates into more than 10% of postpayment income. The opposite is true if payments are regressive. If H^{post} is the relative concentration index for postpayment income, Pfähler's index of progressivity, π^{PF}, is defined as

$$\pi^{PF} = -H^{post} \tag{5}$$

which is twice the area between h^{post} and h^{pre}. Note that if the payment system is progressive, so that h^{post} lies above h^{pre} as in Fig. 2, H^{post} is negative and π^{PF} is positive. The opposite is true when the payment system is regressive. Like π^S, π^{PF} ranges from –1.0 to +1.0.

The indices of Pfähler and Suits are related: it can be shown that

$$\pi^{PF} = [t/(1-t)]\ \pi^S \tag{6}$$

where t is, as before, the average payment rate. Thus, as with the Reynolds-Smolensky index, differences in the redistributive effect of progressive payment systems can be broken down into (a) differences in the average payment rate and (b) differences in the departure from proportionality.

Horizontal Equity

This leaves the issue of *horizontal equity* (the requirement that equals be treated equally). It might be defined in terms of the extent to which those of equal ability to pay actually end up making equal payments regardless of, for example, gender, marital status, trade union membership and place of residence. In the Netherlands, different occupational groups are eligible for different insurance schemes. As a result, people with the same income in 1981 could end up paying as little as 2% of their income while others pay as much as 13% depending on their age and employment status (Rutten and Janssen 1987). In this paper we will not look at the issue of horizontal inequity formally using indices but we will comment on changes below (p. 163).

Health Care Financing in the Netherlands Before and After the Proposed Reform

The Current Financing System

The present Dutch health care system can be characterized as a combination of a social insurance system (like the Federal Republic of Germany) and a private insurance model (like the United States). Health care services are being provided predominantly by private organization which operate in an environment of elaborate government regulation.

Health care is financed from three main sources: (a) social insurance contributions, (b) private insurance premiums and (c) direct payments. The fourth source – general taxation – accounts for only about 6% of health care revenues.

Social insurance contributions are of two types. The first is the so-called AWBZ contribution under the Exceptional Medical Expenses Act. It is compulsory for all persons below pensionable age and covers expenses incurred in respect of three types of care, namely "catastrophic illness" (illness requiring long-term institutional care), outpatient mental care and home nursing. AWBZ contributions are a fixed proportion of "premium income", up to a ceiling and are paid by the employer. The second type of social insurance contribution is paid to sick funds to cover short-term care. These contributions are compulsory for wage earners and social security beneficiaries with an income below a certain level. Civil servants employed by provincial and municipal governments are covered by an employment-specific statutory scheme. Both sick fund and statutory insured pay premiums proportional to gross income up to a ceiling. Together, these two groups comprise about 68% of the population. The remaining 32% have to buy private insurance with risk-related premiums. They have the choice to opt out for part of their health care and pay deductibles in return for premium reductions.

Essentials of the Proposed Reform

In the summer of 1986 the Dutch Government appointed an external committee to advise on a revision of the structure and finance of the health care system. The main terms of reference were: (a) to make recommendations on strategies for reducing the burden on the public health care budget, (b) integration of health care and social care provision, (c) improvements to efficiency and flexibility in health care by introducing proper incentives for users, providers and insurers, and (d) a shift of emphasis from government regulation to market and self-regulation.

The essentials of the following proposal have already been subscribed by the government. The entire population will be covered by a compulsory basic insurance scheme. In practice, this means that the present AWBZ scheme will be extended to cover about 85% of all health care costs. However, it will only partly be paid for by a premium in proportion to income (up to a maximum) and partly – which is new – by a fixed premium per insurance policy. About 10% of all health care costs will have to be financed out of these fixed premiums.

The income-related premiums are to be collected by the Tax Office and paid into a central fund. Allocation among insurers will be on the basis of the number of insured but with some adjustment for risk mix. Fixed premiums may vary with the number of insured per household, and out-of-pocket payments with the amount of the deductible. Health care services not covered by the basic insurance (e.g. drugs, physiotherapy, dental treatment) can be covered by supplementary insurance with a fixed premium.

The consequences of the proposals for the degree of progressivity of health care payments are uncertain. On the one hand the extension of the compulsory basic insurance with income-related payments may increase the relative contribution of the higher income groups compared with the present situation. But on the other hand it is unclear whether the payments for supplementary insurance might not offset this effect; if higher income groups also enjoy better health, they may have to pay lower supplementary premiums and/or out-of-pocket expenses. The overall effect may be examined empirically under various assumptions regarding behavioural responses with respect to supplementary insurance purchase and out-of-pocket payments.

Empirical Analysis and Results

Vertical Equity

The empirical investigation is based on data taken from the 1985 Household Expenditure Survey of the Netherlands Central Bureau of Statistics (CBS). We measure a household's "ability to pay" by its pre-tax (i.e. gross) but equivalent income. This means that the reported income is adjusted for household composition using the Netherlands CBS equivalent scale (Schiepers 1988). Because of the relative unimportance of general tax revenues, we examined only the health care financing sources mentioned above.

Baseline Distribution of Actual Expenditures in 1985

Table 1 presents the proportion of total health care payments from each source of finance borne by each decile of equivalent income in the baseline situation. Comparing the first and the last column reveals that the overall financing mechanism is clearly regressive: all deciles, except the two top ones, pay a higher percentage for health care than their income share. This result confirms earlier findings by Wagstaff et al. (1989) for 1984. It can be seen that this result

Table 1. Distribution by deciles of health care payments in the Netherlands in 1985

Income decile	Proportion of pretax income	Proportion of income-related premiums	Proportion of AWBZ	Proportion of direct payments	Proportion of total payments
Bottom	4.5%	6.1%	4.4%	3.3%	5.3%
2nd	6.0%	8.6%	6.6%	4.8%	7.5%
3rd	6.7%	9.4%	7.9%	6.0%	8.5%
4th	7.3%	10.2%	8.5%	6.8%	9.3%
5th	8.0%	10.2%	9.2%	8.4%	9.7%
6th	8.9%	10.4%	9.9%	11.1%	10.4%
7th	10.1%	10.3%	10.8%	10.0%	10.4%
8th	11.9%	11.7%	12.4%	12.9%	12.0%
9th	14.4%	12.0%	14.2%	15.5%	13.1%
Top	22.2%	11.1%	16.2%	21.1%	13.9%
% of total payments		58.6%	27.7%	13.7%	100.0%
Gini/Conc	0.2539	0.0797	0.1895	0.2820	0.1379
Kakwani		–0.1743	–0.0645	0.0281	–0.1161
Reynolds-Smolensky					–0.0266
Suits		–0.1856	–0.0751	0.0188	–0.1270
Pfähler					–0.0291

is mainly due to the regressive pattern in the major source of finance, namely the insurance premiums with a Kakwani index of –0.17. Unfortunately, in this column private and public insurance premiums, which obviously show very different progressivity patterns, cannot be separated out. The Kakwani index for the overall distribution is less negative (–0.06) because the distribution of AWBZ premiums is only slightly regressive and that of direct payments even progressive. But both indices are close to zero, indicating proportionality.

These results are easily understood with some basic knowledge of the dual character of the Dutch health care system. Publicly (sick fund) insured roughly pay a premium in proportion to their salary up to a maximum level. Those who exceed the upper income limit pay premiums to competitive insurers which are not income but risk (mainly age) related. In return for premium reductions they often have substantial deductibles, which implies that they have to pay cash for health services used and higher prices than the sick fund insured. However, as can be seen from Table 1, these higher direct payments do not offset the premium advantage.

This apparently unjust distinction between publicly and privately insured was precisely one of the considerations underlying the reform proposals of the Dekker Committee.

Assumptions Underlying Reform Simulations

The point of departure for both the Committee proposals and the scenarios considered here is that the total health care budget remains the same but that the rules according to which the total burden is distributed across the population may vary. Total health care expenditures in 1985 amounted to 33 640 million guilders. The different scenarios on policy options are described in Table 2. The Dekker Committee's proposal was that 75% of it should be financed out of a *premium proportional to income* (Commissie Structur en Financierung Gezondheidszorg 1987). The remaining 25% minus any direct

Table 2. Characteristics of the different policy scenarios

Policy scenarios	1a	1b	2a	2b	3	4
Ratio income-related/fixed premiums	75/25	75/25	70/30	70/30	62/38	50/50
Income-related premium	12.1%	1.21%	11.3%	11.3%	10%	8%
Fixed premium (including direct payments)	660		793		1005	1319
Fixed premium (excluding direct payments)		417		550		
Current direct payments		Yes		Yes		

payments are to be raised by so-called *fixed premiums*, i.e. a flat rate per adult equivalent (all persons under the age of 18 years are in this context counted as one-half adult-equivalent).

Regarding the extent and distribution of *direct payments* after the reform, some heroic assumptions have to be made. Firstly, it is assumed that the total amount remains constant. Secondly, two assumptions regarding their distribution have been made. The first one implies that the distribution is unaffected by the reform. Admittedly, this is highly unlikely to happen but there are some indications from opinion polls that, at least in the short run, a majority of the population will try to select an insurance policy as close as possible to its present situation. The second one simply assumes that direct payments will be distributed evenly across adult equivalents. They then simply become an extension of the fixed premium.

No attempts have been made so far to improve upon these two crude assumptions because they would require information on income and price elasticities of the demand for health insurance and medical care for various population groups which is currently not available. However, simulations incorporating this type of behavioural reaction are planned in the near future.

In Table 3 the above-described simulations are summarized as scenario 1a (with direct payments included in the nominal premium) and scenario 1b (with direct payments unchanged). The other columns represent mainly variations in the proportional/fixed ratio. Scenarios 2a and 2b are based on the governmental reaction to the committee's proposal suggesting a 70/30 ratio instead of the 75/25 ratio (Dutch government 1988). In addition, we have considered two more drastic deviations (50/50 and 62/38) in scenarios 3 and 4. It can be seen that the repercussions for the proportional and the nominal premium are more substantial in the latter two cases.

The expectations regarding the progressivity of the distributions resulting from these scenarios are fairly obvious: the higher the share of the proportional

Table 3. Summary of progressivity index values for the various scenarios

		Baseline	Dekker Committee		Government		Other
	Policy scenarios	0	1a	1b	2a	2b	3
Progressivity indices	Kakwani	–.116	–.111	–.078	–.122	–.088	–.140
	Reynolds-Smolensky	–.027	–.026	–.019	–.028	–.022	–.032
	Suits	–.127	–.120	–.088	–.131	–.098	–.148
	Pfähler	–.029	–.028	–.021	–.030	–.024	–.034

premium, the more progressive the financing structure. Under the (heroic) assumption that the direct payments will be distributed equally per adult equivalent (scenarios 1a, 2a, 3 and 4), only the Dekker proposal implies some reduction in the degree of regressivity. Both the governmental proposal and especially the two scenarios with a larger share of fixed payments show a shift towards a more regressive payment system. If, however, the other assumption regarding direct payments is adopted, i.e. that their distribution will remain the same as in the baseline situation, then both scenarios 1b and 2b imply a substantial reduction in regressivity. This is, of course, a consequence of the fact that in the current situation the privately insured have higher direct payments than the publicly insured. It is clear that if in the future the direct payments for health care were to become inversely related to income, this would tend to reinforce the degree of regressivity.

All of these findings seem to be fairly insensitive with respect to the choice of progressivity index. The patterns of the index values for the measures of Reynolds-Smolensky, Suits and Pfähler are very similar to that of the Kakwani index, though it appears that the two indices which are based on the area between the pre- and postpayment income concentration curves (Reynolds-Smolensky and Pfähler) generally show smaller absolute values.

Horizontal Equity

Clearly, under a system which states that households with equal income per equivalent adult have to pay an equal proportion of that income for health care, the extent of horizontal equity has to increase compared with the situation described above. Two important violations of this principle have been incorporated in the Dekker proposal. The first is the maximum income level up to which premiums are levied proportionally: households with higher income levels all pay the same (maximum) premium. The second is the fixed premium and possibly the associated direct payments. Without a good measure of horizontal inequity and reliable estimates of the direct payment distributions it is therefore hard to say whether, on the whole, the extent of horizontal inequity will be reduced after a reform.

Conclusions

Given the ongoing status of the research presented above, the results and their interpretation are to be considered as tentative. We have used instruments developed in the tax literature to investigate the degree of progressivity of the Dutch health care system. Household expenditure survey data for 1985 were used as the benchmark with which to compare situations possibly arising in the future as a result of the planned Health Insurance Reform. Overall, we found the financing structure to be regressive, implying that higher income deciles account for a smaller share of total health care payments than their share of total earned income. Under various assumptions regarding the nature of the reform and (absence of) behavioural reactions to it, postreform payment distributions were simulated. Resulting changes were quantified by means of progressivity index calculations. The forecasted effects of the scenarios that most closely represented policy document proposals turned out to be extremely sensitive to the assumptions made regarding the (future) distribution of direct payments. But, obviously, a higher reliance on fixed premiums per adult equivalent than on premiums proportional to income increases the degree of regressivity of the health care financing system.

It is envisaged that, before this type of calculation can usefully be fed into policy discussions about reform, some further refinements and improvements are in order.

Firstly and, most importantly, some elements of the proposed reform have not adequately been built in. The major omission seems to be the potentially redistributive effect of the Central Fund allocations to insurers according to risk mix. Depending on the amount of subsidy given indirectly to nominal premiums paid by "bad risks", the real, i.e. net of subsidy, distribution of the fixed nominal premiums may be less regressive than shown in the tables in the Appendix. Secondly, it hardly needs to be re-emphasized that the "de facto" non-reaction assumption regarding behavioural responses on insurance reform should at least be supplemented with realistic alternative assumptions.

If these requirements can be met in future work, then we believe that these "what if" calculations can play an instructive role in discussions on how to reshape Dutch health care to make it both more efficient and more equitable.

Acknowledgments. The authors would like to thank the COMAC Health Services Research Committee of the EC and the Dutch Ministry of Health for financial support and the Dutch Central Bureau of Statistics for access to the data from the 1985 Household Expenditure Survey.

Appendix

Table 4. Distribution of health care payments in scenario 1a

Income decile	Proportion of pretax income	Proportion of income-related premiums	Proportion of fixed premiums	Proportion of total payments
Bottom	4.5%	3.7%	9.2%	5.0%
2nd	6.0%	6.4%	11.0%	7.6%
3rd	6.7%	7.9%	11.2%	8.7%
4th	7.3%	8.7%	10.9%	9.2%
5th	8.0%	9.3%	10.7%	9.7%
6th	8.9%	10.0%	10.2%	10.0%
7th	10.1%	10.8%	9.4%	10.5%
8th	11.9%	12.5%	9.0%	11.6%
9th	14.4%	14.2%	9.1%	12.9%
Top	22.2%	16.5%	9.2%	14.7%
% of total payments		75.2%	24.8%	100.0%
Gini/Conc	0.2539	0.2000	–0.0291	0.1432
Kakwani		–0.0539	–0.2830	–0.1108
Reynolds-Smolensky				–0.0256
Suits		–0.0663	–0.2834	–0.1201
Pfähler				–0.0277

Table 5. Distribution of health care payments in scenario 1b

Income decile	Proportion of pretax income	Proportion of income-related premiums	Proportion of direct payments	Proportion of fixed premiums	Proportion of total payments
Bottom	4.5%	3.7%	3.3%	9.2%	4.4%
2nd	6.0%	6.4%	4.8%	11.0%	6.9%
3rd	6.7%	7.9%	6.0%	11.2%	8.1%
4th	7.3%	8.7%	6.8%	10.9%	8.8%
5th	8.0%	9.3%	8.4%	10.7%	9.4%
6th	8.9%	10.0%	11.1%	10.2%	10.2%
7th	10.1%	10.8%	10.0%	9.4%	10.5%
8th	11.9%	12.5%	12.9%	9.0%	12.0%
9th	14.4%	14.2%	15.5%	9.1%	13.6%
Top	22.2%	16.5%	21.1%	9.2%	16.0%
% of total payments		71.9%	13.1%	15.0%	100.0%
Gini/Conc	0.2539	0.2000	0.2819	–0.0291	0.1764
Kakwani		–0.0539	0.0280	–0.2830	–0.0776
Reynolds-Smolensky					–0.0189
Suits		–0.0663	0.0186	–0.2834	–0.0877
Pfähler					–0.0214

Table 6. Distribution of health care payments in scenario 2a

Income decile	Proportion of pretax income	Proportion of income-related premiums	Proportion of fixed premiums	Proportion of total payments
Bottom	4.5%	3.6%	9.2%	5.3%
2nd	6.0%	6.4%	11.0%	7.8%
3rd	6.7%	7.9%	11.2%	8.9%
4th	7.3%	8.7%	10.9%	9.4%
5th	8.0%	9.4%	10.7%	9.8%
6th	8.9%	10.0%	10.2%	10.1%
7th	10.1%	10.8%	9.4%	10.4%
8th	11.9%	12.5%	9.0%	11.4%
9th	14.4%	14.2%	9.1%	12.7%
Top	22.2%	16.5%	9.2%	14.4%
% of total payments		70.2%	29.8%	100.0%
Gini/Conc	0.2539	0.2008	–0.0291	0.1323
Kakwani		–0.0532	–0.2830	–0.1217
Reynolds-Smolensky				–0.0281
Suits		–0.0656	–0.2834	–0.1305
Pfähler				–0.0301

Table 7. Distribution of health care payments in scenario 2b

Income decile	Proportion of pretax income	Proportion of income-related premiums	Proportion of fixed premiums	Proportion of total payments	Proportion of total payments
Bottom	4.5%	3.6%	3.3%	9.2%	4.7%
2nd	6.0%	6.4%	4.8%	11.0%	7.1%
3rd	6.7%	7.9%	6.0%	11.2%	8.3%
4th	7.3%	8.7%	6.8%	10.9%	8.9%
5th	8.0%	9.4%	8.4%	10.7%	9.5%
6th	8.9%	10.0%	11.1%	10.2%	10.2%
7th	10.1%	10.8%	10.0%	9.4%	10.4%
8th	11.9%	12.5%	12.9%	9.0%	11.8%
9th	14.4%	14.2%	15.5%	9.1%	13.4%
Top	22.2%	16.5%	21.1%	9.2%	15.7%
% of total payments		67.2%	13.1%	19.8%	100.0%
Gini/Conc	0.2539	0.2008	0.2819	–0.0291	0.1659
Kakwani		–0.0532	0.0280	–0.2830	–0.0880
Reynolds-Smolensky					–0.0215
Suits		–0.0656	0.0186	–0.2834	–0.0977
Pfähler					–0.0238

Table 8. Distribution of health care payments in scenario 3

Income decile	Proportion of pretax income	Proportion of income-related premiums	Proportion of fixed premiums	Proportion of total payments
Bottom	4.5%	3.5%	9.2%	5.6%
2nd	6.0%	6.4%	11.0%	8.2%
3rd	6.7%	7.9%	11.2%	9.1%
4th	7.3%	8.7%	10.9%	9.6%
5th	8.0%	9.4%	10.7%	9.9%
6th	8.9%	10.0%	10.2%	10.1%
7th	10.1%	10.8%	9.4%	10.3%
8th	11.9%	12.5%	9.0%	11.2%
9th	14.4%	14.2%	9.1%	12.3%
Top	22.2%	16.6%	9.2%	13.8%
% of total payments		62.0%	38.0%	100.0%
Gini/Conc	0.2539	0.2023	–0.0291	0.1145
Kakwani		–0.0516	–0.2830	–0.1395
Reynolds-Smolensky				–0.0320
Suits		–0.0643	–0.2834	–0.1475
Pfähler				–0.0338

Table 9. Distribution of health care payments in scenario 4

Income decile	Proportion of pretax income	Proportion of income-related premiums	Porportion of fixed premiums	Proportion of total payments
Bottom	4.5%	3.3%	9.2%	6.2%
2nd	6.0%	6.4%	11.0%	8.7%
3rd	6.7%	7.9%	11.2%	9.6%
4th	7.3%	8.8%	10.9%	9.9%
5th	8.0%	9.4%	10.7%	10.1%
6th	8.9%	10.0%	10.2%	10.1%
7th	10.1%	10.8%	9.4%	10.1%
8th	11.9%	12.5%	9.0%	10.7%
9th	14.4%	14.3%	9.1%	11.6%
Top	22.2%	16.7%	9.2%	12.9%
% of total payments		49.6%	50.4%	100.0%
Gini/Conc	0.2539	0.2057	–0.0290	0.0874
Kakwani		–0.0482	–0.2830	–0.1666
Reynolds-Smolensky				–0.0377
Suits		–0.0614	–0.2833	–0.1733
Pfähler				–0.0392

References

Central Statistical Office (1981) The effect of taxes and benefits on household income, 1979. Econ Trends 327:104–131

Commissie Structur en Financierung Gezondheidszorg (1987) Bereitheit tot veranderung (Willingness to change). Staasuitgeverij, The Hague

Dutch government (1988) Veranderung verzekerd (Changes assured). Governmental letter to Parliament, March 7, 1988

Gottschalk P, Wolfe B, Haveman R (1986) Health care financing in the US, UK and the Netherlands: distributional consequences. 42nd congress of the International Institute of Public Finance, Athens

Hurst J (1985) Financing health care in the US, Canada and Britain. Kings Fund, London

Kakwani NC (1977) Measurement of tax progressivity: an international comparison. Econ J 61:139–142

Lambert PJ (1985) Tax progressivity: a survey of the literature. Institute for Fiscal Studies, London (Working paper no. 56)

Lambert PJ, Pfähler W (1988)

Ministry of Health, Welfare and Cultural Affairs (1988) Changing health care in The Netherlands. Rijswijk, p 90

Pfähler W (1983) Measuring redistributional effects of tax progressivity by Lorenz curves. Jahrb Nationalökonomie Stat 198:237–249

Reynolds M, Smolensky E (1977) Public expenditures, taxes and the distribution of income: The United States, 1950, 1961, 1970. Academic, New York

Rutten F, Janssen R (1987) An economic view of inequality in health care. In: Scientific Council for Government Policy (ed) The unequal distribution of health care. (in Dutch) The Hague

Schiepers JMP (1988) Huishoudensequivalentiefactoren volgens de budgetverdelingsmethode (Family equivalence scales). CBS Social-economische Maandstatistiek 3:28–36

Suits D (1977) Measurement of tax progressivity. Am Econ Rev 67:747–752

Wagstaff A, Van Doorslaer E (1989) Measuring the progressivity of the Dutch health care financing system. EC Cost Containment Project, working paper no 4, University of Limburg, Maastricht

Wagstaff A, Van Doorslaer E, Paci P (1989) Equity in the finance and delivery of health care: some tentative cross-country comparisons. Oxford Rev Econ Policy 5:89–112

Incentives to be Healthy: An Economic Model of Health-Related Behaviour

S. Birch and G. Stoddart

Introduction

As policymakers around the world struggle to find ways of controlling the increasing demands on health care systems, attention has been extended to non-health-care influences on population health status. This increasing policy interest in environmental and behavioural influences on health status is probably the result of inter alia:

1. Observed continuing differentials in health among population subgroups (in particular social classes) despite alleged improvements in access to health care (Royal Commission on the National Health Service 1979; UK Department of Health and Social Security 1980; Whitehead 1988)
2. An increasing acceptance that the effect of health care on health status *at the margin* is low in developed economies, both in absolute terms and relative to the marginal impact of other social programmes (i.e. flat of the curve medicine; McKeown 1976; Auster et al. 1969; Enthoven 1980)
3. Observed differentials in health status among "the affluent classes" (Marmot 1986; Marmot and Morris 1984), suggesting that poverty per se is not the only causal factor of health status differentials and hence that considerable reduction or elimination of health differentials will require more than just antipoverty programmes

Nevertheless this shift of attention away from how health care can be used, or its production reorganised to improve health service performance, and towards how individual and societal behaviour can be changed to improve population health status, appears to have had little impact on health economics research. Research interests appear to remain concentrated on the analysis of health *care* (i.e. "downstream") problems, whether at the level of the individual *procedure* or the health care *system*. What has become known as the "topic" of health economics (Culyer 1981) might therefore be more accurately described in most cases as health care economics (Evans 1984).

The primary objective of this paper is to consider what the discipline of economics has to offer in understanding the causes of health-status differentials. We develop a model of individual behaviour, based on an extension of existing economic theory, and consider its potential for use in predicting differentials in life styles and identifying efficient policies for reducing health-status differentials with particular reference to health-related behaviour.

The context of the paper is to emerging policy debate in Canada concerning inequalities in health across income groups and the role of incentives in the determination of life styles. Recognition of non-health-care influences on health status in Canadian policy debate goes back at least to the Lalonde report (Lalonde 1974). Yet it is only in the past few years that the reduction of inequalities in health status has been identified as a major challenge facing Canadian policymakers (Health and Welfare Canada 1986). Our concern is that this policy debate could learn from the United Kingdom experience by avoiding simple "single cause – single effect" type explanations that implicitly underlay policies of health care provision free at the point of delivery (e.g. United Kingdom National Health Service, Canadian Medicare) and instead focus on multifactorial models of health-related behaviour.

The Black Report (UK Department of Health and Social Security 1980) highlighted the weaknesses (and consequences) of following this single cause – single effect approach by emphasising the unequal distribution of various other factors which may be determinants of health. Notwithstanding this, we argue that the policy recommendations contained in the report were based on an *implicit* model which took a similarly restrictive approach to behaviour determination. In particular the observed poorer health status of less affluent groups is *assumed* to be caused by their lower incomes and knowledge, and the provision of more income and/or education is consequently *assumed* to generate behavioural changes which enhance health status.

In this paper we focus attention on the determinants of health-related behaviour (i.e. "upstream" problems), defined as behaviour which, although undertaken primarily for reasons other than the impact on health status, nevertheless has an impact, either positive or negative, on the health status of the individual undertaking the behaviour. We examine whether the analytical tools of economic theory can be applied to the determination of individual behaviour in order to predict the differential incidence of health-related behaviours across social groups and the consequential differentials in health status ceteris paribus.

We do not suggest that the economic model to be developed can provide explanations of all observed behavioural patterns. Indeed we shall begin to draw upon the subject matter of other behavioural sciences as part of the analysis. Further we argue that the economic methodology, when applied broadly to encompass features of the sociological and psychological literature, can be used to explain *some* of the observed differentials in ways which have not to date been recognised or identified, in either the health economics literature or the policy debate.

Our goal is to model the behaviour of the "victims" of poor health as opposed to "blaming" them for the consequences of their behaviour. If the reduction of inequalities in health in society is to be adopted as an important social goal, then more attention should be paid to ensuring that life style *incentives* to individuals are consistent with this goal. Otherwise unhealthy life styles among subgroups of the population may simply reflect behavioural patterns which are in the *best interests of these groups*, even though they are inconsistent with social goals, and may appear irrational to observers isolated from the influences which generate the behaviour.

Understanding Inequalities in Health: A Postwar Perspective

In general, concern with inequalities in health has tended to generate policies aimed at the provision of health care services. In the United Kingdom, postwar concern with equality of opportunity was reflected, inter alia, in the introduction of the National Health Service (NHS) in 1948.

The objective of the NHS was to ensure that

> every man, woman and child can rely on getting . . . the best medical and other facilities available; that their getting them shall not depend on whether they can pay for them, or any other factor irrelevant to real need.
>
> *(Ministry of Health 1944)*

The method by which this objective was to be achieved was essentially the removal of user prices at the point of service delivery. Such an approach, it was believed, would lead to previously unmet needs (the "iceberg" of sickness) now presenting for health care and hence a gradual reduction in total health care needs.

Although the basic approach of removing or reducing price barriers to health care consumption was adopted by many other western industrialised countries, the policy was not based on an explicit behavioural model but on implicit *assumptions* that:

1. The price of health care was the only (or at least primary) barrier to access to health care

2. Access to health care was the only (or at least primary) barrier to access to health
3. Improvements in health status would generate considerable improvements in wellbeing

By removing the price barrier, less affluent members of society would have equal opportunities to choose consumption bundles involving similar levels of health care consumption as more affluent groups and would in fact choose these bundles. Consequently they would achieve similar levels of health status as members of these more affluent groups.

These implicit assumptions have been challenged and shown to be invalid in numerous studies. In the case of the first assumption, Le Grand (1978) found that although poorer groups in society had greater rates of utilisation of NHS Services in the United Kingdom than more affluent groups, the differential rate of utilisation did not correspond to the differential rate of self-reported morbidity. Similarly Bucquet and Curtis (1986) found that the greater incidence of self-reported morbidity for particular conditions in manual workers in three London boroughs was not reflected in higher rates of consultation for these conditions. In other words, poorer groups used health care services less per unit illness (or need) even though the services were free at the point of delivery. One explanation of these observations is that the cost of using the service to the *individual* (i.e. the opportunity cost or shadow price) exceeds the price at point of delivery. Removing the price barrier of health care therefore deals with only one element of the total barrier to health care utilisation.

The second assumption was challenged by McKeown (1976), who showed that the major improvements in health occurring over the past 200 years had less to do with improvements in access to health care and were more closely associated with improvements in dietary practices and sanitary reforms. In earlier work, Auster et al. (1969) used multiple regression analysis of cross-sectional data to show that education and smoking behaviour were more powerful in explaining interstate variations in United States mortality rates than the availability of health care services. The correlates of health, which were interpreted by the authors as determinants of health, appeared to be multiple, health care being just one such determinant, and by no means the most important one.

The validity of the third assumption is challenged by the observed differential response to information concerning the adverse health effects of smoking. Although the results of studies suggest that individuals in all groups now accept that reducing smoking reduces the risk of illness and death, less affluent groups show much less response to the information (Townsend and Davidson 1982; La Vecchia et al. 1986; Pierce 1989).

Recognising the limitations of the single cause – single effect framework underlying the NHS approach to reducing health inequalities, the authors of the Black Report recommended a comprehensive list of policies aimed at improving the incomes and knowledge of poorer groups in society in order that they might:

1. Have a greater understanding of the broader determinants of health and therefore make more informed (and by implication, efficient) decisions concerning consumption bundles
2. Have sufficient resources to adopt the consumption patterns required to attain the health levels of more affluent groups

Although these recommendations constitute a much broader approach to understanding factors which influence population health status and the distribution of health throughout society, the report fell into the same "policy trap" as the founding fathers of the NHS over 30 years previously. Policy recommendations were based on *assumptions* concerning the response of individuals to the proposed policies, without reference to any underlying behavioural model. In other words, it continued to use a single cause – single effect approach, albeit in a wider framework than previously. Hence it assumed that giving the poor more money and exposing them to information on health risks would lead them to behave (i.e. choose consumption bundles) in similar ways to more affluent groups. If these poorer groups then choose to spend the extra income in different ways (e.g. more cigarettes and hamburgers instead of jogging shoes and fresh vegetables), the single cause – single effect explanation falls down. The model is then unable to *challenge the view that, in the presence of similar knowledge about health risks and sufficient resources to achieve a healthy life style (i.e. similar opportunity sets), poorer groups simply choose to follow less healthy life styles, and by implication lower levels of health and earlier deaths. If this is the case, inequalities in health become much less important to policymakers concerned with equating opportunities*, as opposed to outcomes (i.e. actual health improvements), and focusing attention on health as opposed to wellbeing, i.e. the impact of health on individual utility.

Although the lack of any behavioural model represents a fundamental limitation of the Black Report, it is worth noting that the proposals emerging from the report are remarkably consistent with the comparative static predictions of the existing approaches to the demand for health in the economics literature.

Most of the economic literature on the demand for health is based on the model and related work of Grossman (1972) and uses the household production theory (Becker 1965). Under this approach individuals use marketed and non-marketed resources to produce commodities in the household in combinations which maximise utility. Health capital is one such commodity which is produced from inputs of own time and health care inputs and which generates (utility-bearing) flow of health.

The first-order conditions for utility maximisation derived from the model imply that individuals continue to invest in health capital until the benefit of the flow from additional health capital equals the opportunity cost of its production (i.e. the familiar condition of marginal benefit equals marginal cost). Grossman's main interests did not lie in modelling health-related behaviour as defined in this paper (activities having impacts on health but undertaken primarily for non-health reasons) but in understanding and estimating the relationships between health status, health care utilisation (which Grossman interpreted as health care demand), wages rates, education and age.

Issues of joint production were introduced briefly in the final section of the work. In particular some inputs in household production functions were modelled as entering the health capital production function, where they have a negative marginal productivity, as well as entering the production function for which they are primarily used (and hence have a positive marginal productivity). For example cigarettes enter the production function for relaxation and the health capital production function. The effect on the first-order conditions is to increase the marginal opportunity cost of relaxation by an amount equal to the impact of the marginal production of relaxation on health capital.

The purpose of this section of Grossman's analysis was not to identify and explain correlations between socioeconomic variables and health-related behaviours, but to show more generally how a negative income elasticity of health does not imply that health is an inferior good – merely that the income elasticity of commodities with health-detrimental inputs (such as relaxation by smoking) exceeds the income elasticity of health capital production. The corollary of this, however, is that if individuals or groups differ in their patterns of health-related behaviour, it is the result of differences in income elasticities. No consideration is given to *why* income elasticities differ but the implication, as with the implicit framework of the Black Report, is that groups *choose* different consumption bundles per se and hence the different income elasticities are a reflection of different utility functions.

Although the original Grossman work has generated considerable further research (see Birch 1987), most of this has focused on refining or improving the specification of the model or the estimation of the derived equations. Little attention has been paid to the determinants of health-related behaviour or alternative approaches to modelling such behaviour. Muurinen (1982) introduced "environmental" variables as influences on the rate of depreciation of health capital stock. In other words, such influences "used up" scarce health capital (use-related depreciation).

This had the advantage of allowing for adverse impacts on health occurring even in periods when health capital production was zero (i.e. health care consumption zero in terms of the Grossman model). Muurinen later expanded the environmental variables category to include "hazardous consumption and production activities". While this "use-related" depreciation approach to health-related behaviour provides a more general method of including interrelationships, it was not a primary focus of the analysis and was not endogenously determined.

A feature of the demand for health research which deals more directly with the issue of health-related behaviour is the specification of the education-health relationship. The relationship between health and education has been the subject of a large number of empirical studies (e.g. Grossman 1972; Grossman 1975; Shakotko and Grossman 1981). However, our interest lies in the alternative conceptual foundations of the relationships. While Grossman's initial work modelled education as enhancing the technical efficiency of household production (i.e. producing greater outputs from a set of given resource inputs) (Grossman 1972), an alternative approach used in later studies is that education enhances the allocative efficiency in terms of the choice between production processes.[1] In other words, more educated individuals are more aware of the adverse health effects of certain activities and hence are in a better position to make informed decisions between health-detrimental and health-neutral methods of production *of a given commodity*. In this case more educated individuals have healthier life styles ceteris paribus because of their greater knowledge.

However, the important point here is that the prediction is based on ceteris paribus conditions. To move from here directly to a list of policy proposals of the type suggested in the Black Report *assumes* that providing those individuals who follow unhealthy life styles with health education will lead to their choosing similar consumption bundles (i.e. life styles) as the more educated – and hence back to the single cause – single effect approach. Again no consideration is given to *why* the less educated are observed to *choose* less healthy life styles and their behaviour is not modelled – it is merely assumed that they are subject to the same incentives and constraints as their more educated counterparts.

An alternative approach to explaining the health-education relationship, and by implication, to explaining differentials in health, is that education and health both represent investment activities involving current opportunity costs in return for future returns. Farrell and Fuchs (1982) observed that differentials in the prevalence of smoking between young adults of differing education levels existed before the additional education was received. In other words the additional education could not explain the differential smoking behaviour but

---

[1]The two approaches need not be mutually exclusive as shown by Welch (1970).

was more likely an additional reflection of an underlying third variable which affected the willingness and/or ability to invest in health and education in the same way. They suggested that time preference was one possible underlying variable, the value of which might differ between individuals and thus *cause* the observed differential behavioural patterns.

In separate work Fuchs attempted to measure time preference using individuals' declared preferences between money alternatives occurring now and at points in the future (Fuchs 1982). Although the determinants of time preference were not explored, alternative explanations of genetic transmission of preferences and conditioning early in life were suggested. In the work with Farrell (Farrell and Fuchs 1982), it was suggested that differences in rates of time preference inferred from observed behaviour might be the result of imperfection in the capital market giving rise to unequal access to intertemporal transfers (i.e. differences in time preference *at the margin*). Although this argument implies that observed life style differentials might be the result of differential opportunity costs, the explanation was not based on the prediction of any behavioural model but was generated by post hoc rationalisation of observed behaviour.

A Model of Health-Related Behaviour

In this section a model of health-related behaviour is developed. In contrast to the existing literature on the demand for health, we focus our attention on deriving conditions for the optimal production of commodities which, although having impacts on health status, are primarily consumed for other (utility-bearing) reasons. We conceptualise health status as a quality-adjusted (or equivalent-efficient) time variable which is utility bearing in addition to being a scarce resource for use in other commodity production functions. In other words, illness does not represent time lost (i.e. of no use in other activities) but a reduction in the marginal productivity of time as an input to work, rest and play.

Consider the individual's intertemporal utility function

$$u = u(x,y,h) \qquad (1)$$

where $x = \{x_j\}$

$y = \{y_j\}$

$h = \{h_j\}$

and $j = t, \ldots t + n$

Vectors x and y represent the individual's planned household production of commodities x and y in future periods and h is the vector of health in future periods. Commodity x differs from y in so far as x has no direct impact on quality-adjusted time production, h, but y impacts directly, either positively or negatively on h. This impact may be immediate (e.g. driving while under the influence of alcohol) and/or delayed (e.g. excessive alcohol consumption). The individual is assumed to have some expectation of the time of death based on life expectancy estimates. Uncertainty does not feature in this simple model at present, although the assumption could be relaxed at a later stage (Gafni and Peled 1984). The production of each of the commodities is represented by the following production functions,

$$x_j = x(X_j, T_j^x) \qquad (2)$$

$$y_j = y(Y_j, T_j^y) \qquad (3)$$

$$h_j = h(M_{j-1}, T^h_{j-1}, h_{j-1}, \ldots, h_o, y_{j-1}, \ldots, y_o, N) \qquad (4)$$

Where X, Y and M are market inputs, T^x, T^y and T^h are inputs of efficient time and N is an exogenous endowment variable. Because x and y are commodities in the form of smoking, jogging or watching TV, they are "consumed" as they are produced within the household.

Following Grossman (1972), the individual has a single period full resource constraint, R_j, given by[2]

$$R_j = h_j w_j + v_j = (h_j - T_j^w)\, w_j + p_j^x X_j + p_j^y Y_j + p_j^m M_j; \qquad (5)$$

where w is the marginal opportunity cost of (quality-adjusted) time spent in household production, v is a wealth stock variable, T^w is the quality-adjusted time spent in non-household production and p^x, p^y and p^m unit prices of market inputs x, y and m respectively. Generalising the resource constraint over time gives

$$R^* = \sum_{j=t}^{t+n} \frac{(h_j - T_j^w)\, w_j + p_j^x X_j + p_j^y Y_j + p_j^m M_j}{(1+r)^{j-t}} \qquad (6)$$

Maximising the intertemporal utility function subject to the generalised full resource constraint generates first-order conditions as follows,

$$U_t^x = \varphi\,(p_j^x \; dX_j / dx_t + w_j \, dT_t^x / dx_t) \qquad (7)$$

[2]Derived by substituting the quality-adjusted time constraint
$h_j = T_j^x + T_j^y + T_j^h + T_j^w$
and the income constraint
$I_j = T_j^w w_j + v_j = p_j^x X_j + p_j^y Y_j + p_j^m M_j$
into the expression for full wealth, i.e.
$R_j = h_j w_j + v_j = (h_j - T_j^w)\, w_j + p_j^x X_j + p_j^y Y_j + p_j^m M_j$.

$$U_t^y \sum_{j=t}^{t+n} U_j^h \frac{\frac{dh_j}{dy_t}}{(1+r)^{j-t}} = \varphi\left[\left(p_t^y \frac{dY_t}{dy_t} + w_t \frac{dT_t^y}{dy_t}\right) - \sum_{j=t}^{t+n} w_j \frac{\frac{dh_j}{dy_t}}{(1+r)^{j-t}}\right] \tag{8}$$

$$\sum_{j=t}^{t+n} U_j^h \frac{\frac{dh_j}{dh_t}}{(1+r)^{j-t}} = \varphi\left[\left(p_t^m \frac{dM_t}{dh_t} + w_t \frac{dT_t^h}{dh_t}\right) - \sum_{j=t}^{t+n} w_j \frac{\frac{dh_j}{dh_t}}{(1+r)^{j-t}}\right] \tag{9}$$

Equation 7 is the familiar first-order condition that consumption of x continues until marginal benefit equals marginal cost. Although the first-order conditions in Eq. 8 and 9 are less straightforward in algebraic terms, the interpretation of the conditions is exactly the same. Equation 9 is the first-order condition for the production of health previously derived by Grossman (1972) and reproduced by Muurinen (1982). The interpretation offered by these authors was that health production continues until the sum of the marginal direct (i.e. utility-generating) and indirect (i.e. resource-generating) benefits equals the marginal opportunity cost of health production.

Although the interpretation of the future resource consequences of improved health status as a benefit, as used by both Grossman (1972) and Muurinen (1982), is inconsistent with welfare economics theory (Birch 1987; Birch and Donaldson 1987), this is not crucial to the present analysis. Of more interest to us here is the first-order condition for the production of the health-related commodity, y, given in Eq. 8 which has not previously been derived in the economics literature as far as we are aware. Although the algebra again appears complex, the interpretation is more simple: under utility-maximising assumptions, household production of y continues until marginal benefit (on the left-hand side of the expression) equals marginal cost (on the right-hand side).

The benefit of y production is given by the net effect of the marginal utility of y consumption and the utility consequences of this consumption of y on health status h. It is worth emphasising that both elements of the benefits expression are subjectively determined. The marginal cost of y production, on the other hand, is objectively determined (although the value of the marginal cost depends on the subjectively determined marginal valuation of wealth, φ) and given by the net effect of the opportunity cost of factor inputs and the impact of this consumption of y on future resource constraints (e.g. income-earning capacity).

There are a number of features of the model derived above that are useful in understanding and predicting health-related behaviour. In particular health-related behaviour is endogenously determined and hence is consistent with the rationality assumptions underlying the model. Utility, and in a broader context social welfare, represent more than just health status and consequently *there is an optimal amount of health-related commodity consumption* (and more particularly health-detrimental activities) which a utility-maximising individual engages in. That is to say, unhealthy lifestyles may be in the best interest of the individual *given the distribution of resources in society*. But that is not the same as some population groups choosing less healthy life styles in the face of equal opportunities for health – a point that we shall return to below.

A second feature of the model is that the determinants of health-related behaviour extend beyond the direct utility consequences and opportunity costs of that behaviour. Identified health-enhancing behaviours may involve *competing health risks* which are not equally distributed throughout society. Furthermore these competing risks may generate additional consequences for an individual's resource constraints. For example, accepting advice to stop smoking may lead to increased food or alcohol consumption, both of which have consequences for health risks and resources. Hunt and MacLeod (1987) found that the chances of contracting lung disease at some hypothetical future date were far less problematic to current women smokers wanting to stop smoking than the possibility of gaining weight immediately. Hence changing health-related behaviour often involves trade-offs between health risks both in absolute terms and across time periods (because the timing of the alternative health risks may differ). *Moreover these trade-offs may differ individually or in combination across population subgroups*, implying that differentials in observed behaviour do not necessarily represent differential preferences in the presence of equal opportunities. Existing models of the demand for health have the capacity to explore both of these features. Indeed the approach we have taken is to adopt the basic model of these previous analyses and extend it to the analysis of health-related behaviour. In doing so we argue that it helps to explain and predict observed behavioural patterns.

A third feature of the model is the *dynamic nature of the determinants of health-related behaviour*. In particular the indirect effects of health-related behaviour, represented by the impact of the behaviour on health status and the associated consequences for the opportunity cost of time, occur in future periods. Although the existing models of demand for health incorporate the dynamic nature of the health production process, the data sets used in testing the model's predictions have tended to be cross-sectional and have not considered the impact of expected future values of the consequences of health production, other than by using present values as proxy variables. As a result, implications arising from the dynamic aspects of the model have not been fully explored. Our analysis of health-related behaviour using the current model considers explicitly the individual's utility of expected future health consequences and the expected impact of such consequences on future resources resulting from the marginal production of health-related commodities.

Implications of the Model

The model developed in the previous section emphasises the multifactorial nature of the determination of health-related behaviour. In particular the determinants of health-related behaviour can be grouped under four main categories: the marginal valuation of the health-related commodity; the marginal valuation of health consequences arising from the commodity's consumption; the expected marginal opportunity cost of future (quality-adjusted) time; and the real resources of the individual. We shall take as given and equal across all individuals the marginal valuation of the health-related commodity at each level of consumption (i.e. equal preferences for the commodity per se). Under the current model, observed differentials in behaviour are consistent with this assumption. The observed differentials may be explained by differences in the values of some of the other determinants of health-related behaviour as identified in the following comparative static predictions.

Increases in the real resources of individuals will generate an increase in the consumption of all non-inferior commodities ceteris paribus as the marginal utility of wealth, φ, falls. The income support proposals of the Black Report would, under this line of argument, enable the less affluent members of society to pursue similar patterns of consumption to the more affluent groups. Whether or not this actually occurs depends on the relative levels of the other determinants of health-related-behaviour, as is highlighted by the model. In other words, the ceteris might not be paribus and while income support may enable the poorer groups to pursue similar consumption patterns (i.e. life styles) it may not be in the individual's best interests (i.e. individual utility may not be maximised) to do so. Assuming for the moment that underlying preferences are the same then only if the life style *incentives* facing the individuals are also the same across population groups should we expect to observe similar behaviour given similar resources.

The same limitation applies to policies aimed at changing relative and/or absolute prices of health-related commodity inputs. Such policies essentially take a societal viewpoint and apply it to individual behaviour without considering life style decisions from the viewpoint of the individual, i.e. in the context of the incentives and constraints facing the individual. We do not suggest that such policies have no merit, but that on the basis of an explicit behavioural model they are not the panacea for observed differentials in health-related behaviour. We should not be surprised, therefore, if poorer groups use such income supplements to increase their consumption of health-detrimental commodities.

Another policy instrument which features prominently in both the policy proposals of the Black Report and associated reports, and the demand for health literature, is the provision of additional education. It is implied that if only the less healthy groups of society had better knowledge of interrelationships between behaviour and health then, provided their resources were sufficient, they would make more efficient (i.e. healthier) life style choices. In terms of the present model an increase in education would improve the accuracy of individual's perceptions of the impact of current behaviour on future health and consequently lead to changes in life style corresponding to behavioural patterns followed by the more educated group ceteris paribus.

Improved knowledge of life style-health relationships increases *dh/dy* and hence increases the marginal benefit and reduces the net marginal opportunity cost of health-enhancing behavioural patterns (and reduces marginal benefits and increases marginal opportunity costs of health-detrimental patterns). As with the income support proposals, the success of this policy depends crucially on the ceteris paribus assumptions holding. Again the proposed policy is essentially *enabling* less educated groups to behave in different ways without considering whether it is in the individual's best interests to respond to the improved information. For example, information concerning the adverse health effects of smoking has been widely disseminated. Yet, as was mentioned above, the published data on smoking prevalence show consistently that reduction in smoking prevalence associated with this information provision has been highly concentrated in the more affluent and more educated groups in society (Townsend and Davidson 1982; Pierce 1989).

It does not seem plausible to explain this observation in terms of large sections of the population not understanding or not believing the information. A far more plausible explanation would seem to be that, while reducing smoking is in the best interests of the more affluent groups in society, the same may not be the case for members of the less affluent groups under current circumstances. Hunt and MacLeod (1987) provide support for this type of explanation in the context of alcohol abuse in Scotland. Many problem drinkers tended to give up drinking of their own accord once the drinking begins to pose a problem *for them* as opposed to for other people.

Consideration of the other determinants of health-related behaviour as identified in the model helps us to understand why this might be the case. In particular the model emphasises the investment nature of the life style-health relationships. Consequently individual decisions concerning life style choices depend not only on the relative costs of inputs in alternative commodity production functions, but also on the perceived value of the future returns to that behaviour.

Farrell and Fuchs (1982) suggested that differentials in the rates of time preference are connected with observed differentials in the levels of investment behaviour undertaken (see above). Such differentials in time preference might reflect differentials in preferences for present and future consumption per se between subgroups of the population, in which case they would be of little interest to policymakers concerned with promoting equal *opportunities* for health. Alternatively they might reflect differentials in access to intertemporal transfers (e.g. imperfections in the capital market) in which case policy instruments would be required to promote equality of opportunity. In terms of the present model a reduction in r, the marginal rate of time preference, would increase the impact of future health consequences of life style and the associated resource consequences of life style choice. So for example in the first-order condition for health-related behaviour (Eq. 8), with $dh/dy > 0$, a reduction in r increases the marginal benefit and reduces the marginal opportunity cost of the (health-enhancing) behaviour while the opposite effects occur if $dh/dy < 0$ (i.e. health-detrimental behaviour).

Differences in the rate of time preference at the margin generate differences in the present values of future effects of *equal future value*. Marginal benefits of health-related behaviour would also be affected if the future value of the returns to the behaviour differed across individuals. In other words *incentives* to adopt healthy life styles may differ. In terms of the model derived above, an increase in U^h, ceteris paribus, increases the marginal benefit of health-enhancing behaviour and reduces the marginal benefit of health-detrimental behaviour leading to a substitution of healthier life styles. In a simple model of individual utility maximisation, this effect reflects differentials in preferences for health between individuals. An alternative explanation suggested here is that the individual utility function *is not separable between health and other commodities but the marginal utility of health at any level of health depends on levels of consumption of other commodities which are not equally distributed in society*, i.e. $du/dh_j = f(k_j), f_k > 0$, where k is an input to the utility function complementary to h. Increasing the consumption of such commodities (e.g. social support) would therefore increase the marginal benefits of healthy life styles and generate a substitution of healthy for less healthy behavioural patterns ceteris paribus.

Although the notion of utility functions non-separable in health has not featured prominently in the health economics literature to date, there is a considerable and growing body of research in sociology which emphasises the relationships between health and health-related behaviour on the one hand and social relationships, support mechanisms and coping capacities on the other (see, for example, Antonovsky 1979; Berkman 1984, 1986; Berkman and Breslow 1983; Berkman and Syme 1979; Cassel 1986; Blazer 1982; House et al. 1988; Orth-Gomer and Johnson 1987) which would be consistent with this approach. As Hunt and McLeod (1987) emphasise.

> Health related behaviours are essentially social acts embedded in the structure which defines and delineates reality. Such behaviours are created and maintained by social relations, including those which grow out of the economic and political ethos, and are made possible by norms, values, rules and common history.

In addition it is consistent with the concepts of surplus powerlessness (Lerner 1986) and learned helplessness (Seligman 1975) which appear in the sociological and psychological literature respectively, in which the loss of control, or ability to cope, in one or more areas of life generates a tendency for individuals to give up control in other areas. Hence if support mechanisms break down, individuals may lose the *incentive* to follow health-enhancing patterns of behaviour.

This notion of multiple determinants of the marginal utility of health is therefore consistent with both an extended economic model and contemporary models of individual behaviour in other behavioural sciences. Furthermore it has face validity in that we might expect individuals to be influenced by their expected future social circumstances in determining their consumption portfolios between present commodities and future health.

Finally, consider the impact of an increase in the expected marginal opportunity cost of future (quality-adjusted) time (w in the model). As w increases the net marginal cost of the health-enhancing (health-detrimental) commodity falls (rises) and hence more healthy patterns of behaviour will be adopted ceteris paribus. In other words the current (or potential) lawyer has a greater incentive to avoid future illness from a pure earnings point of view (i.e. the return to healthy behaviour is greater and hence more healthy behaviour is substituted for less healthy behaviour at the margin), as well as from the point of view of any greater expected social support, than the current (or potential) long-term unemployed individual. It is important to note that this effect does not relate to *current incomes*, and hence cannot be addressed by income support policies, but is concerned with the expected value of future (quality-adjusted) time. Providing more income, either now or in the future, to those with lower marginal valuations of future time does not affect the incentive to "produce" (quality-adjusted) time.

Furthermore this effect is separate from increasing the marginal utility of future health by changing the levels of the determinants of marginal utility, although in some cases the two effects may be coincident (e.g. individuals with greater probabilities of future support mechanisms may also have greater expected valuations of future time). Indeed the separate nature of each of the determinants of health-related behaviour is an important feature of the model because it provides an explanation of the heterogeneity of risky behaviour and the clustering of health risks both across and within subgroups of the population.

Summary

> Oversimplification of human behaviour leads us towards descriptions of reality which are considerably at variance with human experience and cast doubt upon the validity of our information and thus upon its applicability.
>
> *Hunt and MacLeod (1987)*

We set out in this paper to consider whether economic analysis could be applied to the determination of individual health-related behaviour and so help avoid oversimplification of explanations of individual behaviour. Our work provides a number of important messages both for economists and researchers of other disciplines interested in understanding differentials in health-related behaviour and the implications for inequalities in health.

The first message is that economic analysis can be applied to the determinants of individual behaviour. *In order to provide a comprehensive understanding of observed behaviour, however, we need to use a broad economic framework and go beyond the traditional boundaries of the contents of economic analysis drawing upon concepts, ideas and subject matter of other behavioural sciences.*

We do not suggest that the rationality assumption underlying the traditional economic approach is applicable to individual decision making. It is sufficient to assume that individuals behave *as if* they were rational economic decision makers. Neither do we suggest that economic analysis in general, or the current model in particular, can provide all the answers. Other approaches, which do not use any rational economic modelling, might perform as well, or even better than the proposed model in explaining and predicting individual behaviour. Indeed uncertainty, risk taking and addiction could be useful extensions to the model. Nevertheless it represents an extension to the current application of economics to life style decision making and provides some insights in understanding the determinants of individual behaviour.

The second message is that *health-detrimental behaviours are not "bad" per se, nor is the consumption of such commodities an indication of irrational behaviour.* The extended economic model derived here analyses behaviour from the individual's point of view explaining behavioural patterns in terms of what is in the individual's own best interests. It is therefore important that policymakers concerned with reducing inequalities in health take this as a starting point and consider the changes required for the individual to alter behaviour in a way consistent with a social objective of reducing inequalities. Indeed the implication behind the analysis is that policies aimed at changing population health status should first consider what the implications are for individual utility. Determinants of health-related behaviour are multiple. Encouraging or forcing individuals to reduce unhealthy behaviour may reduce the wellbeing of those individuals, even in the long term, unless the incentive structures are resource distributions in society are aligned in ways which make such behavioural changes *in the individual's own best interests*. This point is further emphasised by Hunt and Martin (1988), who note that health-related behavioural change, while having impacts on health, often stems from non-health considerations. So, for example, changes in smoking behaviour are often the result of individuals changing jobs or getting married as opposed to considerations of the health implications of the change.

A third message is that *the determinants of the marginal valuation of health may be multiple and extend beyond just pure preferences and the level of health. As such, the relative importance of health to wellbeing may be smaller than generally perceived but, more importantly, may depend on the availability of other, complex social forces which are not distributed equally in society.*

A final message is that taking *a partial view of health-related behaviour, such as that underlying current policy proposals, risks leading to policies which not only fail to achieve their stated objectives but are counterproductive.* For example, income supplements may lead to the poor consuming more of all goods including cigarettes while generally available health education may generate a greater response from the more affluent and healthy groups. Under these circumstances inequalities increase.

The predictions of the model are, as yet, untested. Nevertheless, they are consistent with many observations of differentials in health and health-related behaviours reported in the literature. Furthermore they serve to warn us not to use simplistic answers to complex questions which can lead to premature conclusions being drawn such as "victim-blaming", or preference-based explanations of observations.

In previous work, one of the authors emphasised that, in the context of supplier-induced utilisation, we cannot *blame* providers for responding to incentives presented to them in ways which contravene neither ethics nor regulations (Birch 1988). Similarly we should avoid blaming individuals for behaving in ways which represent rational responses to current incentives as generated by current social forces. The causes of the socially undesirable outcomes, whether it be overutilisation of services or the excessive consumption of tobacco, are the incentives inherent in the system, not the individuals who respond to these incentives.

Acknowledgements. We wish to thank Bob Evans at the University of British Columbia and our colleagues in the Polinomics group at McMaster University for constructive comments on drafts of this paper, and Lori Houghton for translating our handwritten manuscripts into final form.

References

Antonovsky A (1979) Health, stress and coping. Jossey-Bass, London
Auster R, Leveson I, Saracheck D (1969) The production of health: an exploratory study. J Hum Resources 4:411–436
Becker G (1965) A theory of the allocation of time. Econ J 75:493–517
Berkman L (1984) Assessing the physical health effects of social networks and social support. Annu Rev Public Health: 413–432
Berkman L (1986) Social networks, support and health: taking the next step forward. Am J Epidemiol 123:559–562
Berkman L, Breslow L (1983) Health and ways of living. The Almeda County Study. Oxford University Press, Oxford
Berkman L, Syme S (1979) Social networks, host resistance and mortality: a nine year followup study of Almeda county residents. Am J Epidemiol 109:186–204
Birch S (1987) The demand for health: extensions to the human capital model. PhD thesis, University of York
Birch S (1988) Item of service remuneration in general practice in the UK: what can we learn from dentists? Fam Pract 5:265–270
Birch S, Donaldson C (1987) Applications of cost benefit analysis to health care: departures from welfare economic theory. J Health Econ 6:211–225
Blazer D (1982) Social support and mortality in an elderly community population. Am J Epidemiol 115:686–694
Bucquet D, Curtis S (1986) Socio-demographic variations in perceived illness and the use of primary care: the value of community survey data for primary care service planning. Soc Sci Med 23:737–744
Cassel J (1986) The contribution of the social environment to host resistance. Am J Epidemiol 104:107–123
Culyer A (1981) Health, economics and health economics. In: Van der Praag J, Perlman M (eds) Health, economics and health economics. North Holland, Amsterdam, pp 3–11
Enthoven A (1980) Health plan: the only practical solution to the soaring cost of medical care. Addison Wesley, Reading Mass
Evans R (1984) Strained mercy: the economics of Canadian health care. Butterworths, Toronto
Farrell P, Fuchs V (1982) Schooling and health. The cigarette connection. J Health Econ 1:217–230
Fuchs V (1982) Time preference and health: an exploratory study. In Fuchs V (ed) Economic aspects of health. University of Chicago Press, Chicago, pp 93–120
Gafni A, Peled D (1984) The effect of labelling on illness related absenteeism: an economic explanation for the case of hypertension. J Health Econ 3:173–178
Grossman M (1972) The demand for health: a theoretical and empirical investigation. National Bureau of Economic Research, New York
Grossman M (1975) The correlation between health and schooling. In: Terlerkyj N (ed) Household production and consumption. National Bureau of Economics Research, New York, pp 147–211
Health and Welfare Canada (1986) Achieving health for all: a framework for health promotion. Health and Welfare Canada, Ottawa
House J, Landis K, Umberson D (1988) Social relationships and health. Science 241:540–545
Hunt S, MacLeod M (1987) Health and behavioural change: some lay perspectives. Community Med 9:68–76
Hunt S, Martin C (1988) Health-related behavioural change – a test of a new model. Psychology Health 2:209–230
Lalonde M (1974) A new perspective on the health of Canadians, a working document. Government of Canada, Ottawa
La Vecchia C, De Carli A, Pagano R (1986) Educational prevalence of smoking in Italian men and women. Int J Epidemiol 14:279 (letter)

Le Grand J (1978) The distribution of public expenditure: the case of health care. Economic, 45:125–142

Lerner M (1986) Surplus powerlessness. Institute for Labour and Mental Health, Oakland

McKeown T (1976) The modern rise of population. Arnold, London

Marmot M (1986) Social inequalities in mortality: the social environment. In: Wilkinson R (eds) Class and health. Tavistock Publications, London

Marmot M, Morris J (1984) The social environment. In: Holand W, Detels R, Knox G (eds) Oxford textbook of public health, vol 1. Oxford University Press, Oxford

Muurinen JM (1982) Demand for health: a Grossman model. J Health Econ 1:5–28

Orth-Gomer K, Johnson J (1987) Social network interaction and mortality: a six year follow-up study of a random sample of the Swedish population. J Chronic Dis 40:949–957

Pierce J (1989) International comparison of trends in cigarette smoking prevalence. Am J Public Health 79:152–157

Royal Commission on the National Health Service (1979) Report (Chairman: Sir Alec Merrison). Her Majesty's Stationary Office, London

Seligman M (1975) Helplessness: on depression, development and death. Freeman, San Francisco

Shakotko R, Grossman M (1981) An explanation of the dynamic relationship between health and cognitive development in adolescence. In: Van de Gaag J, , Perlman M (eds) Health, economics and health economics. North Holland, Amsterdam

Townsend P, Davidson N (1982) Inequalities in health. The Black Report. Penguin, Hommondsworth

UK Department of Health and Social Security (1980) Inequalities in health: report of a research working group. Department of Health and Social Security, London

UK Ministry of Health (1944) A National Health Service. Cmnd 6502. Her Majesty's Stationary Office, London

Welch F (1970) Education in production. J Polit Econ 78:35–59

Whitehead M (1987) The health divide. Penguin, Hammondsworth

Case Studies

Drug Price Information and Cost-Consciousness of Physicians: Results of a Survey of Belgian General Practitioners

D. de Graeve and G. Carrin

Introduction

Objective of the Study

The Belgian Ministry of Public Health distributes an Independent Drug Formulary (IDF) on a 2-yearly basis. This formulary (called the Gecommentarieerd Geneesmiddelenrepertorium) is edited by a group of prominent experts in pharmacology, brought together by the Belgian Centre for Pharmacotherapeutic Information. It contains scientific information about all drugs marketed in Belgium; it also mentions the brand name, composition, package form, prices per package and reimbursement category. [The NHI reimburses drugs according to their reimbursement category. Drugs of category (a) are totally reimbursed. For pensioners, widows, orphans and invalids, the NHI reimburses 85%, 50% and 40% for drugs of categories (b), (c) and (cs) respectively; for other insured persons, the reimbursement percentages are respectively 75%, 50% and 40%. Drugs of category (d) are not reimbursed.] Daily drug costs and comparisons between those costs for similar therapies are not provided, however. There is also a brief comparison between the relative medical effectiveness of the drugs in similar therapeutic categories; price comparisons are absent, however. This formulary is sent, free of charge, to all Belgian physicians and pharmacists. Students in the last 2 years of their graduate studies also receive a copy.

Cost-containment and cost-consciousness in health care has been one of the recurrent themes in Belgian health policy. Pharmaceuticals occupy rather an important position in the national health insurance budget, viz. 15% of total expenditure in 1984. [Health insurance and drug expenditures (related to employee insurance) amounted to 176.2 billion Belgian francs and 25.8 billion Belgian francs, respectively; see Kesenne and Feltesse (1988).] By far the most important policy instrument to date to contain drug costs is the setting of drug prices by a regulatory body. However, the Belgian Secretary of Public Health has also played a large role in the IDF. (Mrs. W. De Meester was Secretary of Public Health during the period October 1986-May 1988.) In fact, the IDF should send sufficient signals to prescribers about the cost implications of their prescribing behaviour. The latter role should be enhanced if necessary.

The present article reports on a study that prepared a policy decision on this topic. The objective of the study was to assess the effectiveness of current price information in the IDF on cost-conscious prescribing behaviour. The results would constitute a suitable background for future policy decisions on drug cost information to prescribing physicians.

The Survey

Oral interviews were held among a random sample of 491 general practitioners (GPs). First, the survey gathered information about personal characteristics, practice setting and use of various sources of drug information. Secondly, we asked GPs to assess the importance of information on prices of drugs and their reimbursement category in their own prescribing pattern. Other prescribing criteria were also examined such as medical effectiveness, side effects and contraindications, the type of administration of the drug and the reputation of the pharmaceutical company. Thirdly, the method of simulated patients was used to obtain information about prescription costs and to analyse empirically the degree of cost-consciousness. This method consists of presenting GPs a written profile of four patients and requesting them to determine a drug therapy. The patients selected were a patient with high blood pressure, a patient with acute sleeping disorders, a patient with a throat infection and a patient with heart complaints. GPs were asked to prescribe at most two drugs and to mention brand names, method of drug administration, and the package, dosage and length of treatment.

For each simulated patient, a list of potentially useful drugs was established. The list was based upon the Drug Formulary. Half of the GPs in our sample received these particular lists. The other half also received drug price information related to comparable therapeutic categories. By dividing the whole sample into two subgroups, we wanted to investigate whether extra price information would change prescribing behaviour. For each drug, the minimum and maximum daily cost of the drug was presented. Computation of the latter extremes was based on recommendations concerning minimum and maximum dosage in the IDF. Furthermore, the average daily cost was presented graphically, by means of horizontal bars. The latter enabled one to make a visual comparison between prices.

It is important to repeat that in our study GPs were presented uniquely with lists of selected drugs established by a team of experts in pharmacology, who were also responsible for editing the IDF.[1] The selection of drugs consists of those pharmaceuticals that are considered to be comparable in effectiveness, related to the four sickness patterns.

The Stated Importance of Cost Information

Descriptive Analysis

General practitioners were asked to indicate the relative importance of the above-mentioned prescribing criteria. They could indicate whether the criterion was "very important", "important", "unimportant" or "very unimportant".

Effectiveness was seen as the most important criterion: 88% of GPs find this a very important criterion, 9% an important criterion. Undesired effects are very important and important for 53% and 46%, respectively. Contraindications are very important for 60% and important for 37% of GPs. Concerning the method of administration, 15% and 73% find this a very important and important criterion. Prices and reimbursement category are clearly less important than "medical" criteria, 59% of GPs find both criteria important, and 3% and 10% of GPs find the price criterion and reimbursement category very important. The fact that more importance is attached to reimbursement indicates that GPs seem to protect the financial interests of their patients. The criterion of the pharmaceutical company is less important: 80% find the criterion to be unimportant to very unimportant. A summary of responses is given in Fig. 1.

Determinants of the Stated Importance of Cost Information

Method and Hypotheses

The logit regression approach was adopted to explain the stated importance of information on prices and the reimbursement category. The binary dependent variable assumed the value of 1 if the GP estimated the price and reimbursement category to be important, and 0 otherwise. The explanatory variables consist of the physician's age and workload, measures of behaviour with regard to the source of drug information (IDF, other formularies, scien-

[1]We thank especially Professor M. Bogaert of the University of Gent (Belgium) for his contribution and supervision.

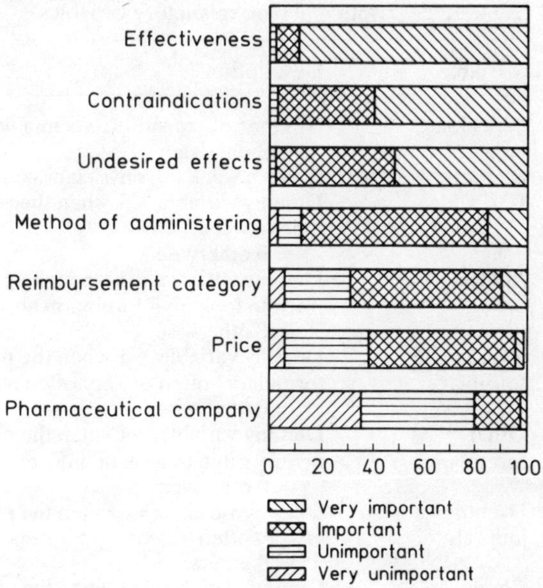

Fig. 1. Relative importance of criteria in prescribing

tific journals, special post-university courses, samples, colleagues, company representatives) and a measure of evaluation of price information in the IDF. A detailed explanation of determinants is given in Table 1.

The first main hypothesis is that physicians with a smaller workload (patient load and scientific work) (especially the young GPs) will pay more attention to prices and reimbursement categories when prescribing. Indeed, those physicians have more time to inspect cost information; the time-price of the cost of learning is indeed smaller. Furthermore, it is evident that, given Belgium's fee-for-service system, physicians with a small workload want to attract more patients. Hence, it is likely that they try to satisfy their patients by attempting to provide them with low-cost health care.

Secondly, the age variable is added to the regression analysis in order to test the hypothesis that, the younger physicians are, the more cost conscious they are. The latter would follow from the fact that they have been educated in a period in which cost containment in health care has become an important policy issue.

Thirdly, we hypothesize that GPs who use the IDF more frequently, and who are thus confronted indirectly with price information, will attach more importance to cost information.

Fourthly, concerning the other sources of information, a number of them ("Medex", "Therapeutic Formulary", "Scientific Journals", "Other Formularies" and "Samples") do not contain any price information. Therefore, we expect that these exert no influence on the stated importance of cost

Table 1. Description of the explanatory variables

Variable	Description
Workload	Number of consultations in a week
Age	Age of physician
Scientific work	Hours a week the physician spends on scientific work
IDF + 5	Dummy variable; = 1 when the physician uses the IDF more than five times a week; = 0 otherwise
Medex	Dummy variable; = 1 when the physician uses the Medex often or very often to look up information about drugs; = 0 otherwise
Therapeutic formulary	Dummy variable; = 1 when the physician uses the "Therapeutic formulary" often or very often to look up information about drugs; = 0 otherwise
Other formularies	Dummy variable; = 1 when the physician uses Other formularies often or very often to look up information about drugs; = 0 otherwise
Scientific journals	Dummy variable; = 1 when the physician uses scientific journals often or very often to look up information about drugs; = 0 otherwise
Courses	Dummy variable; = 1 when the physician uses courses often or very often to gather information about drugs; = 0 otherwise
Samples	Dummy variable; = 1 when the physician uses samples often or very often to gather information about drugs; = 0 otherwise
Colleagues	Dummy variable; = 1 when the physician uses colleagues often or very often to gather information about drugs; = 0 otherwise
Representatives	Dummy variable; = 1 when the physician uses the Medex often or very often to gather information about drugs; = 0 otherwise
Evaluation, information (in general, price, reimbursement)	Dummy variable; = 1 when the physician evaluates the information from the IDF in general, or with respect to the price or the reimbursement category in particular, as good or very good; = 0 otherwise
Evaluation, presentation, reimbursement	Dummy variable; = 1 when the physician evaluates the presentation of the reimbursement information as good as very good; = 0 otherwise
Importance, price	Dummy variable; = 1 when the physician attaches importance or much importance to the price when prescribing; = 0 otherwise
Importance, reimbursement	Dummy variable; = 1 when the physician attaches importance or much importance to the reimbursement category when prescribing; = 0 otherwise

information. It is uncertain whether the remaining sources (courses, colleagues and representatives) mention cost information in a systematic way. Hence, we decided not to formulate a specific hypothesis.

Fifthly, the way physicians evaluate the cost information in the IDF is likely to contribute to explaining physicians' interest in cost information; the greater the appreciation for the current cost information with the IDF, the more cost information is likely to occupy an important position among the prescribing criteria.

Results

Estimation results are presented in Tables 2 and 3. The likelihood ratios reveal that, on the whole, the set of explanatory variables is not apt to explain the stated importance of both price and reimbursement category.

Two variables do appear to have a statistically significant effect, however. First, we deduce from Table 2 that, as age rises by 10%, the probability of

Table 2. Determinants of the theoretical importance of the price: logit estimation results

Variable	Logit coefficient	Significance	Mean value of the variable
Constant	*1.24*	.06	1.00
Workload	–.00	.71	101.06
Age	*–.03*	.02	36.02
Scientific work	.00	.87	5.51
IDF + 5	–.17	.51	.35
Medex	.15	.54	.62
Therapeutic formulary	.00	.99	.27
Other formularies	.14	.57	.45
Scientific journals	.26	.32	.56
Courses	.15	.56	.48
Samples	–.14	.62	.27
Colleagues	.18	.50	.35
Representatives	.01	.96	.55
Evaluation information price	.31	.39	.87
Level of significance of the estimation (maximum likelihood ratio) = .67 (*n* = 335)			

Note: The level of significance represents the change that the value of the coefficient equals 0. Italic coefficients are significant.

Table 3. Determinants of the theoretical importance of the reimbursement category: logit estimation results

Variable	Logit coefficient	Significance	Mean value of the variable
Constant	1.00	.17	1.04
Workload	.00	.97	101.06
Age	–.00	.88	36.02
Scientific work	.00	.91	5.51
IDF+5	.07	.79	.35
Medex	.09	.73	.62
Therapeutic formulary	*–.52*	*.06*	.27
Other formularies	–.05	.85	.45
Scientific journals	.28	.31	.56
Courses	.18	.50	.48
Samples	.15	.62	.27
Colleagues	.29	.29	.35
Representatives	–.04	.88	.55
Evaluation information reimbursement	–.16	.74	.87
Evaluation presentation reimbursement	–.14	.73	.82

Level of significance of the estimation (maximum likelihood ratio) = .88 (n = 335)

Note: The level of significance represents the chance that the value of the coefficient equals zero. Italic figures are significant.

stating the price criterion to be important or very important decreases by 3.6%. This confirms our earlier hypothesis about a negative link between age and cost-consciousness. Secondly, the use of the *Therapeutic Formulary* has a fairly important effect on the stated importance of the reimbursement category. Our formulated hypothesis is therefore not confirmed.

Nevertheless, the significance of the two above-mentioned variables does not prevent us from reaffirming that neither physician characteristics nor the use of information sources is a major determinant of the stated importance of cost information.

Observed Importance of the Price Information in the Prescriptions for Simulated Patients

Descriptive Analysis

Daily costs of prescriptions for the four simulated patients were computed. The latter cost comprises the total daily cost (reimbursement plus coinsurance) of the drug prescribed by the physician, taking account of the package, administration and dosage determined by the physician. Tables 4–7 give the frequency distributions for the daily cost related to the simulated cases. Note that daily costs were only calculated for those prescriptions that contained drugs appearing on the established lists. In the case of hypertension and heart complaints, we have taken account only of the prescription of a maximum of two drugs. In the case of sleeping disorders and throat infection, only the first prescription was used. Indeed, the combination of two antibiotics (in the case of throat infection) or two benzodiazepines (in the case of a sleeping disorder) is useless.

As can be seen from the sample sizes in Tables 4–7, a number of physicians dropped out of the original sample because they did not adhere to the selected drug lists. Analysis of the causes of this behaviour is outside the scope of the present study, however. (It is granted that information on behaviour is lost in this way. However, we inspected the characteristics of the GPs who did not restrict themselves to the selected drug lists. We found the latter were not significantly different from those of GPs who respected the drug lists.)

The first conclusion is that the price differentials per case are substantial. For the patient with hypertension, the daily cost varies from 1.36 to 69.40 Belgian francs. For the patient with a throat infection, the price differential is even greater and varies from 6.70 to 120 Belgian francs daily. In the case of sleeping disorders, one pays from a minimum of 2.07 to 43.68 Belgian francs.

Table 4. Daily cost of the treatment of hypertension

Prices (Belgian francs)	Frequency (*n*)	(%)	Cumulative frequency (%)
≤5	50	13.2	13.2
>5 and ≤10	61	16.1	29.3
>10 and ≤15	86	22.7	52.0
>15 and ≤20	54	14.2	66.2
>20 and ≤25	58	15.3	81.5
>25	70	18.5	100.0
Total	379	100.0	100.0

Table 5. Daily cost of the treatment of a throat infection

Prices (Belgian francs)	Frequency (*n*)	(%)	Cumulative frequency (%)
≤40	22	9.6	9.6
>40 and ≤50	116	50.9	60.5
>50 and ≤60	45	19.7	80.3
>60	45	19.7	100.0
Total	228	100.0	100.0

Table 6. Daily cost of the treatment of sleeping disorders

Prices (Belgian francs)	Frequency (*n*)	(*n*)	Cumulative frequency (*n*)
≤5	36	9.9	9.9
>5 and ≤10	186	51.4	61.3
>10 and ≤15	125	34.6	95.9
>15	15	4.2	100.0
Total	362	100.0	100.0

Table 7. Daily cost of the treatment of heart complaints

Prices (Belgian francs)	Frequency (*n*)	(*n*)	Cumulative frequency (*n*)
≤10	60	17.8	17.8
>10 and ≤20	57	16.9	34.7
>20 and ≤30	139	41.2	76.0
>30 and ≤40	53	15.7	91.7
>40	28	8.3	100.0
Total	337	100.0	100.0

For the patient with angina pectoris, the minimum daily cost is 1.41 Belgian francs whereas the maximum is 82.15 Belgian francs.

Determinants of the Observed Importance

Methods and Hypotheses

The dependent variable is the daily drug cost. The latter is certainly the appropriate variable when analysing the cost of chronic diseases. The daily cost was also retained as a dependent variable for the study of the costs of the two acute illnesses, in order to maintain a comparison with analysis of the two chronic illnesses. However, we accounted for the total cost of acute illnesses by including the length of therapy as an explanatory variable.

In order to explain variations in the cost of prescribing, a multivariate regression analysis was undertaken. Four sets of explanatory variables are considered. *First* there are the physician characteristics: age, workload and scientific work. We hypothesize that their effects on the cost of prescribed medicine are similar to those on the stated importance of cost criteria. The lower the workload and the scientific work, the less the time cost for the physician of informing him- or herself about drug cost information. More information of drug costs is likely to make the physician more alert to the cost consequences of his or her prescribing. We therefore expect a negative effect of these variables of drug costs. As before, we reason that the younger the physician is, the more he or she is likely to be sensitive to cost issues. Hence, a positive effect of age on costs is expected.

The *second* set of variables consists of variables related to the use and content of drug information. It is expected that the more frequent the use of the IDF, the less costly the prescribed medicines; therefore, the dummy variable IDF + 5 is hypothesized to have a negative effect on the daily cost. The dummy variable "price lists" reflects whether the physician has received the comparative price tables or not; we expect it to have a negative impact on cost. Concerning the variables "Medex", "Therapeutic Formulary", "Scientific Journals" and "Samples", we expect these to have a positive effect. Indeed, "Medex and "Therapeutic Formulary" are privately sponsored drug formularies containing no price information whatsoever; "Scientific Journals" and "Samples" do not mention price information either. Hence, physicians will not be stimulated especially to use drug costs as a criterion in their prescribing. It is uncertain whether the remaining sources ("Courses", "Colleagues" and "Representatives") mention cost information in a systematic way, hence our desire not to formulate a specific hypothesis.

The attitudes of physicians with respect to the importance of cost and effectiveness criteria constitute the *third* set of explanatory variables. The hypothesis is that GPs who assess cost criteria as important or very important will also prescribe in a less costly way. Therefore, the coefficients of "Price Criterion" and "Reimbursement Criterion" ought to be negative. We posit that the "Effectiveness Criterion" is linked positively to drug costs. Cost-conscious prescribing implies that one weighs incremental effectiveness vis-à-vis incremental costs. Thus, physicians who judge effectiveness to be important will, ceteris paribus, pay less attention to the possibility of prescribing the cheapest available drugs. The way physicians evaluate the cost information in the IDF is likely to contribute to explaining the use of this kind of information; the higher the appreciation of the current cost information with the IDF, the more cost information is likely to be looked up. We expect the evaluation variables to exert a negative effect on costs.

The *fourth* set of explanatory variables contains treatment characteristics: dosage, length of therapy and prescription of a combination drug. Note that dosage is measured as the difference between the dose prescribed by the GP and the mean theoretical dose suggested in the IDF. One would expect daily cost to depend positively on the dose and the prescription of a combination drug. Length of therapy was included to investigate the possibility of a trade-off between shorter treatments that might be more expensive on a daily basis and treatments that are lengthier but cheaper.

Definitions of the explanatory variables are given in Table 8.

Table 8. Definition of variables

Variable	Description
Price list	Dummy variable; = 1, when the GP received comparative price tables; = 0, otherwise
Effectiveness criterion	Dummy variable; = 1, when the GP finds the effectiveness of the drug an important to very important criterion when prescribing; = 0, otherwise
Dose difference	Dose prescribed by the GP -- mean theoretical dose suggested in the GGR
Combination drug	Dummy variable; = 1, when the GP prescribes a second drug; = 0, otherwise
Length of therapy	Length of the drug treatment

Note: For the explanation of variables not mentioned, see Table 1.
GGR, Gecommentarieerd Geneesmiddelenrepertorium.

Results

From Table 9, it can be seen that the price differences of the prescriptions cannot be explained by physician characteristics, the use of different sources of information and the theoretical importance of prescription criteria. It is important to note here that the presentation of comparative price tables does not influence the prescribing habits of the physicians in the survey. In fact, this is not totally unexpected. Physicians were confronted with comparative price tables in a kind of laboratory experiment. It stands to reason that in such a setting behavioural changes will not be induced immediately.

Only the therapy characteristics have a significant influence on price differentials. First, the daily cost of a prescription increases significantly when physicians combine different drugs in one treatment. Secondly, the difference

Table 9. Influence of physician, practice and therapy characteristics on the daily cost: regression analysis

Independent variables	Coefficients and level of significance			
	Hypertension coefficient sign	Sleeping disorder coefficient sign	Sour throat coefficient sign	Heart complaints coefficient sign
Constant	*14.23 (.00)*	13.78 (.00)	*79.34 (.00)*	*25.55 (.00)*
Workload	.00 (.78)	.00 (.96)	.04 (.10)	.01 (.38)
Age	−.01 (.82)	−.05 (.28)	.09 (.73)	−.07 (.18)
Scientific work	.09 (.53)	−.05 (.54)	−.51 (.38)	.15 (.19)
IDF + 5	1.11 (.34)	−.77 (.27)	2.01 (.69)	*1.96 (.04)*
Medex	1.63 (.14)	.32 (.65)	2.86 (.54)	−.82 (.36)
Therapeutic formularies	.76 (.54)	−.31 (.70)	5.98 (.23)	−.61 (.54)
Other formularies	1.09 (.32)	.18 (.79)	−3.78 (.41)	−.75 (.40)
Scientific journals	1.05 (.38)	−.18 (.80)	1.76 (.72)	−1.43 (.13)
Courses	−.33 (.78)	−.16 (.82)	−3.28 (.49)	1.19 (.22)
Samples	−.78 (.54)	.83 (.29)	−4.40 (.39)	−.45 (.67)
Colleagues	−1.23 (.29)	−.37 (.60)	1.96 (.70)	−.72 (.46)
Representatives	.14 (.90)	−1.28 (.08)	1.26 (.79)	.16 (.87)
Price list	.99 (.37)	.52 (.45)	2.15 (.65)	−.36 (.69)
Price criterion	−1.75 (.16)	.01 (.99)	−8.27 (.11)	.23 (.82)
Reimbursement criterion	−1.12 (.41)	−.86 (.30)	−4.42 (.38)	−1.40 (.20)
Effectiv. criterion	1.17 (.70)	−133 (.62)	−9.85 (.42)	*5.25 (.04)*
Evaluation of information price	.74 (.75)	1.05 (.40)	4.29 (.71)	−1.56 (.32)
Evaluation of information reimbursement	1.09 (.62)	−.92 (.52)	1.52 (.89)	*−3.82 (.04)*
Evaluation presentation reimbursement	−.78 (.65)	1.63 (.15)	−6.37 (.37)	−2.59 (.10)
Dose difference	*6.29 (.00)*	6.80 (.00)	−5.64 (.01)	3.77 (.00)
Combination drug	*12.12 (.00)*	–	–	18.18 (.00)
Length of therapy	–	.02 (.21)	−.87 (.28)	–
$\overline{R}^2$ (sign)	.36 (.00)	.21 (.00)	0.5 (.13)	.70 (.00)
N	269	177	165	241

Note: The level of significance represents the chance that the value of the coefficient equals zero. Italic figures are significant.

between the dose recommended by the IDF and the real dose the physician prescribes has a positive and significant influence on the daily cost of the treatment of hypertension, sleeping disorders and heart complaints. On the other hand, a relative "overdose" of antibiotics results in a cheaper daily cost. This contradiction can be explained by the fact that in Belgium cheaper antibiotics happen to be "safer" in terms of overdose than the more expensive ones. This relationship between relative overdose and daily cost is not a causal one, however.

The regression analysis clearly shows that the profile of "low cost" prescribers is hard to define. Moreover, there does not seem to exist a prescriber who maintains a "low cost" habit across different illnesses.

Conclusions

Our analysis has focused on determinants of, and on possible differences between, stated and observed importance of cost information. It is important to repeat that more than 60% of GPs state that the price is an important criterion. Yet, in reality, Belgian GPs do not seem to pay attention to drug costs when prescribing.

These results are confirmed by international evidence. In fact, a number of authors found that physicians are not very price sensitive (Zelnio and Gagnon 1979; Zelnio 1982), that they lack adequate price information (Lowy et al. 1972; Oppenheim et al. 1981) and do not consider the price to be important when prescribing (Lilja 1976; Babington et al. 1983).

The results of this study lead us to recommend, first, the insertion of comparative price tables, in the IDF. Of course, such tables can only be made when effectiveness and other characteristics of drugs are comparable. In this way, physicians will be induced, more than now, to make cost-conscious drug choices. Physicians are also to be encouraged to reflect upon the impact of dose and combinations of drugs on total cost of prescribing. The feasibility of implementing other measures such as audit (Schroeder et al. 1973), transfer of information by independent representatives (Avorn and Soumerai 1983; Manning et al. 1986; Soumerai and Avorn 1984), postgraduate training courses and economic stimuli can also be investigated.

References

Avorn J, Soumerai S (1983) Improving drug therapy decisions through educational outreach. A randomized controlled trial of academically based "detailing". N Engl J Med 308:1457–1463

Babington M, Robinson L, Monson R (1983) Effect of written information on physicians' knowledge of drug prices. South Econ J 76(3):328–331

Kesenne J, Feltesse P (1988) De Uitgaven van de Ziekteverzekering voor Werknemers van 1945 tot 1986. Dossier 16, Landsbond van Christelijke Mutualiteiten, Brussel, p 96

Lilja J (1976) How physician's choose their drugs. Soc Sci Med 10:363–365

Lowy DR, Lowy L, Warner RS (1972) A survey of physicians' awareness of drug costs. J Med Educ 47:349–351

Manning P, Lee P, Clintworth W, Denson T, Oppenheimer P, Gilman N (1986) Changing prescribing practices through individual continuing education. J Am Med Assoc 256(2):230–232

Oppenheim GL, Erickson SH, Ashworth C (1981) The family physician's knowledge of the cost of prescribed drugs. J Fam Pract 12(6):1027–1030

Schroeder SA, Kenders K, Cooper J, Piemme T (1973) Use of laboratory tests and pharmaceuticals. Variation among physicians and effect of cost audit and subsequent use. J Am Med Assoc 225(8):969–973

Soumerai SB, Avorn J (1984) Efficacy and cost-containment in hospital pharmacotherapy: state of the art and future directions. Milbank Mem Fund Q/Health Soc 62(3):447–474

Zelnio R (1982) Physician's use of the guide to prescription drug costs: an exploration. Drug Intell Clin Pharm 16:874–875

Zelnio RN, Gagnon JP (1979) The effects of price information on physician prescribing patterns – a literature review. Drug Intell Clin Pharm 13:156–159

Joint Price and Quantity Regulation in the Market for Physicians' Services: The Quebec Experiment

L. Rochaix

Introduction

Most countries have adopted some degree of price regulation of the market for physicians' services, with the definition of fee schedules and their regular negotiation. However, price regulation may create a gap between the quantity of services a physician would like to offer at the prevailing fee level (ex ante supply) and the quantity which he or she would provide on purely medical grounds on behalf of the patient (ex ante demand). The excess supply is potentially resorbed by additional/more intensive patient care, while excess demand may be resorbed by care rationing. The adjustment mechanism which predominates in the market for physicians' services clearly is a quantity adjustment.

As a result, regulatory bodies have increasingly developed quantity regulation as a complement to price regulation, first, at the macro level (planning or rationing of health care inputs) to then turn to the microeconomic level (control of physicians' activity rates). The trend here is also clearly away from a retrospective to a prospective basis (the most recent manifestation being the fashion for expenditure caps in the United States, set preferably in terms of incentives rather than constraints.

The object of this paper is to analyse the impact of third party payer joint price-quantity regulation on utilization rates, within the framework of a fixed price model of the market for physicians' services with potential quantity adjustment. In particular, attention will be focused on the rather unique experience of Quebec with expenditure caps, as well as financial incentives and constraints, and the model will be estimated on its highly disaggregated data set on fees and utilization.

Price Versus Quantity Regulation

Evidence on Quantity Adjustment

Generally, empirical research undertaken on the supply of physicians' services has been directed towards the validation of the supplier-induced demand hypothesis (SID) defined by Evans (1974) and according to which physicians have the ability to counter the price reduction following an increase in medical density by a subsequent increase in the volume of services performed. At the root of this discretionary power lies the information asymmetry and the ensuing agency relationship between the physician and patient.

Most econometric test have attempted to establish a positive relationship between medical density and fees (or utilization) and have failed to provide a conclusive test of the existence of SID. [For a review of the literature on empirically testing demand inducement, see Sloan and Feldman (1978); Reinhardt (1978); Pauly (1980); Feldman and Sloan (1988); Rice and Labelle (1988), and the reply by Feldman and Sloan (1988) in the same issue, pointing to the "overwhelming practical importance" of the policy issues raised by demand inducement (p. 621).] Indeed, these tests have suffered from methodological limitations mainly related to the quality of the data (usually aggregate) or the comparability of the geographical areas used in cross-sectional studies. The most important limitation, however, which has cast serious doubt on the possibility of ever defining such a conclusive test, is the identification problem, i.e. the inability to control for changes in explanatory variables other than those included in the regression (especially demand side factors).

Recently, Phelps (1986) proposed an innovative approach to the issue of empirically testing demand inducement which is both pragmatic and potentially more conclusive. It relies on the analysis of the various cost control experiments of the 1980s to study the impact of changes in economic variables such as remuneration systems on physicians' levels of activity. These exogenous changes constitute "natural experiments" and allow a follow-up of the potential modifications in the behaviour of health care providers over time. The identification of quantity adjustments to such changes would support Evans' target income hypothesis which predicts that when physicians' fees fall, in real terms, they will increase their output levels so as to maintain overall income, and vice versa. A number of such studies have indicated a supply response to exogenous changes in remuneration systems, the most recent and conclusive being those of Rice (1984) and Wedig (1989). [See also Holahan et al. (1979) and Berry et al. (1978). Gabel and Rice (1985, p. 595) concluded that "These studies show that freezing or reducing payment levels is not effective in controlling expenditures because physicians respond to increasing the quantity and complexity of the services provided".]

In view of this growing body of evidence on compensating increases in the quantity of services provided, controlling costs by solely controlling fees has increasingly been regarded as a rather ineffective instrument. As a result, prospective payment systems for physicians' services have lately received a great deal of attention in the United States, and expenditure caps are central to the recommendations of the United States physician payment review programme for Medicare (Eisenberg and Kabcenell 1988).

The Quebec experience is unique in this respect in that it constitutes a natural experiment in Phelps' sense which should shed light on the impact of financial variables on physician activity rates, and also gives new insights highly relevant to policymakers on the impact of expenditure caps and more generally the appeal of joint price-quantity regulation over sole price regulation.

The Quebec Experiment

A Brief Outlook on Physicians' Services Regulation in Canada

Canada has adopted a national health insurance system with universal free comprehensive coverage against the costs of hospital and medical care. The system is "federal-provincial" rather than national, and provinces are responsible for matters relating to health. It was implemented in 1957 and was completed in all provinces for hospital care in 1961 and for medical care in 1971.

The general principle is that physicians' associations determine internally both the level and the structure of their own fee schedules. Negotiations with the provincial government are carried out on a "take it or leave it basis", and the process indeed ends with the negotiation of a global amount. A back door was kept open for physicians wanting to opt out of the system, and up until 1984 some provinces even accepted extra billing, i.e. a difference between the standard fee and the price charged over and above, which comes out of the patient's pocket. But these practices have remained moderate across the country and Quebec never actually permitted extra billing: when opted out physicians billed their patients over and above the agreed fee, and the latter could not claim their money back. As a result, the number of physicians who have opted out is less than 1%. (Only about 5% of physicians have opted out, on average, countrywide, and about 5% of total expenditures for insurable physicians' services are charged to patients.)

More importantly, the relative autonomy of the provinces has fostered a variety of expenditure-control methods within Canada, the most effective being those adopted by Quebec. Amongst all the Canadian provinces, Quebec has been the most successful in curbing physicians' expenditure per capita by adopting a more interventionist strategy, combining price and quantity regulation on a prospective basis.

The Quebec Joint Price Quantity Regulation

Quebec physicians are paid directly by the RAMQ (Régie de l'Assurance Maladie du Québec), which acts as the paying agent for Quebec's provincial government. But the fee schedule is negotiated directly between the government and the representatives of the medical profession. What is clearly at stake in this fee-bargaining exercise, however, is the integration of past quantity responses to be closed off in the negotiation, itself becoming "a process rather than an event". [For a thorough presentation of the Canadian experience, see Barer et al. (1986) and for the Quebec experience, Contandriopoulos et al. (1989, 1990).] The 1976 fee agreement is a good example of such a process where loopholes were identified in the fee schedule, and a number of diagnostic tests consequently rebundled in the visit fee, leaving physicians theoretically little room for manoeuvre.

Within this general framework, a prospective global cap has been placed in 1976 on overall GPs' expenditure. An individual target income is negotiated, which when multiplied by the total number of practising GPs yields the global fund earmarked to GPs' services. (The target income being essentially defined as an average income over the GP population, exclusion criteria are set for its calculation to avoid including GPs working on a part-time basis.) The overall rate of fee increase necessary to achieve this income is then worked out (on the assumption of constant quantity of services per GP). However, for certain procedures which either the government or GPs' representatives would want to encourage/curb, specific rates of increase can be negotiated, which should average out (for example, the encouragement of domiciliary care, offset by the reduction of certain diagnostic procedures). Collective overshooting at the end of the period is sanctioned by a reduction of the overall rate of fee increases to be granted in the next period.

As a result, total expenditures can exceed the cap in any particular year, but the collective sanction (in terms of reduced rates of increase of overall fees in the coming year) prevents a cumulative departure from the agreed cap, the overshooting being recaptured in the following years.

The system, however, was potentially unfair since a collective sanction could be brought about by the behaviour of a small group of GPs with high activity rates. Indeed, the implementation of an overall expenditure cap with no corresponding limit on the quantity of services billable by each physician may give rise to free riding. On the one hand, some physicians will continue increasing their activity rates, while the more cost-conscious ones will potentially incur two sanctions, as noted in Lomas et al. (1989): a current income loss coupled with future losses that may arise if fees are adjusted downward to sanction overshooting. As a result, GPs' representatives have accepted the implementation of an individual quarterly gross income ceiling high enough only to affect "workaholic" physicians (about 10%). In practice, the ceiling entails a reduction of 75% of the fee paid by the RAMQ to the physician for any service provided over and above the ceiling.

Inasmuch as fees are regulated, this income ceiling represents de facto an individual cap on the overall quantity of services provided per physician. In this respect the Quebec experience constitutes an example of joint price and quantity regulatory strategy. Furthermore, it creates the conditions of a natural experiment (in Phelps' sense), where the potential responses of health care providers to such incentives and constraints can be followed over time. Within this framework, one of the main questions addressed here is the extent to which joint price-quantity regulation does affect physicians' activity rates, and if so, how.

Modelling the Utilization of Physicians' Services

Introducing Demand-Inducement in Equilibrium Models

Economic models developed to capture the notion of demand inducement are usually based on Green's equilibrium equation (1978), one good example of which is provided by Stano et al. (1985). Crucial to Stano's model is the assumption that regulated fees can create a gap between what physicians are prepared to provide at the going fee and what patients should receive on purely medical grounds and personal preferences. Given the information asymmetry which prevails between physicians and their patients, physicians attempt partially or completely to eliminate the gap between demand and supply in the ex ante sense.

Following Stano, let *D* and *S* represent demand and supply functions in the ex ante sense, and *D* represent the demand which should arise if physicians acted solely in their patients' interest,

$$D = a_0 P^{a_1} Y^{a_2} \qquad a_1 < 0 \qquad (1)$$

$$S = b_0 P^{b_1} MD^{b_2} N^{b_3} \qquad b_1 > O; b_2 > 0 \qquad (2)$$

where *Y* represents income and other independent variables in the demand equation and *MD* and *N* represent respectively the number of physicians and other independent variables in the supply equation. Following Green (1978), let the equilibrium level *Q* of actual utilization be approximated by:

$$Q = D \cdot \left(\frac{S}{D}\right) \qquad (3)$$

where λ represents the proportion of an excess demand (or supply) gap which would be eliminated by a deflation (inflation) of services provided. (If $\lambda = 0$, then $Q = D$ and there is no quantity adjustment. On the contrary, when $\lambda = 1$, there is quantity adjustment which will bring the excess-supply (demand) gap to zero, so that physicians will be on their ex ante supply curve.) In order to measure the amount by which the gap is closed and how intensity changes with changes in supply, substitute Eqs. 1 and 2 are substituted into Eq. 3 to obtain:

$$\log Q = \log D + \lambda(\log S - \log D) \qquad (4)$$

$$\log Q = (1 - \lambda)\log a_0 + \lambda \log b_0 + (a_1(1 - \lambda) + \lambda b_1)\log P + a_2(1 - \lambda)\log Y + \lambda b_2 \log MD + \lambda b_3 \log N \qquad (5)$$

$$\log Q = \alpha_0 + \alpha_1 \log P + \alpha_2 \log Y + \alpha_3 \log MD + \alpha_4 \log N \qquad (6)$$

From the multiplicative form and the assumption that b_2, the elasticity of supply, is unitary, $\hat{\alpha}_3$ is an estimate of λ, the demand shift factor.

Along with the short-run model, the authors propose a long-run model to determine the extent to which market forces drive fees towards competitive levels.

An Adaptation to the Quebec Case

This standard model should be adapted to suit the purposes of the study at hand:

1. Since user prices are zero, ex ante demand is no longer a function of the patient's income, and since fees are fixed the long-term price equation in effect reflects the fee negotiation process defined earlier.
2. More fundamentally, the purpose of the study is not to attribute an increase in the quantity of services to either demand or supply in order to provide a "conclusive" test of the existence of demand inducement [see Auster and Oaxaca (1981) on the identification problem]. Rather, the essence of the argument is that in health care systems where prices are fixed, and entry to the medical profession highly regulated by the State, the exogenous shocks to which physicians are likely to quantity respond are changes in remuneration systems (often in relation to cost control experiments), rather than increases in medical density. [This point has been taken up again recently by Rice and Labelle (1988), in their response to Feldman and Sloan, who tended only to consider as "direct" tests of

demand inducement those which involved medical density as the central explanatory variable.] Consequently, the central variable here is no longer medical density, but exogenous changes in the remuneration system. Earlier results indicated a high temporal correlation between medical density and real fees for medical services, which cannot be accounted for theoretically, and strongly suggest an alternative to testing demand inducement based on changes in remuneration systems rather than on changes in medical density.

Research Design

Justification for Study Design

There are a number of advantages to the chosen time series design (see Campbell and Stanley 1963) compared with previous analyses of physician activity rates, beyond the very fact that the data could be specifically collected for the purpose of the study.

Inasmuch as the price variable is adequately controlled in Quebec (fixed fees and no extra billing), the only behavioural response by physicians to the implementation of financial incentives and prospective payment systems is quantity/complexity adjustments. In order to trace such responses, a highly reliable and disaggregated data set is essential. A number of studies of inducement in the market for physicians' services have often remained limited to the analysis of visits, for lack of information (McCarthy 1985; Wilensky and Rossiter 1983), when results by Rice (1984) have clearly shown that it is perhaps the only area in which physicians do not induce demand!

Such is the case for the Quebec data base, for it is generated for payment purposes, and based on a very precise fee schedule. Furthermore, the data were provided on a monthly basis, which constituted an asset for the study of the impact of a quarterly ceiling on activity rates, and the identification of any downward trend over the quarter. Also, unlike United States studies on Medicare/Medicaid claims, the study does not have to rely on the selection of a particular recipient group in the population of patients.

Beyond these general considerations which have justified the choice of Quebec for such an empirical analysis, the sampling method obeyed the following criteria:

1. The choice of a particular geographical area (Montreal Metropolitan) was justified by its high physician/population ratio (both generalists and specialists), compared with other areas in Quebec, the rationale being that no excess demand should prevail in this area.

2. A cohort design was chosen so as to control for secular trends such as the feminization of the medical profession and to minimize behaviour modifications in the GPs' sample. This design was also important in isolating the results from the effect of another financial incentives policy developed concurrently by the RAMQ in 1982, and which aimed at encouraging young physicians to practise in remote areas. Results from analyses carried out on this policy are available in Contandriopoulos et al. (1986). Existing information ("Les Effectifs Médicaux au Québec", Corporation Professionnelle des Médecins 1986) of a comparative nature between the different regions of the Quebec province shows that GPs included in the cohort were representative (in sociodemographic terms) both of the region and more generally of the province at large.
3. The choice of the study period (1977–1983) was justified with the following reasons:
   a) On the one hand, it represents a homogeneous period in terms of fee structure and organizational setup. It is posterior to the major changes of the 1970s in the Quebec health care system which affected both demand and supply, and had made previous results such as those by Berry et al. (1978) less conclusive. It is also posterior to the major rebundling exercise of 1976, so that the fee schedule structure has remained constant.
   b) This period is characterized by exogenous changes in the remuneration system, which are sufficiently important to encourage quantity responses on the part of physicians. On two separate occasions, the ceiling regulation was removed (for respectively 15 and 9 months), the first period being accompanied by an important tariff freeze, while the second is concomitant with a strike that substantially affected GPs' activity. As for financial incentives, the fee for some procedures such as home visits was nearly doubled over the period.

Methodology

Information Collected

The data were collected by the RAMQ and the Corporation Professionnelle des Médecins (which has the responsibility for quality assurance within the Quebec health care system) and provide information on a cohort of GPs based on all physicians of the area of Montreal Metropolitan, who were fully active in 1974 (the reference year) and for the entire study period: 1977–1983. A total of 677 GPs was selected under these criteria, and a further selection of 571 GPs were carried out in order to reject both high and very low revenue outliers. Nine physicians were rejected, whose income was about C$17 000/ month, i.e. twice the ceiling, as well as 97 GPs whose incomes were actually below the minimum standard used as the exclusion criterion in the calculation of the official target income, and whose main type of practice was clearly not fee for service but salary. The selection was carried out in a representative month (January 1979).

1. Physician characteristics: age sex, university of MD, year of MD, language (French or English), postal code.
2. Annual data from the questionnaire of the Corporation Professionnelle des Médecins: number of hours worked on average per week over the year, percentage of time spent on nine different activities (office care, hospital care, research, teaching, administration, etc.)
3. Monthly data collected by the RAMQ upon payments made to physicians:
   a) Quantity of the 50 most frequent procedures (i) provided by each physician (j) each month (t): Q_{ijt}.
   b) Revenue derived from the quantity of each procedure monthly: R_{ijt}. Note, however, that in the original data, R_{ijt} is already truncated for physicians who are above the ceiling: for those, the official fee P_{it} is progressively reduced, with $P_{ijt} = \alpha P_{it}$, and $0.25 < \alpha < 1$. As a result, available information is $P_{ijt} = R_{ijt}/Q_{ijt}$, where $P_{ijt} = P_{it}$ for those physicians below the ceiling and $P_{ijt} = \alpha P_{it}$ for physicians above. In order to isolate modifications in gross incomes truly resulting from physicians' choices of workloads rather than simply the mere financial sanction entailed by the ceiling, official prices were recovered for the period to recalculate revenues.
4. Additional cross-sectional data were available for the middle of the period (1980), characterizing the physician's area of practice: level of education and revenue of the population served, as well as access measures to services. The data originate from two studies, one on poverty by Wilkins (1985), and the other on the geographical allocation of health care resources by the Direction Régionale des Programme des Services Sociaux in 1980. The linkage was effected between the postal code available for each physician in the sample and the CLSC (Centres Locaux de Santé Communautaire).

Definition of Study Variables

The first step was to select a workable number of procedures out of the 2455 procedures used at least once by a GP from the sample over the period of study. Procedures were selected on the basis of three criteria: the contribution of a procedure to R_{jt} (revenue criterion), the importance of a procedure in the mix (quantity criterion) and the continuity over the period (the procedure must be used at least once in each month). Fifty procedures were chosen as the common set to be analysed for GPs, including both high revenue generating though less common procedures (such as child delivery), and conversely low paid but common procedures (such as the ordinary visit). The advantage of the frequency indicator is to ensure that a procedure remains valid over the entire period, a necessary condition for time series analysis. Overall, this reduction of information to 50 procedures seems highly justified by the fact that 96% of the whole sample's gross revenue is derived from the 50 chosen procedures.

The main difficulty resided in the three dimensionality of the information collected: indeed, beyond the time dimension, there are two cross-sectional dimensions: physicians and procedures. In order to handle these three dimensions at once, the following approach was developed:

Comparisons between physicians with different incomes were made possible by defining three income groups:

1. An income group of 122 physicians above the ceiling or below by no more than 10%, the purpose of the research being to analyse the behaviour of those physicians who gravitate around the ceiling.
2. A low income group of 334 GPs whose income is above a minimum standard but does not exceed the official target income.
3. A middle group of 115 GPs falling between these two classes.

Then, for each of these income groups, analyses were carried out both at aggregate level (i.e. on earnings from all 50 procedures) and on a procedure basis.

Estimation, Results, and Discussion

Results presented here are based on time series analyses of overall activity rates compared across different income groups. Some evidence will also be provided at a disaggregate level for a selected number of procedures. [Some of these results are already available in French in Rochaix and Largeron (1989)].

Specification of the Utilization Equation

Two types of dependent variables were used as proxies for physicians' activity rates, according to the desired level of aggregation: either over all 50 procedures, or at each procedure level.

1. In the first case, the dependent variable is gross individual non-capped real billings per working day of the month, for each of the 4 subgroups defined, derived from fee for service activity on the 50 selected procedures. A correction was introduced into the calculation of real billings to account for variations in the number of working days in each month over the years. In so doing, we ensure that variations in activity levels truly reflect physicians' choices of workloads. Income from other sources (i.e. salaries or lump sum payments for fixed periods of working time in hospital) were introduced into the regressions but coefficients were not found to be significant. In fact, fee for service practice constituted by far the most important of the three income components over the time period: 94.5% in 1978 and 87.8% in 1983 (Annual Statistics, RAMQ). In order to generate a measure of activity rates which takes into account the varying complexity of procedures, each procedure fee was used as a weight in the aggregation over all procedures, using constant 1980 prices. Inasmuch as fees were originally defined in relation to the Californian Relative Value Scale (C*RVS*), they reflect the time and complexity involved in each procedure. Although this weighting system is imperfect because fee levels are also the outcome of a bargaining process, it seems better than a mere aggregation over the quantity of procedures as different as ordinary visits and child delivery, for example. In so doing, we also derive the best proxy for activity rates by suppressing any overall price effect over the period. Four such dependent variables were constructed for each of the four subgroups of physicians (all physicians, high revenue, average revenue and low revenue physicians) corresponding to the individual average real billings per subgroup.
2. In the latter case, the dependent variable was the quantity of each of the 50 procedures considered, used by each of the four subgroups per month.

Two time periods were used: the overall period of 84 months and the capped period which covers 60 months.

The index of medical services (IMS) defined in Barer et al. (1986) was used as independent variable at aggregate level. (An internal index consisting of a quantity-weighted average over the 50 chosen procedures was computed in order to validate this published index. For external comparability, the latter was used in the analysis, although no significant difference was found.) The relative price of each procedure (the official price deflated by the IMS) was chosen at disaggregate level. In so doing, we capture both the general price elasticity of supply in the aggregate equations and evidence of relative price elasticities at procedure level.

Seasonal variations were originally corrected for by introducing standard quarterly dummies. However, preliminary results indicated that variations in activity levels were best accounted for by respecifying the original dummies to focus on holidays in summer (DJuly) and winter (DDec). Interestingly, this finding in itself tempers the view that physicians' workloads are essentially affected by seasonal variations to which they would react passively. In fact, the main source of variation turns out to be holidays, which are predictable, and the result of choices made jointly by the physician and patients.

Finally, dummies were introduced to analyse the impact of exogenous changes in the remuneration system such as tariff freezes or the implementation of a quarterly ceiling on gross individual earnings. The two deregulated periods were identified by separate dummies (*D1* and *D2*). Positive signs for *D1* and *D2* would validate both the hypothesis of target income (a tariff freeze being followed by an increase in quantity/quality) and of a constraint imposed through expenditure caps on high revenue physicians (a deregulation being followed by an increase in activity rates). A third dummy (*D3*) was defined for the analysis of the ceiling over the 60-month period, a negative sign validating the hypothesis that high revenue physicians reduce their activity rates during the 3rd month of the ceiling.

No further demand proxies were introduced in the equations, because demand side factors were mainly controlled for in the actual design of the study. However, cross-sectional information permitted a corroborating analysis which showed that demand variables (mainly revenue and education) were not significant in a regression explaining physicians' individual real billings. Physicians' characteristics on the contrary were important, especially age, sex, hours of work per week and activity types.

In order to quantify the effects of these economic variables and test for their statistical significance, the following reduced form equation was used for the overall period:

$$\ln X_j = \alpha_j + \beta_{1j} DJuly + \beta_{2j} DDec + \beta_{3j} D1 + \beta_{4j} D2 + \beta_{5j} \ln IMS + \varepsilon_j$$

where $j = 1$ to 4 and X_j is the activity rates proxy for each of the four income subgroups defined, at aggregate level. At disaggregate level, X_j is the quantity of each procedure used by the subgroup of physicians ($i = 1 \ldots 50$). For regressions on the 60-month period, *D3* replaces *D1* and *D2* in the equation.

Empirical Findings

The aggregate equation results in Tables 1 and 3 cover the entire study period (84 months) for the four subgroups, while Tables 2 and 4 cover the 60 months during which the ceiling was enforced. All variables are expressed in logarithms so that coefficients can be read as elasticities. In general, the model seems to fit the data rather well. Results were adjusted for autocorrelation by the Prais-Winsten (cf. Maddala 1977) method, which corrects for a first-order autoregressive correlation process.

Evidence on a Backward Bending Physicians "Supply"

The first interesting results in Table 1 are the overall negative (though low) price elasticities of supply, which provide further evidence of a backward bending physician's marginal cost curve.

Table 1. Aggregate equation results over the entire study period: 84 observations

	Income Group			
Independent variables	All revenue	High revenue	Middle revenue	Low revenue
Constant	+11.32	+11.29	+11.71	+11.19
	(33.80)	(32.71)	(31.45)	(30.29)
DJuly	-.29	-.36	-.24	-.26
	(12.61)	(14.89)	(9.05)	(11.65)
DDec	-.07	-.09	-.04	-.07
	(3.08)	(3.80)	(1.55)	(3.22)
D1	+.05	+.05	+.05	+.04
	(2.91)	(3.12)	(2.95)	(2.49)
D2	-.01	+.00	-.01	-.02
	(.59)	(.20)	(.76)	(1.01)
lnIMS	-.23	-.14	-.32	-.25
	(3.22)	(1.93)	(4.07)	(3.23)
R^2	.70	.74	.58	.68
DW unc.	1.90	1.97	2.08	1.81
DW corr.	2.02	2.01	–	1.99
SER	.058	.062	.068	.059

R^2, coefficient of determination, adjusted for degrees of freedom; *DW* corr., Durbin-Watson test statistic for first-order serial correlation, corrected by the Prais-Winsten method for first-order autoregressive correlation process. Absolute *t* values in parentheses, under coefficients (elasticities).

lnQ1 (lnPI1), log of quantity (relative price) of ordinary visit; *lnQ2 (lnPI2)*, log of quantity (relative price) of day home visit; *lnQ50 (lnPI50)*, log of quantity (relative price) of complete visit; *lnQ52 (lnPI52)*, log of quantity (relative price) of complete and major visit. Numbers in brackets under the mean of the dependent variable represent the average share of subgroups' activity allocated to that particular procedure.

Table 2. Aggregate equation results over 60 months: 60 observations

Independent variables	Income Group: All revenue	High revenue	Middle revenue	Low revenue
Constant	+11.28	+11.20	+11.70	+11.17
	(30.17)	(28.76)	(31.96)	(28.07)
DJuly	−.29	−.37	−.25	−.27
	(11.46)	(15.45)	(8.01)	(10.17)
DDec	−.11	−.15	−.07	−.11
	(3.92)	(5.53)	(2.07)	(3.58)
D3	−.03	−.06	−.02	−.01
	(2.12)	(4.35)	(1.08)	(.83)
lnIMS	−.22	−.11	−.32	−.25
	(2.74)	(1.41)	(4.10)	(2.93)
R^2	.72	.80	.57	.68
DW unc.	1.72	1.62	1.97	1.71
DW corr.	1.94	1.96	–	1.94
SER	.056	.055	.066	.059

See Table 1 for key to abbreviations.

These negative price elasticities of supply would not be so surprising if the dependent variable had been derived by deflating the current PQs with the IMS: indeed, if this were the case, as the IMS goes up, constant PQs would decrease. But, by construction, the dependent variable suppresses this overall price effect, so that negative price elasticities of supply are suggestive of a backward bending supply curve. The idea of a backward bending supply is still controversial, but there is a growing body of empirical support for this concept (Mitchell 1984; Wedig et al. 1989). As noted by Wedig et al. (1989, p. 610), "the physician's marginal cost curve can bend backwards because the opportunity cost of the physician's own time plays such a key role in the practice's total cost curve". Furthermore, the fact that elasticities are comparable across income groups in Table 1 would point to sociocultural rather than economic factors which may have increased the opportunity cost of leisure for all physicians over the period. Studies for the Corporation Professionnelle des Médecins indicate that the number of hours worked on average per week has dropped substantially from 52.1 to 48.1 over the period.

Wedig further analyses the adequacy of fee controls when there is evidence of such a backward bending supply, and concludes that "With negatively sloped supply, vigorous price controls would cause a forward movement down along the physician's marginal cost curve, leading to unexpected increases in quantity and/or quality". The results derived from the analysis of the tariff freeze imposed on Quebec physicians support these predictions.

Table 3. Aggregate equation results over the entire study period: 84 observations

Variables	Income Group All revenue	 High revenue	 Middle revenue	 Low revenue
Mean dependent variable lnQ1	11.58 [.28]	10.47 [.29]	9.93 [.27]	10.79 [.27]
Constant	+17.86	+16.95	+18.37	+15.83
	(9.74)	(8.77)	(7.36)	(9.01)
DJuly	–.30	–.33	–.23	–.32
	(10.55)	(10.85)	(7.69)	(10.98)
DDec	–.19	–.19	–.18	–.20
	(6.61)	(6.30)	(6.07)	(6.85)
D1	–.03	–.01	–.05	–.03
	(1.34)	(.60)	(1.37)	(1.37)
D2	–.14	–.12	–.16	–.13
	(4.60)	(3.92)	(3.70)	(4.61)
lnPI1	–.92	–.95	–1.25	–.75
	(3.39)	(3.32)	(3.36)	(2.87)
R^2	.67	.67	.60	.68
DW corr.	2.05	2.06	2.14	2.04
Mean dependent variable lnQ50	11.20 [.38]	10.07 [.39]	9.64 [.41]	10.35 [.35]
Constant	+9.94	+9.73	+7.22	+9.30
	(10.94)	(9.62)	(6.74)	(9.18)
DJuly	–.34	–.38	–.31	–.33
	(14.73)	(14.68)	(11.87)	(13.54)
DDec	–.17	–.16	–.15	–.20
	(7.19)	(6.08)	(5.75)	(8.04)
D1	+.07	+.07	+.09	+.06
	(5.69)	(4.87)	(5.86)	(4.42)
D2	+.01	+.02	+.01	–.00
	(.62)	(1.48)	(.94)	(.39)
lnPI50	+.17	+.50	+.33	+.14
	(1.41)	(.36)	(2.27)	(1.07)
R^2	.71	.70	.64	.71
DW corr.	2.05	2.11	2.02	2.02
Mean dependent variable lnQ52	8.84 [.06]	7.51 [.05]	7.12 [.06]	8.13 [.07]
Constant	+8.64	+5.14	+8.60	+8.35
	(2.66)	(1.70)	(2.30)	(2.25)
DJuly	–.26	–.29	–.23	–.25
	(8.16)	(7.47)	(6.76)	(7.71)
DDec	–.32	–.31	–.32	–.32
	(9.42)	(7.70)	(8.80)	(9.28)
D1	+.08	+.12	+.02	+.07
	(1.73)	(2.87)	(.37)	(1.24)
D2	–.01	+.01	–.03	–.04
	(.29)	(.37)	(.51)	(.61)

Table 3. (*Continued*)

Variables	Income Group All revenue	High revenue	Middle revenue	Low revenue
lnPI52	+.02	+.29	−.17	−.02
	(.07)	(.79)	(.38)	(.04)
R^2	.55	.53	.47	.53
DW corr.	2.40	2.21	2.42	2.43
Mean dependent variable	8.73	7.22	7.21	8.09
lnQ2	[.03]	[.02]	[.04]	[.04]
Constant	+4.25	+1.51	+1.42	+4.69
	(2.78)	(1.22)	(.62)	(3.25)
DJuly	−.16	−.33	−.09	−.14
	(7.01)	(8.70)	(3.49)	(5.96)
DDec	−.06	−.06	−.06	−.05
	(2.54)	(1.68)	(2.37)	(2.14)
D1	+.06	+.10	+.11	+.02
	(1.58)	(3.35)	(2.02)	(.61)
D2	+.05	+.02	+.08	+.02
	(1.19)	(.75)	(1.28)	(.60)
lnPI2	+.59	+.75	+.76	+.45
	(2.93)	(4.63)	(2.51)	(2.36)
R^2	.49	.58	.45	.40
DW corr.	2.39	2.07	2.62	2.18

See Table 1 for key to abbreviations.

The results presented in Table 1 indeed show that physicians have responded positively to a tariff freeze by increasing their activity rates, the coefficient of the *D1* variable being significantly different from zero. These results are important in that they identify quantity responses which cannot be attributed to changes in demand factors or are not blurred by concomitant changes in prices. At this level of aggregation, however, it is not possible to distinguish between a quantity response and a shift towards more complex procedures, but analyses carried out on a procedure basis can provide further evidence on this issue.

Indeed, Table 3 supports the hypothesis of a substitution towards more complex and therefore better paid procedures. For the three procedures chosen to illustrate this phenomenon, we find that the "major visit" (*Q50*) does seem to replace the "ordinary visit" (*Q1*), a trend already identified in Quebec, but which seems to be even more pronounced in times of tariff freeze. This example corroborates Rice's findings that physicians cannot "induce" ordinary visits. But the negative sign of *D1* would be indicative of substitution effects in favour of more lucrative types of visits such as *Q50* or *Q52*.

Table 4. Aggregate equation results over 60 months: 60 observations

Variables	Income Group			
	All revenue	High revenue	Middle revenue	Low revenue
Mean dependent variable lnQ1	11.60	10.49	9.95	10.81
Constant	+18.23	+17.34	+19.08	+16.29
	(8.69)	(8.03)	(6.43)	(8.12)
DJuly	–.33	–.36	–.24	–.35
	(10.85)	(11.39)	(7.91)	(11.08)
DDec	–.25	–.26	–.25	–.25
	(7.27)	(7.22)	(6.91)	(7.03)
D3	–.04	–.06	–.02	–.03
	(2.44)	(3.34)	(1.60)	(1.95)
lnPI1	–.98	–1.01	–1.35	–.81
	(3.13)	(3.14)	(3.06)	(2.70)
R^2	.71	.72	.60	.72
DW corr.	2.06	2.12	2.07	2.03
Mean dependent variable lnQ50	11.19	10.05	9.62	10.34
Constant	+9.30	+9.06	+6.51	+8.75
	(12.83)	(11.57)	(7.69)	(9.47)
DJuly	–.36	–.41	–.32	–.34
	(15.92)	(16.23)	(12.78)	(13.53)
DDec	–.20	–.17	–.17	–.24
	(8.13)	(6.44)	(6.44)	(8.79)
D3	–.03	–.06	–.00	–.01
	(2.23)	(3.85)	(.57)	(1.15)
lnPI50	+.26	+.14	+.42	+.22
	(2.67)	(1.35)	(3.71)	(1.77)
R^2	.80	.79	.74	.79
DW corr.	2.00	2.05	2.02	1.98
Mean dependent variable lnQ52	8.84	7.49	7.13	8.13
Constant	+8.36	+5.12	+7.52	+8.63
	(2.28)	(1.41)	(1.85)	(2.02)
DJuly	–.33	–.40	–.30	–.31
	(10.99)	(10.17)	(9.69)	(8.86)
DDec	–.38	–.39	–.40	–.37
	(10.14)	(8.48)	(10.35)	(8.48)
D3	–.05	–.08	–.07	–.01
	(2.97)	(3.52)	(4.07)	(.84)
lnPI52	+.06	+.30	–.04	–.05
	(.14)	(.67)	(.08)	(.10)
R^2	.55	.56	.50	.48
DW corr.	2.69	2.46	2.58	2.55

Table 4. (*Continued*)

Variables	Income Group			
	All revenue	High revenue	Middle revenue	Low revenue
Mean dependent variable lnQ2	8.71	7.20	7.17	8.08
Constant	+4.09	+1.25	+.48	+4.56
	(2.29)	(.89)	(.19)	(1.55)
DJuly	−.19	−.32	−.13	−.17
	(7.06)	(6.86)	(4.41)	(6.04)
DDec	−.06	−.10	−.06	−.03
	(1.90)	(1.90)	(1.64)	(1.03)
D3	−.01	−.05	−.02	−.00
	(1.22)	(1.80)	(1.10)	(.10)
lnPI2	+.61	+.79	+.88	+.46
	(2.60)	(4.27)	(2.61)	(2.26)
R^2	.49	.53	.42	.44
DW cor.	2.51	2.14	.280	2.29

See Table 1 for key to abbreviations.

More generally, the results at disaggregate level provide evidence against the hypothesis that physicians have simply worked longer hours during the tariff freeze. They may have done so, but they have also shown their ability to react strategically by choosing the most lucrative procedures.

The fact that this freeze period also corresponds to a ceiling deregulation does not invalidate the previous findings. If anything, the deregulation makes the period more comparable to previous instances of tariff freezes. But it becomes difficult to disentangle the two effects, at least at such an aggregate level, for they work in the same direction (i.e. an expected increase in utilization). Finally, the coefficient of the dummy for the second period of ceiling deregulation (*D2*) is not significantly different from zero. The activity reduction related to the strike must therefore have been compensated by an increase in activity for the remaining months of that period.

The comparison of findings across income groups in Table 1 provides further insights into the respective importance of the tariff freeze and the ceiling deregulation: inasmuch as the *D1* dummy is significant for all income groups, this tends to indicate that the former dominates the latter. Indeed, if the converse were true, the activity rates of other income groups should not be affected, or at least less affected than those of high income physicians, who are the real target of this individual ceiling regulation. Further results on the 60 months over which the ceiling was implemented, both at aggregate level (Table 2) and on a procedure basis (Table 4), will provide more evidence on the actual impact of the ceiling on physicians' activity levels.

Evidence on the Impact of Expenditure Caps

Table 2 considers the impact of the quarterly ceiling regulation on physicians' workloads over the 60 months when the ceiling regulation applied and, in particular, on their allocation of working time over the quarter. The general hypothesis to be tested here is whether physicians are totally passive and let the flow of patients who walk through their door determine their activity rates entirely, or whether they can shift part of their workloads over to the next quarter to circumvent the ceiling regulation. There is some informal support for such strategic behaviour from data collected by the Ministry of Health on the percentage of physicians above the ceiling per quarter for the area of Montreal Metropolitan: 11% hit the ceiling for at least one quarter in the year, this proportion remaining constant whatever the quarter, while the corresponding percentage for the four quarters is only 2%.

To see how binding the ceiling is for high revenue physicians, one must find out whether it reduces activity rates through longer holidays usually taken in July or December, or whether it does constrain physicians to reduce their activity beyond these periods. To distinguish between the two cases, *D3* excludes standard holidays, i.e. takes a value of zero for the 1st and 2 months of the ceiling and for July and December, only to capture reductions in activity related to the capping itself. When looking at these results, we reject the null hypothesis of no significant change in activity rates in the 3 month, with a negative coefficient for *D3* significantly different from zero for high revenue physicians only.

In Table 2, low income physicians serve as controls in case the decrease in activity rates in the 3 month of the quarter were a general phenomenon, unrelated to the ceiling regulation. Another control was provided by running a regression with a "fictive" *D3* dummy during the no-ceiling period to see whether the established pattern carried over. Both proofs clearly outlined the atypical behaviour of high revenue physicians, which points to their ability to reduce activity in the 3 month of the quarter and possibly shift some of their activity over to the next quarter.

Also, the fact that other income groups did not experience increases in activity rates in the 3 month of the ceiling (Table 2) suggests that little redistribution took place between physicians (a prime objective of the ceiling regulation), either because high revenue physicians have succeeded in ironing out peaks in demand or because they have passed it on to colleagues within their income group. It must be noted, however, that the cohort design excludes the young physicians who may have joined a practice and would benefit from this redistribution of activity at the end of the quarter. It is therefore difficult to produce entirely conclusive evidence on the redistributive impact of the ceiling across income groups, but it is likely to have been fairy limited.

Finally, Table 4 shows further evidence on physicians' ability to reduce activity and change their mix of services: here, the item of major visit (*Q50*), which had increased significantly for high revenue physicians during the freeze period, is now reduced in the 3rd month of the ceiling while it has remained constant over the 3 months for the other income groups. The same reasoning applies for home visits (*Q2*), when comparing results in Tables 3 and 4 for high revenue physicians versus other income groups.

Evidence on Specific Price Elasticities

Along with the implementation of expenditure caps and fee controls, the Quebec government has agreed to a limited number of financial incentives given to physicians in order to increase the delivery of certain services in excess demand. Regressions run on a procedure basis indicate that, in general, price elasticities of supply did not vary significantly across income groups. Physicians were indeed sensitive to some of these price rises (as in the case of home visits in Tables 3 and 4), although their response was in no way perfectly elastic and varied from one case to another. Consequently, further analysis is required to find out which factors other than financial may also be determinant in physicians' use of particular procedures. In this respect, the complementarity/substitution phenomena between procedures seem an interesting research avenue. Such a study is currently under way at the GRIS and should provide further evidence on physicians' responses to financial incentives.

Conclusion

The analysis focused on three aspects of third-party payer regulation as developed in Quebec: fee controls, expenditure caps and financial incentives for specific procedures. The results provide evidence of a backward bending supply over the whole period, with a significant increase in activity rates and in complexity of procedures during the tariff freeze period, which would further support the hypothesis of income targeting behaviour. Expenditure caps were shown to be constraining high revenue physicians in their allocation of effort over the quarter and in the actual mix of services provided. Finally, some positive price elasticities of supply were found for certain target procedures, although the response was selective.

More generally, the analysis of the various sets of incentives and constraints facing Quebec physicians shows that they behave strategically and have the discretionary power necessary to shape demand according to criteria other than purely medical ones. However, the fact that it manifests itself in instances such as tariff freezes (see Van Doorslaer and Geurts (1987) for an original test of demand inducement based on this reasoning) suggests that the ability to manipulate demand was not fully exploited previously, a possible indication of physicians' disutility in using their discretionary power for ethical reasons.

Acknowledgements. The author is greatly indebted to A.P. Contandriopoulos and A. Lemay (GRIS, Université de Montréal, Quebec), and to J.D. Hey (Department of Economics, University of York, UK). Also, our thanks are due to the RAMQ, in particular P. Bossé and the Corporation Professionnelle des Médecins for providing the data and to M. Rodrigue from the Féderation des Médecins Omnipraticiens du Québec for his advice.

References

Auster R, Oaxaca R (1981) Identification of supplier-induced demand in the health care sector. J Hum Resources 16:327–343

Barer ML, Evans RG, Labelle R (1986) Fee controls as cost controls: evidence from the frozen north. Milbank Mem Fund Q 66 (1):1–64

Berry C, Brewster JA, Held PJ, Kehrer B, Manheim L, Reinhardt U (1978) A study on the responses of Canadian physicians to the introduction of universal medical care insurance: the first five years in Québec, project report 78–09. Mathematica Policy Research

Campbell DT, Stanley JC (1963) Experimental and quasi-experimental designs for research. Houghton Mifflin, Boston

Contandriopoulos AP, Fournier MA, Lemay A (1986) Choix dur lieu de pratique: attitudes des médecins résidents et internes due Québec. GRIS, University of Montreal, Montreal

Contandriopoulos AP, Lemay A, Tessier G, Champagne F (1989) Modalités de financement et contrôle des coûts du système de soins: l'exemple du Québec. Sci Soc Santé 7(4):113–137

Contandriopoulos AP, Champagne F, Pineault R (1990) Systèmes de soins et modalités de rémunération. Soc Travail 1:95–115

Direction Générale des Programmes des Services Sociaux, Service de l'Evaluation, (1980) La répartition territoriale des médecins omnipracticiens, des dentistes et des médecins spécialistes

Eisenberg J, Kabcenell A (1988) Organized practice and the quality of medical care. Inquiry 25 (1):561–589

Evans RG (1974) Supplier-induced demand: some empirical evidence and implications. In: Perlman M (ed) The economics of health care and medical care. Wiley, New York, pp 163–173

Feldman R, Sloan FA (1988) Competition among physicians, revisited. J Health Polit Policy Law 13:239–261

Feldman R, Sloan FA (1988) Reply from Feldman and Sloan. J Health Polit Policy Law, 14(3):621–623

Gabel JR, Rice T (1985) Reducing public expenditures for physician services: the price of paying less. J Health Polit Policy Law 9(4):595–609

Green J (1978) Physician-induced demand for medical care. J Hum Resources 13 [Suppl]

Holahan J, Hadley J, Scanlon W, Lee R, Bluck J (1979) Paying for physician services under Medicare and Medicaid. Milbank Mem Fund Q 57(2):183–211

Lomas J, Fooks C, Rice T, Labelle RG (1989) Paying physicians in Canada: minding our Ps and Qs. Health Aff 8:80–102

Maddala GS (1977) Econometrics. McGraw-Hill, New York

McCarthy T (1985) The competitive nature of the primary care services market. J Health Econ 4(2):93–117

Mitchell JB (1984) Why do women physicians work fewer hours than men physicians? Inquiry 21:361–368
Pauly MV (1980) Doctors and their workshops. University of Chicago Press, Chicago
Phelps RG (1986) Induced demand – can we ever know its extent. J Health Econ 5:356–365
Reinhardt U (1978) Comment on Sloan FA and Feldman R competition among physicians. In: Greenberg W (ed) Competition in the health care sector: past, present and future. Aspen Systems, Germantown
Rice T (1984) Physician initiated demand for medical care: new evidence from the Medicare program. Adv Health Econ Health Serv Res 5:129–160
Rice T, Labelle RG (1988) Do physicians induce demand for medical services? J Health Polit Policy Law 14(3):587–625
Rochaix L, Largeron C (1989) Facteurs economiques et pratique médicale au Québec: vers un budget global en ambulatoire. Sci Soc Santé VII(2):45–65
Sloan FA, Feldman R (1978) Competition among physicians. In: Greenberg W (ed) Competition in the health care sector: past, present, and future. Aspen Systems, Germantown
Stano M, (1987) A clarification of theories and evidence on supplier-induced demand for physicians' services. J Hum Res 22(4):611–622
Stano M, Cromwell J, Velky J, Saad J (1985) The effects of physician availability on fees and the demand for doctors' services, Atlantic Econ J 51–60
Van Doorslaer E, Geurts J (1987) Supplier-induced demand for physiotherapy in the Netherlands. Soc Sci Med 24(11):919–925
Wedig G, Mitchell J, Cromwell J (1989) Can price controls induce optimal physician behaviour? J Health Polit Policy Law 14(3):601–620
Wilensky G, Rossiter L (1983) The relative importance of physician-induced demand in the demand for medical care. Milbank Memorial Fund Q 61:252–277
Wilkins R (1985) Données sur la pauvreté dans la région métropolitaine de Montréal. Research Surfacing the Poor. June 1985

Redefining Incentives in Primary Medical Care: The Finnish Demonstration Project

M. Pekurinen, I. Vohlonen, and H. Sintonen

Introduction

How best to organize primary health care services within a publicly operated health system has remained an unresolved question. Despite continuing emphasis in northern Europe upon the primary care as the backbone of an equitable and efficient health care system, there are divergent views as to how primary care should be organized, delivered and remunerated, in particular with regard to general practitioners (GPs).

In Finland, most GPs are salaried employees of the municipal government, with offices in publicly operated health centres serving a geographically defined population. Some GPs also maintain a supplemental private practice.

In Finland, a Personal Doctor Programme has recently been advocated to restructure the primary medical activities of GPs within publicly operated health centres (Vohlonen 1989) and to achieve the clinical advantages and performance incentives of enrolling each citizen on a specific GP's list, but within the broader team-based population responsibility of a health centre.

In order to develop a specific methodology to implement the personal doctor approach, and to explore the costs, effectiveness, efficiency and feasibility of extending it to the entire Finnish population by the early 1990s, a large demonstration project was launched in 1983 and implemented in 1986–1987. This paper reports the main results of an economic evaluation of the Personal Doctor Programme based on this demonstration project.

Background of the Demonstration Project

In the 1960s and early 1970s, the Finnish health care system was very much dominated by the hospital sector. With the enactment of the 1972 Public Health Act, a national planning and state subsidy system for municipal health services was introduced with the explicit goal of developing primary care. Over the subsequent 15 years, this planning and resource allocation process, coupled with the consolidation of non-acute inpatient, clinic care, maternal and child health, and school health activities into health centres, had increased the range and capacity of public primary medical and health services in Finland (Pekurinen et al. 1987).

In the early 1980s, discussions started about restructuring the GPs' role within health centres. Until then, GPs provided services in a variety of separate, vertically administered programmes, often with few links between them, in a service model that in larger cities resembled the early industrial assembly line. While patients received the designated clinical or preventive services, only in the most rural locations would they meet the same GP regularly enough to develop a personal relationship. For the physician, this absence of specified patient responsibility led both, clinically, to less rounded knowledge of the patients' overall situation, and, personally, to a sense of detachment from the patients being served. Both of these outcomes were associated with increasing GP job dissatisfaction (Piri and Vohlonen 1987).

A personal doctor programme was conceived as a way to reduce the organization-caused aspects of these problems. By restructuring primary medical services so that one particular physician becomes the provider of all primary medical services to a patient, policymakers hoped to move from an episodic approach to a more holistic framework for patient care. In 1983, the Ministry of Social Affairs and Health established a steering committee to plan, implement, and evaluate a demonstration project based on the personal doctor concept.

Public health centre as well as private GPs were included, reflecting the relatively high levels of private ambulatory care delivered within the larger Finnish cities. The demonstration project's character also reflected a variety of structural constraints within the public salary and private sector reimbursement systems, as well as the formal responsibilities of the municipal board of health.

Implementation of the Demonstration Project

The demonstration project was planned in 1984–1985 and implemented in 1986–1987 in the four largest cities in Finland. Population panels (total of 165 000 inhabitants), 15 health stations (of which 6 were private physician practices) and 67 GPs (51 public and 16 private) were selected for the demonstration. To ensure comparability, these panels were balanced in terms of age, sex, social characteristics and travel distance to health centres of the populations. An additional 24 GPs working in similar health stations and with similar population panels were selected as a control group to represent the traditional public health centre delivery system.

To assess the impact of different financial incentives, three separate organizational models were designed. Two of the models focused on the publicly operated health centres, while the third was designed for use by the private group practices. The three models differed largely in terms of the physician remuneration system. From the patients' view, all three models were free of charge and designed to be equal in terms of the availability, accessibility and content of services.

Model 1 focused on the list-based reorganization of primary medical functions within public health centres without any alteration of the fixed salary system for GPs. Model 2 involved both the reorganization of primary medical functions and an alteration of the physician salary system within public health centres. The new salary framework had three components: a basic allowance for education and experience, a capitation allowance reflecting the size and age/sex composition of the list of citizens and a coverage allowance reflecting percentage of total list seen during a specified period.

Model 3 focused on the provision of primary medical functions by private GPs, fully funded (unlike most private practice in Finland) by the Social Insurance Institution and administered by the municipal board of health. Private GPs were reimbursed according to the same three components as were public GPs in model 2, with additional amounts to cover costs incurred by auxiliary medical personnel. The distribution of enrolled population among the three models is shown in Table 1.

Table 1. Size of population, mean list size and numbers of doctors by the model in the demonstration of the personal doctor programme

	Model 1	Model 2	Model 3	Total
Size of population	78 402	46 697	39 951	165 050
Mean list size	2 529	2 335	2 497	2 463
Number of doctors	31	20	16	67

Methodology and Results of the Evaluation

General Methodology

The purpose of the evaluation was to assess the impact of the three alternative organizational models on the content, delivery, costs and effectiveness of GP services during the 1986–1987 demonstration period. Given the scope of the demonstration project, the evaluation was designed to cover organizational, administrative and financial consequences as perceived by the various participants: citizens, patients, physicians, auxiliary primary medical and primary health workers, administrators, and local and national public health officials. The assessments were made by a before-after design of the three experimental models and a control model. The three alternative models were compared with each other as well as with the traditional health centre delivery system. To ensure adequate coverage of evaluation, a wide variety of observation units and methods of data collection were used (Table 2).

Here we present in summary form the methodology and central findings on costs and effectiveness of the demonstration project.

Table 2. Integration of the units of observation and methods in the evaluation of the personal doctor programme

Unit of observation (Approximate number of observations)	Method
Population (200 000)	Surveys Registers of visits Hospital discharge data
Patients (130 000)	Surveys Interviews Registers of visits
Visits (390 000)	ICPC register Observations Audit
Doctors (100)	Survey Interviews Registers of work and payment
Personnel (800)	Surveys Interviews Observations
Station (20)	Survey Annual reports Observations

Cost Analysis

The primary aim of the cost analysis was to examine the economic impact of different financial incentives on GP's services. Costs of the services were analysed extensively. The costs were evaluated in terms of the direct costs (payment, social security, etc.) of GPs' labour and administration (GPs' office, auxiliary staff, equipment, etc.) as well as the indirect costs of practice (laboratory examinations, prescriptions, referrals, etc.). Costs were standardized for patients' age, sex and diagnosis. Sensitivity analyses were performed to examine how sensitive the obtained results were to the "prices" and quantities used. The final cost analysis was performed for the 2nd year of the experiment, which was assumed to reflect established personal doctor practice and hence the long-term economic effects of the system as compared with the traditional system.

Direct Costs. Detailed instructions for allocating the direct costs for each GP on a uniform basis were designed for the participating health centres. Health centres collected and reported GPs' labour costs monthly and other direct costs annually. The Social Insurance Institution collected similar data on participating private GPs on a monthly basis.

Direct costs per GP were clearly lower in the experimental models than in the control model (Table 3). Direct costs per visit were lowest in model 3

Table 3. Direct costs per doctor by the model in the personal doctor programme in 1987 (Finnish markka per doctor per year)

	Control	Model 1	Model 2	Model 3
GP's salary	160 888	150 733	170 552	181 669
Other direct costs	305 294	224 651	251 430	207 249
Total direct costs per doctor	466 182	375 384	421 982	388 918
Index (control = 100)	100	81	91	83

Table 4. Direct costs per visit by models in the personal doctor programme in 1987 (Finnish markka per visit)

	Control	Model 1	Model 2	Model 3
GP's salary	49.22	59.53	55.35	62.61
Other direct costs	93.39	88.73	81.60	71.42
Total costs per visit	142.61	148.26	136.95	134.03
Index (control = 100)	100	104	96	94

and highest in model 1 (Table 4). However, the cost difference between the models were small.

Indirect Costs. Evaluation of the indirect costs was based on a sample of visits ($N = 16\,000$) on which detailed quantitative information on examinations, prescriptions, referrals, etc. was collected with a uniform follow-up system specifically designed for the purpose [ICPC register (Aro et al. 1986)]. In order to cost laboratory and X-ray examinations and prescriptions a special stratified sample, representing all cities and models in the programme, was drawn from the ICPC register. All the prescriptions and examinations referred to patients in the sample were scrutinized from patient case records by specialists and costed accordingly.

Referrals to specialist, health centre ward, hospital and physiotherapy were costed using the best available information on relevant average costs assuming equal average costs for all the models. The costs covered only those resulting from the first visit to a specialist or hospital outpatient clinic, but not the costs of hospital inpatient care. It was assumed that GPs cannot influence the follow-up visits to specialist or the decision to admit a patient to hospital.

Table 5. Content of care, age, sex and diagnosis standardized in physician visits 1986 and 1987 according to the ICPC register by study group ($N = 16\,001$)

Treatment (% of patients) (STR)	Control	Model 1	Model 2	Model 3
Laboratory	27.7	24.9	25.5	19.3
examination	100	90	93	68
X-ray or ultrasound (%)	12.4	8.9	10.0	11.5
examinations	100	72	81	91
ECG and other	9.2	6.7	6.7	4.2
electrographic examinations	100	71	71	44
Therapeutic	2.6	3.4	3.9	3.5
discussions	100	124	150	129
Referral to	21.5	28.8	29.0	26.8
same doctor in short period	100	134	137	116
Referral to	4.0	3.7	3.2	1.1
another doctor in short period	100	95	80	25
Referral to	2.9	1.5	4.1	5.2
a specialist (other than GP)	100	52	145	204
Referral to general	5.3	5.7	3.7	2.8
hospital	100	108	68	51
N	4058	5108	3455	3380

STR, standardized treatment ratios (control = 100).

Table 5 suggests that the treatment behaviour of physicians had changed considerably, reflecting the greater continuity of care fostered by the personal doctor approach. The greatest improvements were observed within models 2 and 3.

The indirect costs per visit were about one-third lower in the experimental models than in the control model (Table 6). The cost difference between the models is mainly due to different referral patterns to health centre wards and physiotherapy. Referrals to health centre ward have the greatest impact on the costs. If they are left out the cost difference between the experimental models and the control model is reduced to 10%. If referrals to physiotherapy are also left out the cost difference falls to 6%.

Improved continuity of care in the experimental models may have induced GPs to scrutinize referrals to health centre wards more closely than in the traditional system. It is likely that this reflects a genuine change in GPs' referral behaviour and not just an artifact produced by the follow-up study as a similar change was not observed in the control model.

Table 6. Indirect costs per visit standardized for age, sex and diagnosis by models in the personal doctor programme in 1987 (Finnish markka per visit)

	Control	Model 1	Model 2	Model 3
Laboratory Tests	46.42	34.16	45.29	37.63
Microbiological/ immunological test	4.96	4.46	4.13	3.94
Blood test	32.96	21.68	32.37	25.09
Urine test	6.73	6.07	6.89	5.52
Faeces test	0.29	0.40	0.45	0.30
Histological, etc. test	1.13	1.20	1.20	2.32
Other laboratory test	0.35	0.35	0.35	0.45
X-ray or ultrasound examination	20.39	17.40	21.05	35.39
Other Examinations	9.73	4.53	5.44	6.03
Physical function test	1.61	0.27	0.80	0.40
ECG and other electrographic examination	8.13	4.26	4.63	5.63
Prescriptions	63.05	65.51	61.79	67.38
Referrals	296.20	116.74	188.07	129.16
Physiotherapy	54.52	39.73	53.59	33.26
Specialist	3.75	1.95	7.65	7.05
Health centre ward	208.27	44.63	104.13	74.38
District or central hospital Outpatient clinic	29.42	30.02	21.61	14.41
Home care	0.24	0.36	0.84	0.00
Social worker	0.00	0.06	0.25	0.06
Total indirect costs per visit	435.79	238.34	321.64	275.59
Index (control = 100)	100	55	74	63

Total Costs Per Visit. Performance of the GPs in the experimental models was clearly more economical than in the control model (Table 7). Total cost per visit was on average 28% lower in the experimental models than in the control model. The bulk of the costs were due to referrals and prescriptions. Indirect costs accounted for 67%–75% of the total costs. GPs salary accounted for 15% of the total costs in the experimental models. Sensitivity analyses performed did not significantly alter the relative cost differences between the experimental models and the control model nor between the experimental models.

Total Costs Per List. Costs per GP's list were estimated for a standard population of 2000, generating 4000 GP visits in a year. Four estimates were derived for each of the models based on different assumptions about the percentage of all visits made to the personal doctor, referred to as success rate below. In the basic option it was assumed that all visits are made to the personal doctor. In alternative options utilization of parallel services was accounted for and only some of the visits were assumed to be made to the personal doctor (Table 8). The estimation method allowed for the flexible reimbursement system applied in models 2 and 3.

Potential economic gains from the personal doctor programme appear substantial (Table 9). The economic gains are an increasing function of the success rate of the programme. If the success rate of the personal doctor

Table 7. Costs per visit standardized for age, sex and diagnosis by models in the personal doctor programme in 1987 (Finnish markka)

	Control	Model 1	Model 2	Model 3
Direct costs per visit	142.61	148.26	136.95	134.03
Indirect costs per visit	435.79	238.34	321.64	275.59
Total costs per visit	578.40	386.60	458.59	409.62
Index (control = 100)	100	67	79	71

Table 8. Estimated costs of a personal doctor programme in a population of 2000 inhabitants by models with various assumptions about the success rate of the programme (million Finnish markka)

	Control	Model 1	Model 2	Model 3
Success rate 18%	2.12	1.96	2.03	1.99
Success rate 32%	2.12	1.84	1.97	1.89
Success rate 35%	2.12	1.81	1.95	1.87
Success rate 100%	2.12	1.25	1.65	1.41

Table 9. Estimated cost savings of implementation of the personal doctor programme in a population of 2000 compared with the traditional primary medical care system (Finnish markka)

	Cost savings	
	FIM	%
Success rate 18%	120 000	6
Success rate 32%	220 000	10
Success rate 35%	240 000	11
Success rate 100%	680 000	32

programme is 18%–35% it was estimated that 6%–11% of the resources used in the traditional health centre system could be saved or released for other uses. These estimates exclude the costs of hospital inpatient care. Assuming that every fourth patient referred to the hospital outpatient clinic is admitted to hospital, about 8%–12% of the resources could be saved.

Effectiveness

Several measures were used to get a rough idea about the quality and effectiveness of care in various models.

Quality of GP's Performance. Patient surveys of the reference population at the beginning of the demonstration indicated that the most commonly perceived problem of primary medical services was lack of empathy on the part of physicians. The quality of GP's performance was measured in personal interviews by asking the patients, to what extent they perceived service readiness, polite behaviour, clinical competence and empathic attitude among the GPs. The results in Table 10 indicate that there were no major differences in the perceived quality of GP's performance between the models. However,

Table 10. Perceived quality of GP's performance during the most recent visit in 1987 according to patient interview surveys by study groups

Performance is good (% of patients)	Control	Model 1	Model 2	Model 3
Service readiness	81.8	80.9	87.8	91.6
Polite behaviour	86.5	85.5	88.7	95.0
Clinical competence	71.4	78.2	79.1	78.2
Empathic attitude	70.8	76.4	74.8	81.4
N	198	108	117	128

in terms of clinical competence and empathic attitude, there seems to be a slight tendency to the advantage of the experimental models.

Patient Satisfaction. Before the experiment, about 60%–65% of the patients were very satisfied with the visits to the GP. During the experiment in 1987, this proportion was 72% in the control model and about 75%–87% in the experimental models – again a small tendency to their advantage.

Quality of Treatment Process. The quality of treatment process was assessed by using a medical audit-type approach based on patient interviews, medical records and laboratory tests. Hypertension and old-age diabetes were used as tracer diseases in the assessment. The preliminary results suggest that the treatment given in the experimental models was at least equally good in quality as that in the control model.

Health Status and Health-Related Quality of Life. Three methods were used to measure how the health status and health-related quality of life of the patients in various models changed over a certain period. First, the patients visiting a GP in August 1987 were given a self-administered questionnaire of a generic 15-dimensional measure of health-related quality of life (15D). The dimensions included were moving, intellectual or mental functioning, seeing, hearing, eating, communicating, sleeping, breathing, eliminating, working, social participation, depression, distress, pain and perceived health. Each dimension was divided into four to five discrete levels or descriptive statements, by which more or less of the attribute was identified [(Sintonen and Pekurinen 1988, 1989), for an earlier 12-dimensional measure, see Sintonen (1981) and Mooney (1986)].

The dimensions and their levels form an enormous number of combinations or profiles – states of health-related quality of life. A value component attached to the states is scaled so that the "best" state receives a value of 1 and the "worst" (being dead) a value of 0. The derivation of the value component is based on an assumption that the value of a state for an individual is a function of (a) the value he or she places on the level of each dimension and (b) the relative importance or weight he or she attaches to each dimension. If an additive aggregation rule is assumed, the value of state H for individual i is thus

$$v_H^i = \sum_j^m I_j^i \, w_j^i (x_j)$$

where I_j^i = a positive constant for the jth dimension, representing the relative importance the individual attaches to it (j = 1,2,..., m), and

$w_j(x_j)$ = a numerical function on the jth dimension, representing the value the individual places on various levels on the dimension.

The individual is thus faced with a two-stage valuation task. The value component applied in this study was based on the average values elicited by a magnitude method from a sample of 80 hospital inpatients.

In August 1987, a 15D score was determined for 1815 patients. A new 15D questionnaire was sent in March 1988 to about 1700 of them (about 100 did not give their address in the first round), of which, a follow-up 15D score could be calculated for 1231 patients. The three major reasons for dropout were refusal, change of address and death. The final sample consisted of only 611 patients, about whom we know their 15D score both in August 1987 and in March 1988 as well as the model they belonged to. However, the final sample did not differ from the total original sample of 1815 patients in terms of gender mix, average age or average 15D score in August 1987.

Second, the subjects were asked to assess both in August 1987 and in March 1988 their overall health status on a 0–100 ratio scale, where a score of 100 represented complete health. The final sample now consisted of 542 patients with data on their overall assessment in both points of time and the model they belonged to.

Third, in March 1988 the subjects were requested to assess whether their health status was now better, similar or worse than in August 1987, when they visited a GP and when the first measurements were made.

Table 11 shows the average changes in 15D score and overall assessment between August 1987 and March 1988. In August 1987, the average 15D score in the different models varied between 0.86000 and 0.9095, but the differences were not significant. By March 1988, there was on average a small improvement in the 15D score in all models, but the differences in the improvements between the models were not statistically significant.

The average overall assessment in August 1987 in the different models varied between 0.6529 and 0.7481, but the differences were not significant. Apart from model 1, there was on average a small improvement in the assessment by March 1988, but the average changes between the models were

Table 11. Average change in the patients' 15D score and overall assessment between August 1987 and March 1988 by models (SD in parentheses)

	Control	Model 1	Model 2	Model 3
Change in 15D score	0.0095 (0.0819)	0.0003 (0.0762)	0.0013 (0.0719)	0.0057 (0.0686)
N	134	210	122	145
Change in overall assessment	0.0397 (0.1868)	–0.0061 (0.1962)	0.0143 (0.2152)	0.0123 (0.1972)
N	114	180	109	139

not statistically significant. The correlation between the 15D scores and overall assessments was 0.698 in August and 0.753 in March.

Although there are no significant differences in the average changes between the models, changes at the individual level might still be significant, for example, due to possible differences in the patient characteristics. In order to check this, variation in the individual changes was explained by the following simple regression model:

$$y = a_0 + a_1S + a_2A + a_3L + a_4M_1 + a_5M_2 + a_6M_3 + e$$

where y = change in patient's 15D score or overall assessment between August 1987 and March 1988,
S = patient's sex (female = 1),
A = patient's age,
L = patient's initial 15D score or overall assessment in August 1987,
$M1, M2, M3$ = dummy variable for models 1, 2 and 3 (e.g. M1 = 1, if the patient belongs to model 1, otherwise 0),
$a_1, \ldots, a_6$ = parameters to be estimated, and
e = residual term.

It is assumed that the change in the individual's 15D score or overall assessment is primarily explained by his or her age, sex and state at the beginning of the study period. If, after controlling for these variables, the change in the state of the patients of an experimental model (1, 2, or 3) differs essentially from that of the control model, the regression coefficient of the model dummy should deviate significantly from 0.

Table 12. Regression coefficients and their *t*-values of he models explaining the individual variation in the change of 15D scores and overall assessments

Variable	Model for 15D score Coefficient	*t* value	Model for overall assessments Coefficient	*t* value
Constant	0.2807	8.82	0.5336	12.40
Sex (*S*)	0.0020	0.33	–0.0167	1.04
Age (*A*)	–0.0009	5.98	–0.0037	9.11
Initial level (*L*)	–0.2602	8.46	–0.0044	11.73
Model 1 (*M1*)	–0.0062	0.80	–0.0376	1.79
Model 2 (*M2*)	–0.0081	0.92	–0.0324	1.38
Model 3 (*M3*)	0.0006	0.07	–0.0184	0.82
R^2	0.116		0.235	
F	13.159		27.240	
df	(6,601)		(6,533)	

Table 13. Percentage of patients who regarded their health status in March 1988 as better than, similar to or worse than in August 1987

	Better	Similar	Worse	Total
Control	13.2	62.0	24.8	100.0
Model 1	15.9	57.7	26.4	100.0
Model 2	13.0	64.2	22.8	100.0
Model 3	24.3	54.9	20.8	100.0
Total	16.7	59.3	24.0	100.0
$\chi^2 = 9.49$	df = 6			

The explanatory power of both models, although rather modest in absolute terms, is highly significant in the light of the *F* test (Table 12). In addition to the constant term, age and initial state are the only variables whose coefficients differ significantly from 0. This also implies that in none of the experimental models do the changes in health status and health-related quality of life deviate significantly from those in the control model.

This result is also affirmed by Table 13, which shows the distribution of patients by models with respect to felt change in health status between August 1987 and March 1988. The distributions do not differ significantly from each other.

All three methods of measuring changes in health status and health-related quality of life consistently suggest that no different development took place in these respects in the various models during the period under study. Strictly taken the changes in the state of patients cannot be equated with the effectiveness of the models and care given in them – the study design simply leaves most of the threats to internal validity uncontrolled. More reliable conclusions would imply more detailed data on what has happened to the patients between the measurements, what and how much care they have received and how many resources have been devoted to their care.

Job Satisfaction. In general, all personnel groups in the experimental models reported an improvement in their overall job satisfaction. The greatest improvement was observed among GPs in model 2. This may also be reflected in a considerably reduced sickness absenteeism of the personnel observed in all experimental models. However, in one respect the GPs in all three models experienced an increased job dissatisfaction, namely due to psychological stress associated with the increased dependence of patients.

Policy Implications of the Demonstration Project

Three key conclusions can be drawn from the personal doctor demonstration project which may be of particular interest to policymakers in publicly operated health systems. First, the level of both patient and staff satisfaction showed overall improvement in all three models of the personal doctor programme. The demonstration also suggests that reorganizing primary medical services on a personal doctor basis is capable of improving the quality of care within health-centre-based delivery systems.

Second, costs per visit and per list were clearly lower in the experimental models than in the control model. On the other hand, the quality and effectiveness of care in the experimental models were at least as good as in the control model, in some respects better. Taken together, these results imply that the personal doctor approach may be more productive and efficient than the traditional health centre delivery system.

Third, publicly employed GPs are at least as productive and efficient as private GPs when given the same performance incentives by an equivalently structured reimbursement framework. This suggests that, contrary to recent conventional wisdom, public GPs can provide as high quality and as cost-effective patient care as private GPs once the impediments created by inappropriately bureaucratic administrative structures have been eliminated.

In Finland, the results of the evaluation have led to specific policy proposals to the national government. First, the appropriateness of the 1985 policy decision to extend the personal doctor programme to the entire Finnish population in the early 1990s has been reaffirmed and reinforced. Second, a three-part physician remuneration system, similar to that employed in models 2 and 3, has now been proposed as the basis for all public GPs' remuneration.

Perhaps needless to say, the results of an evaluation like this should be viewed cautiously, and that is what we have tried to do. It has not been possible to assess the long-term impacts of the personal doctor programme, which might differ from the short-term effects reported here. It is also hard to say to what extent the results are specific to Finnish society and whether they can be generalized to other societies.

References

Aro S, Hagman E, Vohlonen I (1986) Kansainvälinen perusterveydenhuollon luokitusjärjestelmä lääkärissäkäyntien tarkastelussa. Suom Lääkäril 32:3050–3056

Mooney GH (1986) Economics, medicine and health care. Wheatsheaf, Brighton

Pekurinen M, Vohlonen I, Häkkinen U (1987) Reallocation of resources in favour of primary health care: the case of Finland. World Health Stat Q 40(4):313–325

Piri P, Vohlonen I (1987) Työtyytyväisyys avosairaanhoidon henkilökunan keskuudessa. Sosiaalilääk Aikak 24:287–296

Sintonen H (1981) An approach to measuring and valuing health states. Soc Sci Med 15C:55–65

Sintonen H, Pekurinen M (1988) 15D: A 15 dimensional measure of health. Health economists' study group meeting. Brunel University, July 18–20, 1988

Sintonen H, Pekurinen M (1989) 15D – Askel kohti yleistä terveyteen liittyvän eläämäänlaadun mittaria. Sosiaalilääk Aikak 26:85–96

Vohlonen I (ed) (1989) Personal doctor program: data, results, and conclusion of the Finnish study. National Board of Health, Helsinki, (publication no 50)

Hospital Financing in Spain: Incentives and Equity

M. Casas and E. Spagnolo

Introduction

In times of increasing economic restrictions on health services, the developed countries have adopted, in recent years, a wide range of measures oriented towards the containment of hospital expenditure, the most important fraction of health expenditure. Many authors have discussed the various hospital finance systems, showing the advantages and inconveniences and positive and/or negative incentives of each that require systems of control. However, it seems generally accepted that there is a close relationship between costs incurred by a hospital, and the type and volume of patients which it treats (case mix).

The level of development reached by instruments for measuring case mix, and especially the application of the diagnosis-related groups (DRGs) as a form of payment for hospital admissions by Medicare in the United States (Schweicker 1983), have supplied new elements to the debate surrounding hospital financing. The payment for hospital inpatients based on a fixed charge per hospital day, traditional in Spain, continues to evolve, although with certain corrections intended to lessen the inconveniences of this system.

A number of different tariffs are in use, usually determined in a way that reflects hospital structure, and which try to recognize the differences in hospital complexity, theoretically related to the case mix attended to by each hospital. In Catalonia, the Catalonian Institute of Health (ICS) fixes a range of tariffs per Basic Unit of Care (UBA), equivalent to 1 day of hospitalization, but at the same time specifies a maximum value for hospital average length of stay (LOS), and a maximum number of UBAs/year. The first of these limits is intended to correct for the stimulus to prolong LOS, implicitly contained in the payment system, and thus to optimize economic return.

In spite of an abundance of literature concerning the good and bad aspects of this system, in the absence of sufficiently detailed information about hospital production it has not been possible to assess these theoretical criticisms. Now that the description of case mix differences in Catalonian hospitals is possible, we may compare these case mix differences with those produced by a range of theoretical models of hospital financing. DRGs, described elsewhere (Fetter et al. 1980), have been used to measure case mix, as they had been previously validated in local data bases.

Objectives

Diagnosis-related group based information from five hospitals has been obtained, and all these hospitals are treated as a single multihospital system, for the purposes of presenting a theoretical exercise permitting an approximation to the potential impact of four different hospital financing models. The objective is to analyse differences in economic distributions between the five hospitals, produced by four theoretical models for the financing of hospital inpatient services, and to compare them with the observed case mix differences.

Materials and Methods

The data base used consists of all hospital discharges from five general hospitals in Catalonia during 1987, with a total of 58 259 records. The data were processed by microcomputer, using dBaseIII, Epiinfo and SPSS. For the grouping into DRGs, the Grouper PC software, version 3.0 (1985), from the University of Yale was used. The five hospitals included are all general hospitals, three of them in the city of Barcelona, and the remaining two in nearby cities. The size of hospital varies from 151 to 929 beds. For the economic distribution among hospitals, four models were used:

Model 1. Payment per hospital day with tariffs differentiated according to levels. The tariff corresponding to that fixed by the ICS in 1987 was taken for each hospital, and varied from 11 595 to 18 700 pesetas.

Model 2. Payment per day of stay with a single tariff used for all the hospitals. The tariff taken was the weighted mean per hospital day based on the total budget employed in 1987 for inpatient treatment in these hospitals.

Model 3. Payment per patient. Patients were classified by means of the DRGs. In the absence of information on costs per DRG, the average LOS was used as an estimate of the cost, parameters which other authors have demonstrated to be well correlated (Luke 1979).

The combined set of five hospitals for which data are available is used as the standard to obtain relative weights per DRG. The relative weight per DRG is obtained as the ratio between average LOS for each DRG and the global average LOS in the standard. This therefore represents the relative average LOS of each DRG with respect to the global average LOS in the standard.

Model 4. Payment per case using a relative weight per DRG according to costs. In the absence of cost information per DRG in our environment, the relative weights taken were those used by Medicare in 1988 (U.S. Federal Register). They express the relative cost of each DRG as a fraction of the mean global cost.

The total amount obtained with model 1 is distributed among the five hospitals according to the other three models. The four percentage distributions resulting are compared by means of a chi-square and a pearsonian correlation. The mean charge per patient in each hospital is calculated according to each model, and the relative average charge per patient resulting in each hospital with the different models. Case mix is described by means of a case mix index: the ratio between the average LOS that a hospital would have had were it to treat its patients in each DRG with the average LOS of the standard, and the average LOS of the standard.

Given that the use of the available set of data as the standard could cause problems due to its small size and the different weight of each hospital within the set, we have also calculated the case mix index using 1985 hospital discharge data from Maryland. Using model 1, resultant average charges have been calculated for certain high volume DRGs. These charges were then adjusted for the average LOS and average tariff per hospital day of the global data base, in order to see the effect of these two factors on the final resultant charge per hospital. To achieve more robust estimates of the average LOS after such adjustment, we first excluded those cases with a length of stay which exceeded a certain value (determined as the third quartile plus 1.5 times the absolute difference between the first and third quartiles).

Results

The resulting percentage of economic distribution among the five hospitals according to the four financing models is shown in Fig 1. The maximum differences are found between model 1 and the others. Table 1 shows the ratios between the economic percentage attributed to each hospital with the different models. As an example it should be interpreted as follows: hospital A would get 1.10 times more budget with model 2 than with model 1, or 10% more; 5% more with model 3 and 5% less with model 4. A chi-squared test of the distribution across the five hospitals, comparing the models in pairs, shows significant differences in all cases. Using the p levels, the pairs of models can be ordered from greatest to least similarity as follows:

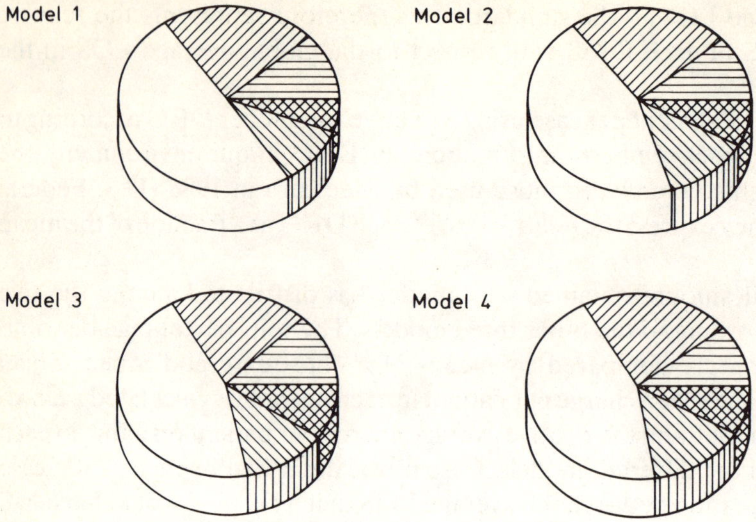

Fig. 1. Percentage economical distribution in five hospitals according to four theoretical models

1. Model 3 – Model 4: $p < 8 \times 10^{-8}$
2. Model 2 – Model 4: $p < 6.2 \times 10^{-8}$
3. Model 2 – Model 3: $p < 5.8 \times 10^{-8}$
4. Model 1 – Model 4: $p < 2.9 \times 10^{-8}$
5. Model 1 – Model 3: $p < 9 \times 10^{-11}$
6. Model 1 – Model 2: $p < 3 \times 10^{-15}$

Table 2 presents Pearson correlation coefficients between the four models, the values being close to 1 ($p < 0.001$) in all cases. Models 1 and 2 are the most similar, as expected, since both are related to the number of hospital days. Following on, the next most closely correlated are models 3 and 4, both of which are per case payment models. Model 1 shows successively decreasing correlations with model 3 and model 4 respectively.

Table 3 shows the average payment per patient obtained for each hospital according to the four models. Table 4 presents the relative charges corresponding to the values in Table 3; it can be seen that the variations from one model to another are very different depending on the hospital, a fact which is also evident in Table 1.

Table 5 presents the case mix indices for the five hospitals, according to two standards. In both cases the same hospitals turn out to be more or less as complex as the standard, although there are some small differences between the two series. The case mix indices using global average LOS as the standard

Table 1. Differences between percentage economic distribution in five hospitals according to four theoretical models

	Model 1 Per hospital day, charge/level	2 Per hospital day single charge	3 Per case DRG weighted by LOS	4 Per case DRG weighted by Medicare costs
Model 1 Per hospital day, × charge/level				
A	1	1.10	1.05	0.95
B	1	0.96	0.90	0.94
C	1	0.91	0.91	0.92
D	1	1.20	1.18	1.26
E	1	1.41	1.75	1.64
Model 2 Per Hospital day, single charge				
A	0.91	1	0.96	0.86
B	1.04	1	0.94	0.98
C	1.10	1	1.00	1.01
D	0.83	1	0.98	1.05
E	0.71	1	1.24	1.16
Model 3 Per case DRG weighted by LOS				
A	0.95	1.04	1	0.90
B	1.11	1.06	1	1.04
C	1.09	0.99	1	1.00
D	0.85	1.02	1	1.07
E	0.57	0.80	1	0.94
Model 4 Per case DRG weighted by Medicare costs				
A	1.06	1.16	1.11	1
B	1.07	1.02	0.96	1
C	1.09	0.99	1.00	1
D	0.80	0.95	0.94	1
E	0.61	0.86	1.07	1

Table 2. Pearson correlation coefficients (*r*) among the four models

	Model			
Model	1	2	3	4
1	1.0	0.9997	0.9972	0.9965
2	–	1.0	0.9969	0.9969
3	–	–	1.0	0.9981
4	–	–	–	1.0

Table 3. Average payment per patient in five hospitals according to four financing models (pesetas)

	Model			
Hospital	1	2	3	4
A	174.539	195.197	187.353	168.424
B	203.460	198.596	186.496	194.574
C	206.187	183.856	184.794	185.398
D	127.733	156.002	153.051	163.675
E	97.139	139.615	173.735	162.528
Overall	179.718	179.718	179.718	179.718

Table 4. Relative mean payment per patient

	Model			
Hospital	1	2	3	4
A	0.97	1.09	1.05	0.94
B	1.13	1.10	1.04	1.08
C	1.15	1.02	1.03	1.03
D	0.71	0.87	0.85	0.91
E	0.54	0.78	0.97	0.90

Table 5. Case mix indexes with two standards: global for the five hospitals (*A*) and Maryland 1985 (*B*)

Hospital	A	B	A–B
A	1.05	1.09	–0.04
B	1.04	1.04	– .00
C	1.03	1.05	– .02
D	.85	.82	+ .03
E	.97	.99	– .02

give, logically, the same values as the indices obtained with model 3, so that in Table 4 this series can be compared with the other three.

Table 6 presents the mean actual charges per hospital obtained with model 1 for eight of the most common DRGs. Important differences can be seen, even in pathologies of low complexity. Thus, tonsillectomy (DRG 60), inguinal or femoral hernia (DRG 162) and appendectomy (DRG 167) (all are without complications and are for adult or young patients) show a range of charges from 1 to more than double.

Given that such charges are influenced by both average LOS and the specific tariffs of each hospital, results are presented with these charges standardized by both variables for two pathologies. In Tables 7 and 8 it can be seen that for DRGs 162 and 60 the differences found in payments could be due either to the average LOS produced in each hospital for these patients or to the tariffs which the hospitals receive.

Discussion

The four economic distribution models tested are conceptually different. Models 1 and 2 are based on a per diem basis and models 3 and 4 on payment per patient, according to two different estimates of the relative cost of each type of patient. The correlations among the four models confirm the greater

Table 6. Average payment of eight high volume DRGs (geometric means) in five hospitals

	Hospital				
DRG Label	A	B	C	D	E
039 Lens procedures with or without vitrectomy	108.025	127.038	146.608	126.126	–
060 Tonsillectomy and or adenoidectomy only, age 0–17	29. 204	19.636	29.172	27.163	11.595
088 Chronic obstructive pulmonary disease	173.734	167.506	135.762	159.159	80.237
098 Bronchitis and Asthma age 0–17	139.464	138.307	208.318	141.141	87.774
140 Angina pectoris	124.346	99.376	135.575	110.565	68.063
162 Inguinal and femoral hernia procedures age 18–69 without CC	112.346	99.376	135.575	110.565	68.063
167 Appendectomy without complicated principal diagnosis age <70 without CC	81.503	86.058	81.719	92.956	52.989
373 Vaginal delivery without complicating diagnoses	60.345	62.494	70.181	57.193	–

CC, Complications and/or comorbidities.

Table 7. Diagnosis-related group 162: inguinal and femoral hernia procedures, age 18–69 years, without complications or comorbidities (excluding outliers); Deviations of mean payments between hospitals and global differences (pesetas)

Hospital	Average payment[a]	Differences			
		Total	Average stay difference	Charge difference	Interaction
A	115.475	–11.884	1.833	–13.523	–194
B	103.645	–23.714	–26.172	3.094	–636
C	144.738	17.379	1.667	15.509	203
D	112.885	–14.474	10.502	–23.073	–1.903
E	71.193	–56.166	–25.005	–38.773	7.612
Overall	127.359	—	—	—	—

[a]Arithmetic mean.

Table 8. Diagnosis-related group 60: Tonsillectomy and/or adenoidectomy only, age 0–17 years, without complications or comorbidities (excluding outliers): Deviations of mean payments between hospitals and global differences (pesetas)

Hospital	Average payment[a]	Differences			
		Total	Average stay difference	Charge difference	Interaction
A	29.502	–837	2.668	–3.221	–284
B	20.490	–9.849	–10.335	737	–251
C	30.855	516	–2.834	3.695	–345
D	27.163	–3.176	2.834	–5.946	–64
E	11.595	–18.744	–13.669	–236	–4.161
Overall	119.605	—	—	—	—

[a]Arithmetic mean.

similarity between models 1 and 2, on the one hand, and between models 3 and 4 on the other. The difference between models 1 and 2 results from there being, for model 1, different tariffs for each hospital, whereas model 2 uses a single tariff.

The introduction of differential tariffs is an attempt to recognize the different costs incurred by the hospitals by virtue of their differing structural complexity, as an estimate of the range of complexity among patients treated. Both models implicitly invite prolongation of stay and the choice of pathologies with a lower intensity of resource consumption in order to optimize the economic gain from each admission. With tariffs scaled according to levels, differences are introduced in the incentives for each hospital. Those with higher tariffs, that is, the more complex hospitals, could attempt to maximize their income by treating less costly pathologies, generally the simpler ones.

In model 3 the relative cost is estimated by the relative average LOS per DRG with respect to the global average LOS. The average LOS can be regarded as a somewhat inexact estimate of cost, but has frequently been used following the demonstration of good correlation between the two variables by several authors (Luke 1979). Model 4 used the relative weights per DRG employed by Medicare (US Federal Register), which we assume to be an estimate of costs incurred in that environment. In both cases it is possible for there to be incentives for the choice of more profitable pathologies for each hospital, and for the minimization of resource consumption, and of average LOS. Besides, in this case, there will also be greater pressure on the relatively less efficient hospitals.

As we have seen, the models are different, and it is not therefore surprising that they yield different distributions. It is more interesting to analyse the type of differences yielded, and their relationship with the case mixes of the hospitals. Hospitals B and C optimize their income under model 1, hospital A under model 2, hospital E under model 3, and hospital D under model 4. This means that the hospitals with the more complex case mix (A, B and C) optimize their income with the models of payment per hospital day, and those with a case mix index below 1 (D and E) with systems of payment per patients, taking the case mix into account. Inspection of the differences yielded by the models compared pairwise reveals that models 3 and 4 appear to be the most similar, although there are some differences, notably for hospital A. Estimates according to relative weights of average LOS in the set of hospitals studied are, as it turns out, similar to those yielded by the relative weights used in the United States, thus showing that average LOS would be a good estimator of cost if the relative cost per DRG in our environment was similar to that in the United States.

Model 2, payment per day of stay at a flat rate for all hospitals, appears to bear a greater similarity to models 3 and 4, which take case mix into account, than to model 1, payment per day of stay with differential tariffs according to hospital structural complexity. These impressions, drawn from the inspection of the relative differences (Table 1) are confirmed by the gradation according to the levels of significance produced by the pairwise comparisons of the models using the chi-squared test, and by the rank of average charges per patient among hospitals according to the different models. In other words, payment through differential tariffs according to hospital complexity yields differences greater than those between case mix, in favour of the more complex hospitals.

Having derived the mean charges per patient in each hospital under each of the four models, and having obtained relative charges with respect to the global mean charge per patient, we observe that model 3 represents, in fact, the case mix index of the hospitals using as standard the average LOS per DRG in the global data base. Model 4 represents the case mix index that we would obtain using the pattern of relative weights employed by Medicare. Under both models, the major differences result for hospital A which experiences a reduction of 0.11 in its index, suggesting that this hospital ought to have a greater proportion of those DRGs associated with greater average LOS in the global data base, but which do not necessarily correspond to DRGs of elevated cost in the United States.

The repercussions, for the various hospitals, of the model used are not the same, hospitals C and E suffering the greater impact. Thus hospital C, which optimizes its income under model 1, would lose 8%–9% of its income with any of the other models; and hospital E would increase its income by between 64% and 75% if it were to be financed by one of the systems based on a per patient payment. An equal difference of 4% of the total budget available means different fractions for each hospital budget.

In order to evaluate the impact at another level, the mean charges are presented according to the various models for eight pathologies, some of which are surgical pathologies of low complexity but high volume. Notable variations can be seen between the hospitals, which exceed a ratio of 1:2 in several instances. From an analysis of deviations of actual payment for two surgical pathologies of low complexity, inguinal or femoral hernia, and tonsillectomy, one can glimpse all sorts of possibilities: hospitals which receive less payment for their greater efficiency (lower average LOS) such as hospital B for DRG 60; hospitals favoured by a higher tariff and their relative inefficiency (greater average LOS) such as hospital C for DRG 162; others with a low tariff that minimize the impact through a greater average LOS, such as hospital D for DRGs 60 and 162; and hospitals penalized by their tariff and at the same time by admission of short duration (hospital E for both DRGs).

The examples exhibited are cases of low complexity, as has been mentioned, and it is to be expected that the more complex hospitals would handle the more costly and complex pathologies. However, the repercussions will depend on the relative weight of these simpler pathologies in the total number of cases treated. For those hospitals included in the study, the percentage of patients with a relative average LOS in the global data base greater than 2.5, or a relative weight in Medicare of 3 or more, reaches only 3% in the highest case. In contrast, the proportion of patients in groups with a lower relative weights is similar in all the hospitals, and it is in these groups of low complexity that the greatest differences in income are seen when payment is per day of stay and with a range of tariff levels.

Several authors have shown differences between the costs of teaching hospitals and non-teaching ones, among which there are also differences of case mix. All concur with the finding that a few DRGs are responsible for the case mix differences between teaching and non-teaching hospitals. However, there are discrepancies in the results with regard to the role played by case mix in explaining the cost differences. Thompson et al. find that case mix explains 70% of the cost differences between teaching and non-teaching hospitals. Frick et al. find that case mix explains only 25% of the mean highest cost per case in teaching hospitals. And Garber et al. identify 12 DRGs that alone account for the greater part of the cost differences between teaching and non-teaching hospitals.

We may conclude that the various economic distribution models presented yield important differences in economic terms for the individual hospitals. At the same time, existing formulas for payment per day of stay with differential tariffs according to hospital structural complexity apparently favour those hospitals with the more complex case mix and penalize those with a simpler case mix in a manner more exaggerated than the actual case mix differences in themselves would suggest. Hospital complexity therefore appears to be a poor estimate of case mix complexity.

The foregoing refers to income received by the hospitals for admission of patients. It is clear that other hospital activities (accident and emergency services, outpatient services, etc.) represent an increasing proportion of the activity, and therefore of the evolution of costs incurred. On the other hand, differences in income are not synonymous with costs incurred by the hospitals.

All this points to the need for a major study of case mix differences, and their role in determining the costs incurred by the hospital. In our environment the lack of cost information, and the small number of hospitals with case mix data, makes it impossible to go much more deeply into an analysis of these differences. However, the need to contain costs, the impact on individual hospitals of financial options and the incentives for inefficiency in the actual payment system make this subject one of the most important for the improvement of hospital efficiency, and equity among hospitals. Similarly, the continual improvement of hospital information systems in Catalonia should support a major investigation in this field.

References

Fetter RB, Shin Y, Freeman JL, Averill RF, Thompson JD (1980) Case mix definition by diagnosis-related groups. Med Care 18:2 [Suppl]

Frick AP, Grisez-Martin S, Shwartz M (1985) Case mix and cost differences between teaching and non teaching hospitals. Med Care 23:4

Garber AM, Fuchs VR, Silverman JF (1984) Case mix costs and outcomes: differences between faculty and community services in a university hospital. N Engl J Med 310:1931
Luke RD (1979) Dimensions in hospital case mix measurement. Inquiry 16:38
Schweicker RS (1983) Report to Congress: Hospital Prospective Payment for Medicare. Washington DC; USPHHS 3
US Federal Register (1987) V 52, N 169, Sep 1
Thompson JD, Fetter RB, Shin Y (1978) One strategy for controlling cost in university teaching hospitals. Med Educ 53:167

Prevention and Compensation of Work-Related Injuries and Diseases in France: Contribution of Insurance Economics*

T. Schneider and F. Fagnani

Introduction

Economic analysis of occupational risk management deals with insurance economics and health economics. As regards occupational injuries and diseases, the primary aim of society must be prevention and, moreover, from the workers' point of view, it seems necessary to achieve the highest possible safety level (Morgenstern 1982). Nevertheless, it has to be recognized that there are safety levels beyond which preventive measures cannot reasonably be expected. Therefore, the economic theory of prevention has to take into account the concepts of adequacy, equity and efficiency to examine the workers' compensation system and to determine health policy related to occupational risks (Bequele 1982).

Taking into account both the limitation of global resources to implement prevention actions and technical constraints, various safety levels appear related to industrial activities. These levels are regularly improved and depend on the historical, economic and social context of industrial activities. Because of the variation in risk perception and tolerability, public policies must be able to cope with risks that become unacceptable and to adopt new safety levels. Such a situation characterizes prevention policies related to occupational risks as well as environmental hazards (Russel 1984). In practice, a definition of tolerability of risks may be empirically defined related to various industrial activities and setting (public, workers, etc.). Finally, it is possible to define social optimum as the more efficient use of prevention and compensation resources under the constraints of risk tolerability.

Taking into account both social perception of risks and economic constraints, public authorities may be driven to determine health objectives or standards in the field of occupational injuries and diseases. These objectives

*This work has been partly supported by the French National Fund (CNAMTS).

are defined in view of promoting prevention policies in the various industrial activities and kinds of risk exposure to reach an optimal utilization of prevention resources (Laffont 1985). Moreover, these objectives involve a breakdown of occupational risks between the different industrial activities and wage earners.

Beyond this definition, public authorities have to establish the incentives to reach such a social optimum. Nevertheless, without any constraint, market regulation does not correspond to social optimum, which is defined at the social level. Therefore, it is necessary to implement prevention policies by regulations or to introduce an economic incentive to promote prevention policies at the workplace. Such a management consists more specifically in establishing a relationship between economic profitability of the firm and social optimum (Appel and Borba 1988; Zelenka 1979).

This paper presents an economic analysis of the workers' compensation system in France, which is an efficient incentive mechanism to promote prevention policy. This system affects employers' behaviour and, referring to insurance economics, the incentives provided within it play a major role in achieving a minimization of the total of prevention and compensation costs.

In principle, the French system of compensation for occupational injuries and diseases combines two separate objectives: first, to insure that the victims are duly compensated and second to encourage companies to put into action preventive measures (Dupeyroux 1984; Kessler 1986). Generally speaking, employees do not have to demonstrate the employers' liability and risk incidence is used to determine employer's contribution for the compensation system. Actually, as mentioned before, it is necessary that public authorities defined global prevention objectives and then introduce economic incentives or regulations to achieve them (Zelenka 1979). But there is not perfect coincidence between employers' objectives (their objectives concern essentially the economic profitability of the firm) and social objectives (concerning health policy and socially acceptable level of safety). As long as the marginal cost of a preventive action is lower than the marginal benefit of this action, the insurance system for compensating occupational risk enables the safety level to be improved at the workplace. Although prevention is the first objective, adequate compensation must be provided for workers whose injury was not prevented. In such a context, it is necessary to determine the optimal financial contribution of employers (Worrall 1983; Worrall and Appel 1985).

Different solutions could be used by public authorities to define the financing of the compensation system: insurance mechanism, regulations, penalties, etc. But this paper deals with the main question concerning both the contribution of different industrial activities (e.g. comparison between service activities and activities in the building industry: 80% of injuries occur in the metallurgical and building industries) and the contribution of past, present and future generations. Structural evolution of industrialized countries contributes to modify health policy for occupational risks, because the accident frequency has stagnated in these countries but, simultaneously, new hazards resulting from chemical products are being discovered. Therefore, new objectives should be determined regarding social optimum and, more specifically, it seems necessary to take into account this new situation for the definition of incentive mechanism which should be able to promote safety level corresponding to new hazards (Danzon 1987).

The object of this paper is to point out that the compensation system depends on the level of acceptability of the risk by the public and the national authorities and that moreover this system is able to provide an incentive mechanism in preventing further injuries.

Recent Evolution of the French National Fund

Compensation and Prevention Objectives

In 1985, 36.5 billion French francs (U.S. $6 billion) were spent on the workers' compensation programme in France, corresponding to 13.5 million wage earners.[1] These expenses were paid entirely by employers and represented approximately 10% of the global expenses of the Health Insurance Fund (CNAMTS).

Compensation and prevention objectives were simultaneously and complimentarily defined when the compensation system was created in 1946. When the number of workers of a firm is more than 300, the rating method constitutes one of the most important elements of the incentive mechanism to promote protection measures: the calculation of employer's rate (related to the contribution to the compensation system) depends directly on the compensation cost of injuries or diseases. Because of the financial impacts of injuries and diseases, the firm can combine health objectives and its economic profitability. Referring to insurance economics, employers try to find the safety level which minimizes their own costs. The optimal situation corresponds to the safety level which equalizes marginal cost of prevention and marginal benefit due to the reduction of compensated risk (Eeckhoudt and Calcoen 1989; Ehrlich and Becker 1972).

[1] In France, the whole working population corresponds to approximately 25 million people. But various occupational groups are not involved in the workers' compensation programme (e.g. civil servants, self-employed artisans and businessmen, agricultural workers and the unemployed). Moreover, there are specific programmes for the compensation of miners and railway and electricity production firm employees.

Employers' rates are determined in order to penalize firms where occupational injuries or diseases are frequent and important (NCCI 1981; Ruser 1985). This situation corresponds to a traditional insurance system where the premium increases with the compensation of the risk. In 1985, the annual frequency was 5 injuries with permanent disability and 50 injuries with temporary disability per 1000 wage earners. The average unit cost paid by the firm was 200 000 French francs (U.S. $33 000) per injury with permanent disability and 10 000 French francs (U.S. $1700) per injury with temporary disability.

French Workers' Compensation

In the French system, the Social Security contribution for workers' compensation paid by a company depends upon it size, the number and severity of occupational injuries and diseases expected within the firm and/or its domain of activity (Dupeyroux 1984). There are two types of payments made by Social Security to the victim: temporary support (for medical expenses and absence from work) and, as far as permanent health consequences are concerned, a pension designed to compensate for the loss of earning from permanent partial disability (PPD). Disability pensions represent the main part of the total budget of the compensation system.

Every year, all firms are notified of their contribution rate (Tc) and overall rate for the coming year. This rate takes into account not only all the risks incurred by the workforce (industrial injuries and diseases) but also flat rate charges and general charges to cover administrative costs. Only the factor referring to the risks of industrial injuries and diseases is specific to the type of company, the rest being fixed every year by the Social Security and applying to all employers. So, the determination of the contribution rate corresponds to Eq. 1:

$$Tc = [(Nb \cdot UCYP \cdot \alpha) + c] \cdot (1 + \beta) \tag{1}$$

where:

- Nb = number of injuries and diseases occurring during the last reference period
- $UCYP$ = pension unit cost per year
- α = capitation coefficient
- C = coefficient concerning administrative costs
- β = instrumental variable

However, the method of calculation depends on the size of staff. For a business with less than 20 employees, the risk is considered to be entirely collective, meaning that a change in the number of injuries or diseases does not directly affect the rate; only a general tendency to rise or fall in all companies of the same type will alter the rate. For firms with 20–300 workers, there is a weighting between the collective risk and the individual risk. The closer the workforce is to 300, the more the individual aspect predominates. Finally, for firms with more than 300 employees, only the effective risk counts. So, the level of risk and the rate of contributions can be an incentive for these firms to put into practice preventive measures.

Based on statistics concerning the frequency and incidence of a given injury or disease, the firm should be able a priori to work out the cost of the compensation which it might be called upon to pay. Insofar as the amounts at stake seem to be non-negligible, such calculations should encourage the management to balance the cost of compensation against the possible costs of preventive measures to reduce the level of risks in the company. In theory, every increase in the compensation paid to victims should push the firm to put safety measures into action if the marginal cost of prevention is lower than the marginal compensation cost (Chelius 1982).

Paradoxical Effects of the Financial Method of the Compensation System

During the past 10 years, the cost of compensating workers has not decreased although the frequency of occupational injuries and diseases has decreased rapidly in the same period because of both prevention policies and change in the structure of the working population (Fig. 1). One of the reasons for such an imbalance is that permanent disability pensions represent the main expenditure of the compensation system. Moreover, no capitalization exists to insure

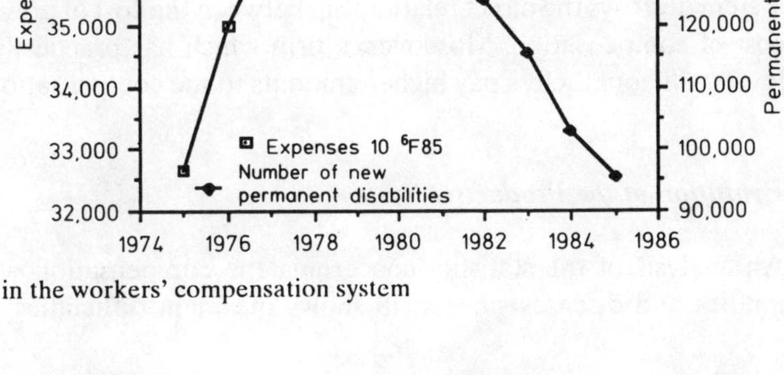

Fig. 1. Changes in the workers' compensation system

the payment of these pensions (nowadays, there are 1.7 million pensions compared with 100 000 new cases of permanent disability every year).

During the 1960s and 1970s, the workers' compensation system encouraged firms to adopt safety measures. Until 1968, increases in the working population ensured the financial balance of the fund. (It should not be noted that all funding is based on annual contributions for injuries or diseases in the current year.) But since the 1970, the need to balance the overall income and outgoings of the system has disturbed the incentive for prevention in breaking the direct relationship between the cost of prevention and of compensation. In fact, the employer's contribution has increased and during the same time occupational injuries have decreased. The workers' compensation system is in a difficult financial position: it must take into account demographic modifications, the evolution of the productive system and its crisis.

The difficulties related to the financing of the National Fund in France have implied different modifications of the calculation methods of employer's rate:

1. The first solution is an increase in the minimum rate which concerns all firms without taking into account their new occupational injuries and diseases; from Eq. 1, we get the minimum rate $T_{\min} = C \bullet (1 + \beta)$ and thus an increase in the instrumental variable β induces an increase in the minimum rate.
2. The second solution consists of varying the unit cost of new injuries or diseases; this solution corresponds to a modification of the "capitation coefficient" α.

Because of the difference between the evolution of new injuries and the increase in pensions, the second solution could disturb economic incentives towards prevention: the firm's contribution could increase even if protection measures were implemented.

In fact, these two solutions have been used during the past 10 years in France to satisfy the financial objectives of workers' compensation, which depend on new demographic evolutions and modifications of industrial labour. The constraint of maintaining year to year financial stability of the system destroys the direct relationship between the cost of prevention and the cost of compensation. Moreover, a firm which has practically reduced risk levels will nonetheless pay higher amounts to the compensation fund.

Evolution of the Productive System

An analysis of the statistics concerning the compensation of occupational injuries and diseases since 1948 shows the main difficulties related to the financial evolution of the system and predicts the evolution for future years (CNAMTS). After the Second World War, the development of production systems induced substantial and constant growth of the population of wage earners, with increases at the rate of 2.5%/year. Since 1974, however, this evolution has halted (Fig. 2).

Since 1974, occupational injuries and traffic injuries related to work have decreased every year: in 1974, there were 1 150 000 occupational injuries with temporary disability compared with 730 000 in 1985 (e.g. an annual decrease of 3.3%; Fig. 3); permanent disabilities present a similar trend: 120 000 occupational injuries with permanent disability in 1974 compared with 74 000 in 1985 (Fig. 4). As far as occupational diseases are concerned, the situation in quite different: the "social" compensation of several diseases has increased during the past 10 years, but the total number of occupational diseases is still marginal compared with occupational injuries (e.g. occupational diseases represent less than 5000 new annual cases). Nevertheless, the average unit cost of permanent disability per occupational disease is twice as important as the cost per occupational injury: 500 000 French francs paid by the firm per disease with permanent disability compared with 250 000 French francs per disease with occupational injury.

The recent decrease in occupational injuries is a consequence of the prevention policies of both firms and public authorities (concerning metallurgy activity and building activity) and of the evolution of the population of wage earners (e.g. decrease in wage earner population in activities in which injury

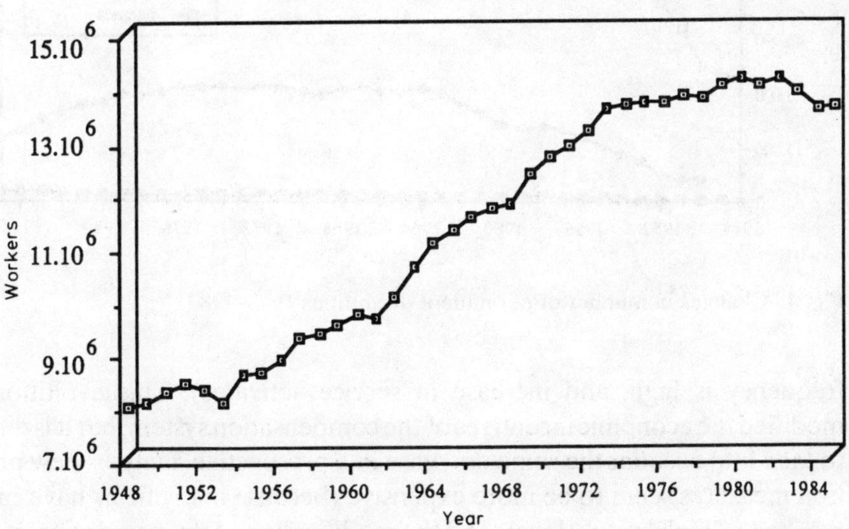

Fig. 2. Changes in worker population 1948–1985

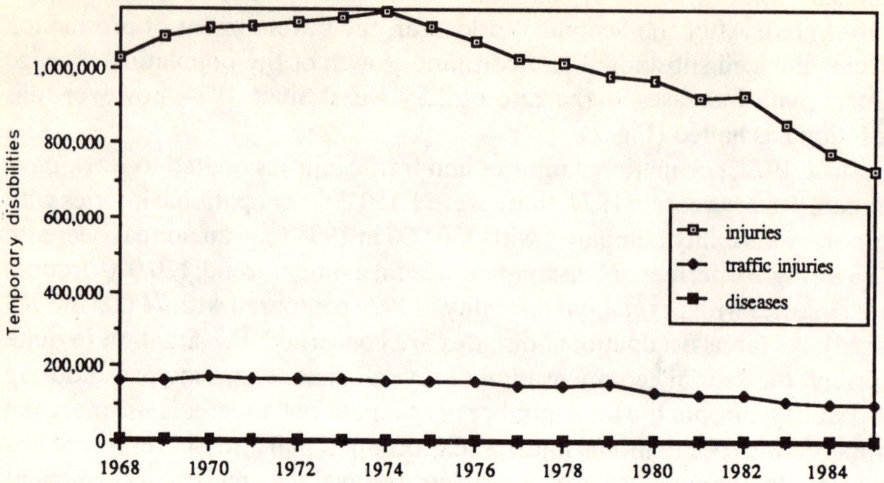

Fig. 3. Changes in number of temporary disabilities 1968–1985

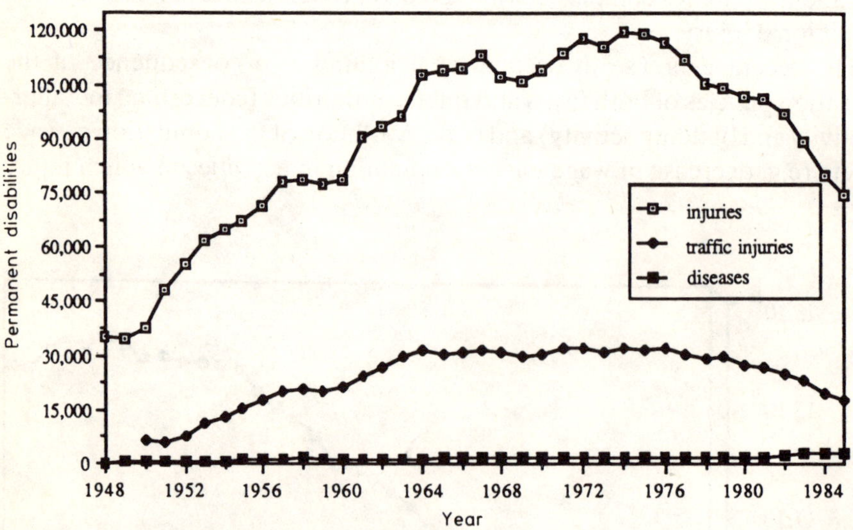

Fig. 4. Changes in number of permanent disabilities 1948–1985

frequency is high, and increase in service activities). This evolution has modified the economic incentives of the compensation system, but it is difficult to take into account the same decrease in a prospective analysis: new protection measures seem to be more expensive (because many firms have rapidly reached a "high" safety level) and the modification of the population of wage earners will be certainly less intensive for the next 10 years.

Evolution of Workers' Compensation Expenses

In this context, it is necessary to define new financial procedures concerning the National Fund in France: nowadays, the calculation of the employers' rate will not provide an equilibrium between the overall income and outgoings of the system without modifications to the minimum rate or/and the unit cost of injuries.

There are three types of expense the National Fund has to provide for in France: temporary disabilities, permanent disabilities and administrative costs (including transfer of expenses between different social security systems). Figure 5 shows the evolution of the workers' compensation expenses.

In addition to the increase in inflation, structural differences have appeared between these different types of expense. One of the most important developments has been the increase in permanent disability pensions, which represent more than 50% of overall expenses in 1985; in contrast new cases of occupational injury have decreased rapidly. Moreover, such difficulties will not be resolved during future years without a real modification of the employers' rate as the demographic evolution of pensioners involves a growth of expenses related to permanent disabilities.

The financing of the National Fund in France is integrated in the Social Security system and therefore is based on the principle of expense "distribution" among the various categories of firms (Kessler 1986). But each new injury or disease with permanent disability involves expenses over several years and frequently over several decades. In fact, there is no "capitalization"

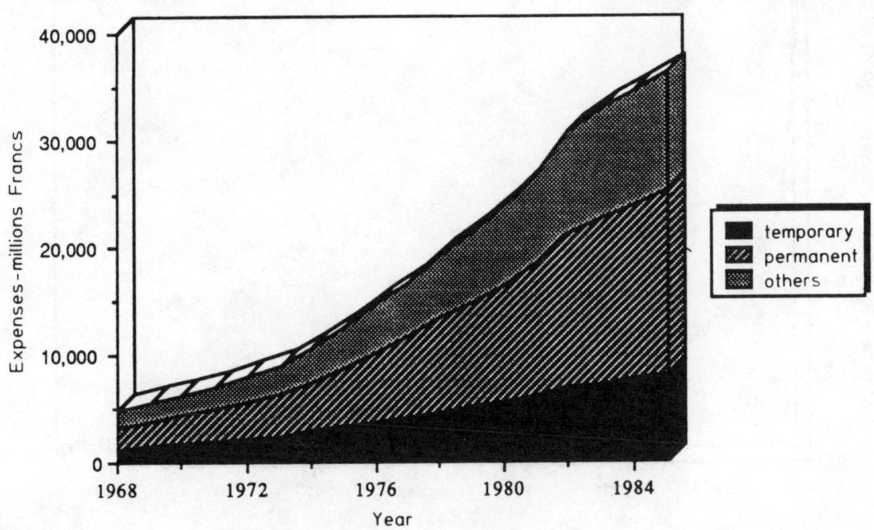

Fig. 5. Changes in expense claims 1968–1985

related to these expenses and, finally, every year, it is necessary to include the financing of all pensioners in the determination of the employers' rate.

At the present time, the calculation of employers' rates has two main objectives: to promote an insurance mechanism between the different firms and to maintain the financial stability of the system. Taking into account the demographic evolution of the system, a disequilibrium appears between the increase or stagnation in the number of pensioners and the decrease in new injuries and diseases with permanent disability. As with all pension systems, the workers' compensation system must take into account the evolution of the ratio between number of pensioners and new permanent disabilities (Babeau 1985). In fact, the financing of the compensation system depends on these new cases: the annual employer's contribution is calculated taking into account the new injuries and diseases. Since the creation of the system, this ratio has always decreased: such a situation shows that the financing of the system has never been well established and economic and demographic developments during the past decade have aggravated this problem. Figure 6 shows the evolution of the ratio between new cases and pensioners with permanent disability (a degree of incapacity of more than 10%).

Finally, prospective analysis concerning the financing of the National Fund in France needs to investigate both the evolution of the compensation system without modification (e.g. how to combine the minimum rate and the unit cost of injuries to determine the financial equilibrium of the system) and the application of various approaches for the calculation of the employer's rate

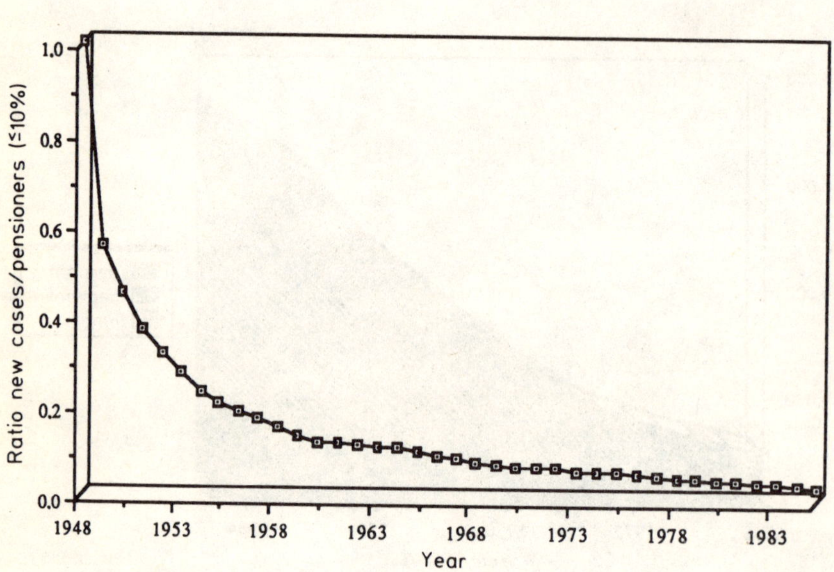

Fig. 6. Changes in ratio of new cases: pensioners (with incapacity rate ≤ 10%)

(e.g. mutualization of pension expenses concerning injuries and diseases since the creation of the Social Security system, and capitalization for compensation of new permanent disabilities; Gollier 1987). These various scenarios modify the safety incentive mechanism and it seems necessary to analyse for each scenario, on one hand, how the firm should satisfy social health objectives and its profitability objectives and, on the other hand, how public authorities should promote prevention policy based on workers' compensation (Laffont 1985). Specific questions concerning occupational cancers must be resolved: nowadays, the compensation system appears too inefficient of manage prevention policy for occupational cancers.

Prospective Analysis of the French National Fund

During the past decade, different modifications of the calculation of the employers' rate have been adopted (1982, 1984, 1988) to satisfy the financial objectives of the French National Fund. But these modifications are preliminary and others should be adopted in the future. Moreover, mutualization and capitalization principles[2] should be discussed, as other pension systems do, because of the number of pensioners (Gollier 1987). Related to this discussion, one of the most important problems concerns the repartition of the financing between different industrial and service activities.

In this context, the evolution of the main parameters of the French National Fund has been defined in collaboration with Social Security experts. Since the beginning of the 1980s, occupational injuries have decreased rapidly (approximately 7%/year) and occupational diseases have increased (5%/year). These developments have been extrapolated for the next decade, which indicates both an intensification of prevention policies of firms and better compensation for occupational diseases (e.g. new hazards must be taken into account). Such a situation is characteristic of industrialized countries and indicates the main evolution of occupational safety during the next decade (Morgenstern 1982). Moreover, the present financial mechanism of the compensation system is inadequate in this new situation: employers' rate are defined on the experience-rating principle, but, for example, occupational diseases only appear several years or decades after the exposure to toxic substances at the workplace. Therefore, an economic incentive related to the employers' rate is not an efficient method of promoting prevention policy.

[2]In a "mutualization system", the current year's expenses are paid out from contributions made in the same year, while in a "capitalization system" some reserves are accumulated and placed on the financial markets.

Using the above assumptions, the simulated evolution, between 1986 and 1995, of new causes of permanent disability compared with the total number of pensioners in the National Fund is presented in Fig. 7. Nevertheless, in addition to this global simulated tendency, there are various evolutions: comparison between 1985 and 1995 of figures concerning new cases shows both a decrease in the total number (86 855 new cases in 1985 and only 46 831 in 1995) and a modification related to the repartition between injuries and diseases (occupational diseases concerned only 4% of the new cases in 1985 compared with 10% in 1995).

Future evolution of the number of pensioners reveals the importance of demographic factors: the proportion of severe disabilities increased (61% of the whole number in 1985 compared with 72% in 1995). Moreover, difficulties appear to reduce the cost of compensation related to past injuries and diseases. If recent developments of various parameters used in the simulation models are confirmed (injuries and disease rates, evolution of wage earner population, etc.), the total number of pensioners is only divided by 2 in 2009 (e.g. 24-year period) and by 10 in 2027. Such a situation proves that, without a capitalization mechanism for pensions, the financing of the compensation system corresponds to both new cases and the past situation concerning injuries and diseases. Therefore, the incentive principle of the system becomes more and more difficult to apply if no modification appears to define the employer's financial contribution.

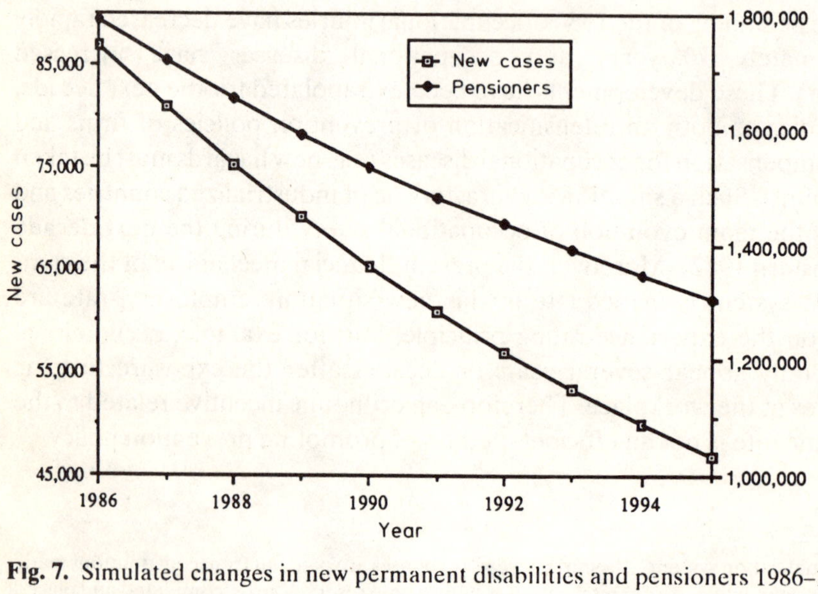

Fig. 7. Simulated changes in new permanent disabilities and pensioners 1986–1995

Figure 8 shows this evolution: the average employers' rate decreases because of the considerable decrease in injuries during the next 10 years. Nevertheless, for a specific firm, if there is no significant decrease in injuries because of limited effects of prevention policies or of the necessity to take into account a long period between implementation of prevention measures and reduction of injuries, the calculated rate is not favourable for the firm (such a type of rate is called "fixed rate" here, because we suppose that the same number of injuries and diseases occurred each year).

Finally, the present financing method of the compensation system is no longer able to promote prevention policies, for each type of firm, because of various evolutions of occupational risks. During recent decades, the main objectives of prevention policies concerned occupational injuries and moreover fatal injuries. Nowadays, the considerable decrease in injuries and the increase in occupational diseases indicates new objectives and implies a redefinition of the employer's financial contribution.

Without modification, expenses of the National Fund will be distributed differently between the various economic activities: because of the increase in expenses related to past injuries, the employers' rate concerning activities with a "high level" of risk will decrease by 40% during the next 10 years while the rate concerning activities with "low level" of risk will only decrease by 20%. Furthermore, if one were to make the hypothesis that there are no occupational injuries and diseases, it appears that effects of past pensioners really "persist" during the next decade even if expenses related to temporary disabilities disappear in that case. Figure 9 presents evolutions of pensioner

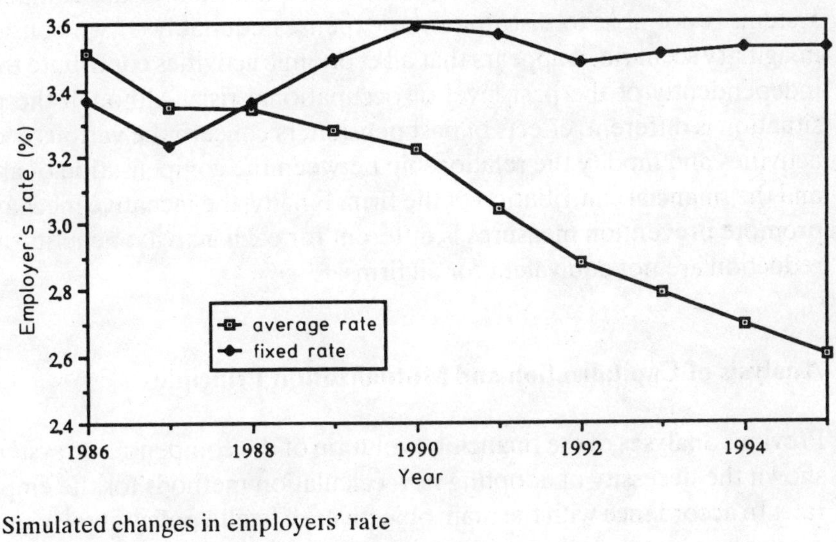

Fig. 8. Simulated changes in employers' rate

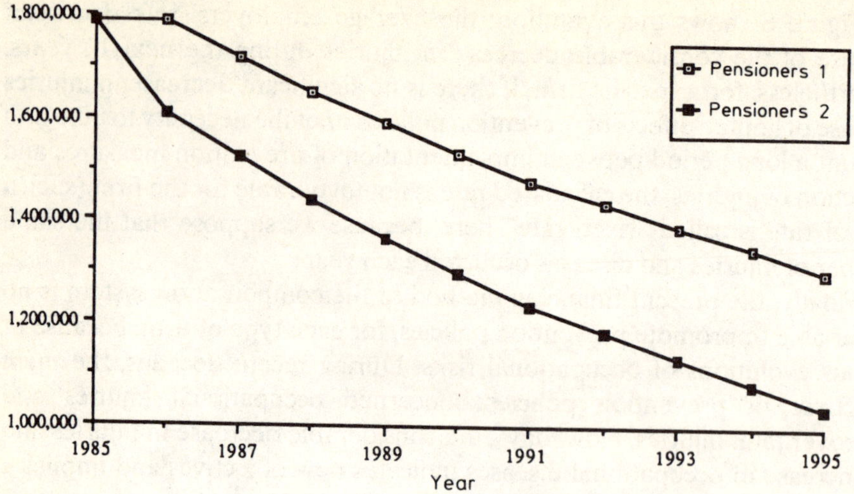

Fig. 9. Simulated changes in numbers of pensioners

numbers in this scenario (called "pensioners 2") compared with extrapolation of the present situation (called "pensioners 1").

Differences between the two scenarios are not great: only 40% more in the present situation compared with the imaginary scenario. Such a simulation confirms the significant effect of past pensioners on the global expenses of the compensation system. The financing of the system must take into account this demographic effect. Moreover, the present calculation of the employers' rate, which is defined to maintain the financial equilibrium of the compensation system, is not able to distribute the expenses equitably. If we consider the imaginary scenario, it appears that all economic activities contribute the same independently of the past level of occupational risk. Although the present situation is different, effects of past pensioners concern the various economic activities and modify the relationship between the compensation of an injury and the financial contribution of the firm. Finally, the incentive mechanism to promote prevention measures is different for each activity: benefits of injury reduction are not equivalent for all firms.

Analysis of Capitalization and Mutualization Principles

Previous analyses of the financing evolution of the compensation system have shown the necessity of adopting new calculation methods for the employers' rate. In accordance with the main objectives of health policy at the workplace, it seems necessary: (a) to distinguish expenses related to past pensioners and the cost of new injuries paid by the firm and (b) to use a specific calculation method for occupational diseases capable of establishing a real incentive for prevention policy of the risk from toxic carcinogens.

Economic Incentive for Occupational Injuries

Referring to insurance economics, the employer tries to find the safety level which minimizes costs. Finally, if no specific regulation is introduced related to exposure to hazards, the only benefit due to the reduction of risk concerns the employer's financial contribution to the National Fund. Therefore, it is easier for public authorities to determine two parts of the employers' contribution for the financing of the system: the first related to the expenses of past pensioners, and the second to capitalize compensation of new occupational injuries. Such a situation allows the main objectives of the compensation system to be satisfied but is not easy to introduce. The main problem of this financial mechanism concerns the constitution of the capitalization fund (Gollier 1987). At the beginning, firms must pay for both past pensioners and future compensation which is capitalized in this case. During the 1st decade, the global contribution of employers will increase and moreover will affect the share of expenses between the various economic activities.

Finally, this principle appears necessary and corresponds to the present tendency of all pension systems (Babeau 1985). But in the case of the workers' compensation system, the financing of the expenses related to past pensioners implies a political decision:

1. Is it preferable to distribute these expenses among all activities independently of their level of risk?
2. Or is it better to consider that the financial contribution must be based on past contributions?

A prospective scenario has been studied taking into account both capitalization of pensions related to new permanent disabilities and mutualization of past pensions. Figure 10 shows the new financing method of the compensation system, where "*k*" represents the "capitation coefficient". This value depends on the financial capacity or acceptability of employers for their contribution to the National Fund. In such a context, the analysis concerning expected life of workers with permanent disability reveals that pension is paid during an average period of 32 years. Taking into account the interest rate, it seems enough to capitalize an equivalent of 25 times annual pension. Thus, we consider that pensions related to past injuries are supported by a mutualization

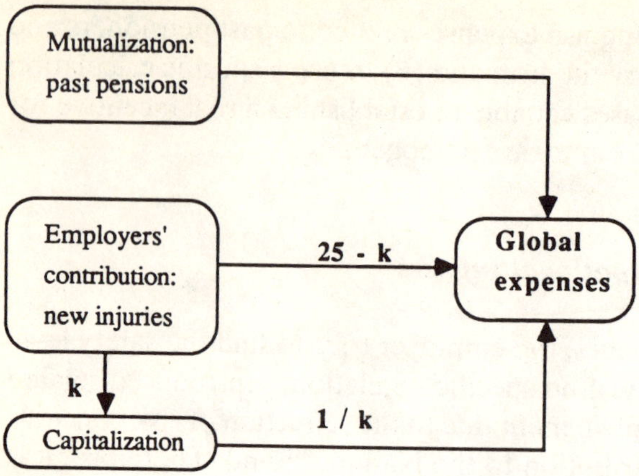

Fig. 10. The capitalization principle

system, while employers' contributions concerning new injuries are partly capitalized.

The application of such a system is relatively dependent on the demographic evolution of pensioners. Therefore, this modification of the financing system is completely subordinated to the financial market. These fluctuations could be significant and disturb the efficacity of the capitalization principle because of the long period taken into account. Finally, it is possible that the capitalization principle, considered as the better solution for the financial repartition between generations (Gollier 1987), is a false solution: difficulties in the financial market could transfer present expenses to future generations.

If we consider the introduction of the capitalization principle for the 1988 budget of the National Fund, employers' rate increase rapidly during subsequent years. The average rate rises by more than 10% between 1987 and 1988. Such a simulation shows the financial effects of the "capitalization fund" constitution (Fig. 11). Therefore, although this increase should establish a better financing method taking into account the transfer between generations, introduction of mutualization related to past pensions would affect the distribution between various economic activities. The employers' contribution rate in activities with a high level of risk would decrease and the inverse situation would appear for activities with a low level of risk.

Finally, taking into account the advantages and disadvantages of the present situation and prospective analysis concerning the capitalization principle, the new financing methods of the compensation system must combine capitalization and mutualization. Such a solution is probably capable of improving the incentive mechanism to promote the prevention policy and to

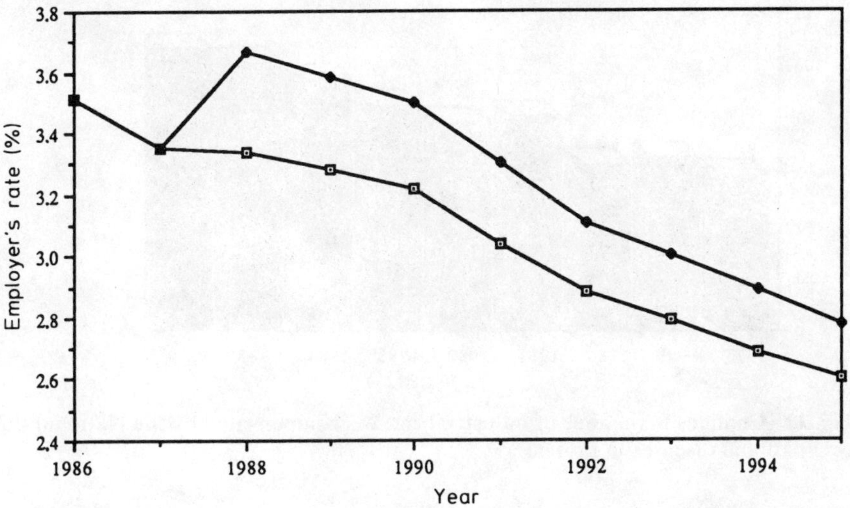

Fig. 11. Comparison of employers' rate with or without capitalization. ▫, without capitalization; ◆, with capitalization

establish the financing method of the compensation system according to the contribution of various generations. Therefore, prospective analysis must take into account the evolution of economic activities and demographic variations and moreover the evolution of compensation and social acceptability of occupational risk (Barrot 1988). But nowadays, such considerations receive no attention.

Employers' Contribution for Occupational Diseases

The system of compensation for occupational diseases presents a limited incentive for prevention. The first difficulty concerns the latency between exposure and recognition of occupational disease. Moreover, occupational exposure can be combined with various exposures which are non-work related. The question is: Who must pay compensation and how much?

One of the most difficult problems is that of industrial cancer. In 1987, exposure to 12 substances and processes gave the right to compensation for cancer as an occupational disease by the National Fund in France. The number of cases of industrial cancer compensated for the first time in 1985 was only about 100. Moreover, the number of industrial cancers compensated for has increased by less than 10%/year since 1978. Figure 12 demonstrates this evolution between 1978 and 1986.

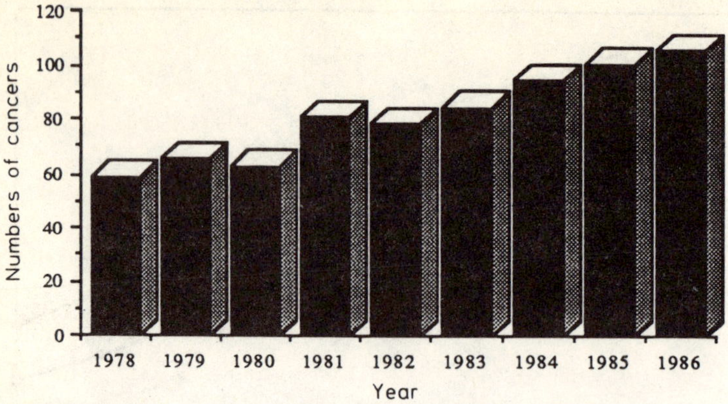

Fig. 12. Changes in number of industrial cancers compensated by the National Fund as occupational diseases in France

Industrial cancer induce an average cost of about 2–3 million French francs (= U.S. $300 000–400 000). So, industrial cancers compensated for the first time in 1985 represent approximately between 200 and 300 million French francs (= U.S. $30–40 million) paid by the firms.

In practice, the incentive for prevention is not so evident, even if these insurance cost are important. Many problems exist: the problems of recognizing an occupational cancer and the latency of this disease (Goldberg and Hémon 1988). At the moment, the system "protects" itself against the appearance of carcinogenic risks because the recognition of the disease as work related is not so evident. The practical difficulties of knowing (particularly in retrospect) whether exposure to carcinogenic substances in the workplace has occurred and the scientific uncertainties which make it difficult to determine the origin of a cancer combine to justify a partial denial of the problem. In 1985, only 101 industrial cancers was compensated for the first time. This figure must be compared with 6000 deaths from cancer every year which might be connected with previous exposure at work, as calculated by applying "conservative" estimations made by epidemiologists to the French situation (Doll and Peto 1981; Oudiz and Le Galès 1988).

Changes in the system of compensation for occupational diseases with respect to cancer could also help to provide an economic incentive for firms to implement preventive action. Referring to the past record of a firm when calculating its contributions is not really applicable to a disease like cancer. It would be a good idea to produce financial incentives to prevention by basing the calculation of contributions on both the past history of the firm but also on its present situation with respect to the risks it carries (like the bonus-malus loading system for insurance). A criterion for the present situation would be the levels of exposure of the workforce to toxic or carcinogenic substances. It follows that a change in these levels would entail a similar change in contributions. In addition, in the case of cancer the question arises of the relative importance or work-related factors among the genetic, life style and environmental factors which might be the cases of the disease. The present system of recognition based on "presumed origin" is therefore inappropriate. Seeking to quantify the extent of responsibility of the work-related factor among all those involved in the aetiology of cancer has led to the concept of "partial attribution". General acceptance of this would increase the number of compensated cancers but, at the same time, only part of the cost of the illness would be borne by the employer. However, the integration of this concept into the system of compensation depends on a political consensus between all the social groups concerned (Appel and Borba 1988).

Conclusion

In this paper, we have essentially discussed the influence of the financial allocation of responsibility for occupational injuries and diseases. More specifically, we have shown that various modifications of the compensation system are necessary in the next few years to provide incentives for employers. Nevertheless, attention should be focused on the problem of determining criteria of optimality. Thus, the main question is to establish health policy which is socially acceptable. In accordance with public economics (Laffont 1985), the first object is to define safety levels for occupational exposure and then to provide incentives for employers with a distinction between injuries and diseases.

Acknowledgment. The authors thank Lise Rochaix for her comments on the first version of this paper.

References

Appel D, Borba PS (eds) (1988) Workers' compensation insurance pricing. Kluwer, Boston

Babeau A (1985) La fin des retraites?. Hachette, Paris

Barrot R (1988) Le dommage corporel et sa compensation: pratique médico-légale et judiciaire. Litec, Paris

Bequele A (1982) The economic analysis and evaluation of working conditions: methods, problems and issues. Working conditions and Environment Department, ILO, CONDI-T

Chelius JR (1982) The influence of workers' compensation on safety incentives. Industrial Labor Relations Revi 35:235–242

CNAMTS (1968–1981) Statistiques de l'année

CNAMTS (1982–1986) Carnets statistiques

Danzon P (1987) Compensation for occupational disease: evaluating the options. J Risk Insurance LIV (2):263–282
Doll R, Peto R (1981) The causes of cancer. Oxford University Press, Oxford
Dupeyroux J-J (1984) Droit de la sécurité sociale, 9th edn. Dalloz, Paris
Eeckhoudt L, Calcoen F (1989) Eléments de microéconomie. Editions Universitaires, Brussels
Ehrlich I, Becker GS (1972) Market insurance, self insurance and self protection. J Polit Econ 80"623–648
Goldberg M, héemon D (1988) Epidémiologie des cancers professionnels: quelle recherche?. Rev Prévenir 16:43–53
Gollier J-J (1987) L'avenir des Retraites. L'Argus, paris
Kessler D (1986) Sur les fondements économiques de la Sécurité sociale. Rev Fr Aff Soc 1
Laffont J-J (1985) Théorie des incitations et économie publique. Recherches économiques et sociales, Commissariat général du Plan, service des études et de la recherche no 15, La documentation française, pp 171–180
Morgenstern F (1982) Deterence and compensation. International Labour Office, Geneva
National Council on Compensation Insurance (1981) ABC's of experience rating. NCCI, New York
Oudiz A, Le Galès C (1988) Prévention des cancers professionnels: problèmes et perspectives. Collection grandes enquêtes en santé publique et épidémiologie. INSERM, Paris
Ruser JW (1985) Workers' compensation insurance, experience rating, and occupational injuries. Rand J Econ 16(4):487–503
Russell LB (1984) The economics of prevention. Health Policy 4:85–100
Worrall JD (ed) (1983) Safety and the workforce: incentives and disincentives in workers' compensation. ILR Press, New York
Worrall JD, Appel D (eds) (1985) Workers' compensation benefits: adequacy, equity and efficiency. ILR Press, New York
Zelenka A (1970) The contribution of social security to accident prevention: influence on prevention of the methods of financing employment injury insurance. Document OAPC/1979/D.2, ILO